Managing Medicine

a survival guide

EDITORS:
Di Sanderson
John Brown

ASSOCIATE
EDITORS:
Peter Moore
Lorraine Foster
Helen Jones
Mike Pedler

FOREWORD:
Dame Rennie
Fritchie

FT

FINANCIAL TIMES
Healthcare

FT HEALTHCARE
a Division of Pearson Professional Ltd
Maple House, 149 Tottenham Court Road,
London W1P 9LL, UK
Telephone: +44 (0)171 896 2424
Fax: +44 (0)171 896 2449
http://www.fthealthcare.com

First published 1997

A catalogue record for this book is available from
the British Library

ISBN 0–443–05655–2

© Pearson Professional Ltd 1997

Publisher: Mark Lane
Project Manager: Brenda Wren
Copy edited by: Patricia MacColl, Cupar
Indexed by: June Morrison, Helensburgh

Typeset by Saxon Graphics Ltd, Derby
Printed by Bell and Bain Ltd, Glasgow

Contents

Contributors

Kath Aspinwall
Senior Lecturer, Centre for Education Management and
Administration, Sheffield Hallam University, Sheffield

Margaret Attwood
Consultant in Individual and Organisational Learning, Bury
Farmhouse, Felsted, Great Dunmow, Essex

John Brown
Senior Lecturer, Department of Social Policy & Social Work,
University of York, Heslington, York

Seamus Carey BSc (Econ) Hons Postgrad Dip (Labour law) MIPD
Organisation Development Consultant, Provider Supporter Unit,
Belfast, Northern Ireland

Charles Collins MA MB BChir CHM FRCS
Consultant Surgeon, Taunton and Somerset Hospital, Musgrove
Park, Taunton, Somerset

Elizabeth Duncan MB ChB MRCGP DRGOC
General Practitioner, The Surgery, Bellshill, Lanarkshire

Bill Evers
Main Street, Huby, York

Anna Firth
Management, Disablement Services Centre, Northern General
Hospital NHS Trust, Sheffield

Amanda Flood RGN
Clinical Specialist in Urology, Taunton and Somerset Hospital,
Musgrove Park, Taunton, Somerset

Lorraine Foster RGN Dip ISHM
Clinical Audit Research Manager, Scunthorpe and Goole Hospitals
NHS Trust, Scunthorpe, North Lincolnshire

Pauline Fryer BS MIPD
Director of Human Resources, Scunthorpe and Goole Hospitals
NHS Trust, Scunthorpe, North Lincolnshire

John Gatrell BA (Hons) PGCertE FIPM MIMgt
Deputy Head, Bournemouth University Business School,
Bournemouth

Jacqueline Goldberg MD FRCS(Glas)
Consultant Surgeon, Law Hospital, Carluke, Lanarkshire

Huw Griffiths
Consultant Clinical Pathologist, Huddersfield Royal Infirmary,
Lindley, Huddersfield

Ian Gunn MB ChB FRCPath
Consultant Biochemist, Law Hospital, Carluke, Lanarkshire

Graham M Horne BA
Director, West Yorkshire Central Services Agency, Leeds

Bob Hudson
Senior Research Fellow, Community Care Division, Nuffield
Institute of Health, University of Leeds, Leeds

Neal Jolly MD
General Practitioner, Lepton Surgery, Huddersfield

Helen Jones
Director, Centre for Leadership Development, Innovation Centre,
York Science Park, Heslington, York

Surrinder Kaur RN RM ADM DipN MTC/Cert BA(Hons) Dip NHS
Management
Professional Development Nurse, City General Hospital, Stoke on
Trent, Staffordshire

Donald MacLean
Consultant Anaesthetist, Law Hospital, Carluke, Lanarkshire

Hugo Mascie-Taylor MD
Medical Director, Leeds Health Authority, Wentworth House,
Harrogate

James McCallion
Consultant Geriatrician, Law Hospital, Carluke, Lanarkshire

Alastair McGowan FRCP FFAEM
Consultant in Accident and Emergency Medicine, St James's
University Hospital, Leeds

Peter Moore MD FRCS
Consultant General Surgeon and Director of Clinical Practice
Development, Scunthorpe and Goole Hospitals NHS Trust,
Scunthorpe, North Lincolnshire

Julia K Moore FRCA MBA
Consultant Anaesthetist, Wirral Hospital, Upton, Wirral

Liz Murphy BSC MBChB MRCP
Consultant Physician, Law Hospital, Carluke, Lanarkshire,
Scotland

Stuart Peacock
Lecturer, Health Economics Unit, Monash University, Melbourne,
Australia

Mike Pedler
Partner, Learning Company Project and Visiting Professor,
Department of Health Studies, University of York, Heslington,
York

Christopher Potter PhD FHSM FIPD
Senior Lecturer, Epidemiology and Public Health Medicine,
University of Wales College of Medicine, Cardiff

Stephen Prosser MA MIHSM
Chief Executive, NHS Staff College Wales, Maes Y Gwernen Hall,
Morriston Hospital NHS Trust, Swansea

David L Sackett
Consultant General Physician, John Radcliffe Hospital, Oxford;
Director, NHS R&D Centre for Evidence-Based Medicine, Oxford

Diana Sanderson
Senior Research Fellow, York Health Economics Consortium,
University of York, Heslington, York

Andrew Short
Consultant Paediatrician, Huddersfield Royal Infirmary, Lindley,
Huddersfield

Paul Smith
Director of Planning, Bradford Health Authority, Shipley, West Yorkshire

Grant Urquhart
Consultant Radiologist, Department of Radiology, Southern General Hospital, Glasgow

Paul Watson MA MB BChir MPH DCH MFPHM
Director of Acute Services, Cambridge and Huntingdon Health Authority, Fulbourn Hospital, Fulbourn, Cambridge

Anthony White PhD FRCS MB BS AKC MHSM
Consultant Otolaryngologist, Royal United Hospitals NHS Trust, Bath; Visiting Professor, Bournemouth University Business School, Bournemouth

Sheila Williams
Training and Development Consultant, Wheatley Wood Farm, North Wheatley, Retford, Nottinghamshire

Tony Winkless BA MPhil AFBPsS FIPD
Occupational Psychologist, The Coach House, Splash Lane, Peterborough, Cambridgeshire

Foreword

In writing this foreword I must declare a personal belief at the outset. That is, for our Health Services to be of the best, most effective benefit for those who need them, there must be a stronger input from clinicians in defining, developing and managing them.

This can be done in a variety of ways. Working upstream in the thinking and decision-making process rather than downstream, and having to live with the consequences. This means contributing at the earliest possible stage to the strategic thinking of Health Authorities. This is a leadership role which requires time and skill to influence in advance of action.

Some will want to be more directly involved in a mainstream way. Taking on a managerial role for different periods of time during their careers. In order to do this it will be important to broaden Nursing and Medical training at the earliest stages and for continuous managerial audit to be available, as well as skill modules and broader learning experiences to be developed.

I believe it is essential for Doctors, nurses and people in allied professions to be actively aware of current trends and issues and the potential impact of these on clinical practice in order to be effective professionals. This doesn't happen automatically. It requires interest, time, processes, skills and a willingness to be part of a larger continuing learning process.

The National Health Service is made up of so many different parts which need to move together in harmony. The pyramids are a magnificent example of engineering. They are also an example of human co-operation and the bringing together of people with different skills, and the organisation of those skills into the creation of a single beautiful whole.

I am quite sure that in addition to a vision and professional expertise there was also strong, effective management.

The National Health Service too can be a beautiful entity, but we need to invest at the right level, at the right time, in the right place, with the right people, if we are going to make it work. This means good management as well as first class professionals.

Dame Rennie Fritchie

The policy framework: selected issues

INTRODUCTION
Diana Sanderson   John Brown

Ever since the National Health Service and Community Care Act 1990 laid the foundations for the development of health care through the 1990s, hardly a week has gone by without part of the media reporting on some aspect of the work of the NHS. Often this has been critical and interpreted within a political agenda. Health issues figured prominently in both the 1992 and the 1997 election campaigns.

Against this backdrop of intense media scrutiny and political posturing, the overall emphasis for health care in the late 1990s was outlined in the White Paper *The National Health Service: A Service with Ambitions* (HMSO, 1996). Five strategic objectives were identified.

- ensuring that there is a well informed public;
- developing a seamless service;
- decision making to be knowledge-based;
- creating a highly skilled and trained workforce;
- providing a service that is responsive.

Four priority areas are seen as raising particular issues when pursuing such objectives:

- primary care;
- information;
- professional development;
- managing quality

It is these objectives and priority areas that provide the immediate policy context for the chapters in this section, as well as providing the framework for the book as a whole. There is a difference, however, between Section One and the other two sections.

While the emphasis throughout the book is upon providing practical guidelines – in essence a 'survival guide' – the authors of

Section One provide an overview of selected issues that does not necessarily draw upon particular local intitiatives. Instead, the emphasis is more upon introducing the selected issues in a way that, while providing practical insights, assists the reader in appreciating the broader policy parameters of delivering health care.

In the first chapter **John Brown** addresses the possible impact upon medicine of changes effecting the role and contribution of other professional groups that are part of the multi-disciplinary team. Initiatives are considered that are beginning to blur traditional occupational boundaries, with a particular emphasis placed upon education and training. The point is made that without care the multi-disciplinary mix can become a multi-disciplinary maze.

The following chapter, by **Bob Hudson,** outlines and assesses developments in contracting and commissioning within the NHS. After a hesitant start in the early 1990s, when contracting and commissioning was still a new, if not novel, initiative, the various issues that were raised have been aproached in an increasingly sophisticated manner. The chapter reflects this increasing sophistication and provides a succinct introduction for all those seeking to understand the processes involved with this pivotal part of the internal market.

In a similar vein, **David Sackett** addresses the issues surrounding the increasing emphasis and momentum around evidence-based medicine. As a term that is increasingly heard compared to only a short time ago, the chapter provides an essential definition. Together with a historical appreciation of the development of evidence-based medicine, the case for its adoption is presented along with practical suggestions on where to find additional information.

The final two chapters both emphasise the importance of resource and capital in the NHS.

Stuart Peacock identifies recent developments in resource allocation and budget setting within the NHS drawing upon the extensive experience gained tackling such issues by the health economists working at the University of York. The implications of the York models are considered together with the policy choices concerning the construction and use of the national formula.

In the final chapter of the Section **Diana Sanderson** considers capital investment in the NHS. Current initiatives are placed in the context of the shortcomings associated with the pre-1991 system. Among contemporary developments the move towards consolidating and increasing the role of the Private Finance Initiative is assessed, with the key issues identified for all those considering pursuing this possibility.

1. Medicine and the multi-disciplinary maze

John Brown

Introduction

When the National Health Service (NHS) was introduced in 1948 four principles guided the design and delivery of health care: ensuring equality of access, promoting equity in treatment, developing a comprehensive local service, and guaranteeing that health care was free at the point of delivery. Over the years each principle has tended to become enshrined as axiomatic in debates and discussion about health care. In such circumstances, even though various policy initiatives have subsequently undermined the position adopted by the founders of the NHS, it can be easy to forget that each of the principles addressed specific problems faced by the country prior to the outbreak of the Second World War.

In the 1940s, only employed men had any form of state cover for meeting the costs of health care. Known by the colloquial term of being 'on the Panel' the arrangements for this cover dated back to the reforms introduced by the Liberal government of Lloyd George at the beginning of the twentieth century. Cover was restricted to the employed man, with the result that others in the family, women, children, the elderly and the unemployed, were excluded from any form of state insurance to help meet the costs of health care. At the same time, the benefit level did not necessarily mean that access to treatment, other than that offered by the general practitioner, was covered. For more costly treatments, and certainly for chronic conditions, the ability to pay rather than medical need determined access to treatment. In the large voluntary teaching hospitals the impact of the depression in the 1920s had served to highlight their parlous financial situation. The teaching hospitals established with endowments could not, even with the development of the Lady Almoner to means-test patients' ability to pay, begin to meet the true costs of treatment. Hospital facilities, whether located in teaching hospitals or in Poor Law Infirmaries, were also unevenly distributed. The range and quality of health care that was available was very much determined by where the person lived.

It is against this backdrop that accounts of the creation of the NHS highlight the crucial contribution of the medical profession to the process of negotiation and accommodation between various health interests and the politicians. Although these accounts do not necessarily portray the medical profession in a positive light, then, as now, clinicians were a major force in debate. In recent years, however, alongside the clinicians and politicians has been seen the emergence of managers as a third major force. Not surprisingly, contemporary issues are discussed in the form of a clinician – manager dialogue, which can often be accompanied by confrontation.

One possible reason is that the sheer volume and pace of developments can be interpreted, and positions adopted, in terms of a clinician – manager conflict as managers are readily seen as part of a broader political process for 'controlling health professionals'.[1] The danger of such a stance, understandable as it may be, is that it is all too easy to forget that there are other players involved with health care. One lesson to be drawn from the establishment of the NHS is that at a time of change it is imperative to adopt a broad view and look at how changes affect all players, and not just focus on those who are major players in the manoeuvring, to promote overtly the interests of service users. Clinicians are one part of the health team; in discussing issues of medical management it is necessary to consider changes affecting other health professions, especially as this has repercussions for the way that health care is delivered and, ultimately, the contribution of clinicians and the clinical support that they receive.

The importance of considering the health team as a whole is given weight with the overwhelming current political imperative for multi-disciplinary work and inter-professional care. Since publication of the NHS and Community Care Act, 1990,[2] the multi-disciplinary inter-professional dimension has been actively and ceaselessly promoted by the government. Even with the change in government it is highly unlikely that this emphasis in workforce planning will be allowed to wither on the vine.

For clinicians the full impact has yet to be felt, although it is possible to discern a trend for nursing staff to take responsibility for some tasks traditionally performed by junior doctors and also to develop their contribution in the GP's surgery. Although such developments are still modest the nursing profession as a whole is experiencing considerable pressure and facing major upheavals that will have an influence upon the nursing contribution to the clinical team. Inevitably, this will affect the nature of the dialogue between clinicians and managers, and will most likely be reflected in changes in the boundaries between different health care professions and the settings in which they practise. Four key initiatives, in particular, will play a crucial role:

1. the continuing commitment by government to the introduction of occupational standards
2. the introduction of Education and Training Consortia (ETCs)
3. the integration of nurse education and training into higher education
4. the shift in emphasis from secondary care to a primary care led NHS.

Occupational standards

In 1986 the UKCC submitted proposals for a new approach to nurse training under the title of Project 2000: A new preparation for practice. The proposals signalled a radical break with the past, where students had followed a three-year specialist training and were an integral part of the workforce. The new proposals outlined a scheme, accepted by the government in 1988, whereby all students would undertake an 18-month common foundation programme followed by a further 18 months following a specialist branch programme. Students were also to be supernumerary and not counted as part of the workforce.

The proposals were an attempt to address problems of technological advances and anticipated changes in demographic profiles while, at the same time, grappling with the longstanding problems of recruitment and retention. However, at the same time as the UKCC were submitting their proposals the government outlined plans to introduce a scheme of National Vocational Qualifications (NVQs) that would identify five skill levels, with the highest, Level 5, corresponding at that time to what was seen as the appropriate level for the professions. As the initial emphasis lay upon determining the content of the levels below that of the professional the nursing profession did not become actively involved in discussions. Others were not so hesitant.

NVQs, as one way of determining occupational standards, soon came to be seen by managers as offering an alternative preparation for staff working on particular tasks of health and social care. Once the notion of competence, the measure employed for determining levels with NVQs, carried employer liability protection it became possible to employ non-professionally qualified staff in a range of activities that had previously been the preserve of holders of a professional qualification. The reaction of nursing to the introduction of health care assistants or support workers with NVQ qualifications was immediate and negative. This has led within nursing to an aversion to becoming actively involved in discussions about occupational standards and NVQs.

Such a position has been fuelled by widespread criticism from the industrial, commercial and manufacturing sectors that NVQs are bureaucratic and costly. Academics have also commented that the approach is unduly mechanistic. While these points are given credence by a major review of NVQs currently under way, the public sector has turned to NVQs as offering one solution to staffing problems. In health care this has been aggravated by a concern that Project 2000 nurses are not necessarily 'fit for purpose' for the tasks that they have to undertake and that the preparation is not necessarily value for money. NVQ provides an alternative in a range of areas that costs less and involves employers in a far more direct way in course design. The nursing profession still, however, remains divorced from debates that are currently under way on occupational standards.

In the autumn of 1996 the Committee of Vice-Chancellors and Principals (CVCP) circulated a document asking for comments on establishing occupational standards in three areas of health care activity: health promotion; professions allied to medicine; and complementary medicine. This is part of a national initiative for establishing 'standards in common', which nursing has decided not to become involved with at present. This is not surprising given the profession's lack of enthusiasm in becoming involved with occupational standards initiatives. What is surprising, however, is that this lack of involvement follows unequivocal support from the NHS Executive for occupational standards and NVQs.

In the summer of 1996 the NHS Executive published an Executive Letter[3] outlining planning guidance for education and training. Here the unambiguous comment is made that:

Education purchasers should work collaboratively with NHS managers to: a) encourage greater linkage between vocational and professional qualifications and promote increased uptake of NVQ/occupational standards based training and opportunities for staff in support worker roles; b) encourage the integration of occupational standards within new and existing courses and education programmes, in particular as a 'common language' for shared learning.

Moreover, this is not confined to support worker roles: 'The NHS Executive encourages statutory and professional bodies to explore the integration and use of occupational standards within new and existing health professional education programmes'.[3]

While occupational standards are not likely to impinge directly upon medicine for some while, it is a development that nursing cannot afford not to be involved with at present. As the largest group of employees in the NHS, the problems of recruitment and retention, issues of continuing professional development, and concerns over Project 2000 ensure that nurses in an increasingly pressured health service have a high political profile. Managers have to staff services with qualified personnel — if there are not sufficient nurses, for whatever reason, they will look elsewhere for alternatives and substitutes.

These can be found not just with the deployment of support workers but from other occupational groups who have embraced the necessity of incorporating occupational standards into their training and education programmes. Physiotherapy and occupational therapy are representative of the professions allied to medicine which have been involved with the development of NVQ programmes. At a broader political level there has been a review of the statutory base of such professions with the proposal, yet to be accepted by government, that the present Council for the Professions Supplementary to Medicine be replaced with a Council for Health Professions. The change in terminology for the body does not preclude the inclusion at some future date of nursing, nor indeed medicine.

While this may seem an outlandish proposition to some, and would require appropriate changes in statute, there is no denying that the introduction of occupational standards is beginning to blur boundaries based upon traditional patterns of demarcation as managers seek to staff adequately the service that they provide. This blurring of boundaries has been reinforced with the introduction of a body, the Education and Training Consortia, that has the potential to move towards an integrated workforce policy for all non-medical health care workers.

Education and Training Consortia

In the spring of 1996 the management of the NHS underwent a major change with the abolition of the 14 Regional Health Authorities that had effectively survived since the introduction of the NHS in 1948. They were replaced with 8 Regional Offices

whose officers became part of the Civil Service. This was well publicised and, for many working within the NHS not directly
involved at Regional level, the changes probably went ahead with
little impact save for the fact that joint commissioning was also
given the green light as part of the package of changes introduced
at that time. Yet the package also contained proposals to establish
Education and Training Consortia (ETCs); although the great
majority of staff within the NHS probably have little appreciation
or knowledge of their introduction, these could prove to be the
biggest single influence upon professional preparation, practice
and deployment since the NHS was created.

Publication by the NHS Executive of two Executive Letters in
1995 provided the outline and rationale for the ETCs.[4,5] These new
bodies, answerable to the Regional Education Development Group
that each Regional Office will establish, have total responsibility
for all preparation of non-medical health care workers. In essence,
through the contracting process it will be possible, depending
upon circumstances and area of activity, to mix different combina-
tions of professional workers. For example, whereas there may
have been contracts in the past for 10 nurses this could now be
adjusted to 5 nurses, 3 physiotherapists and 2 occupational therapists. As the ETCs will also have an advisory role for medical training there is being established a body that is in a position to begin
to outline and implement an integrated workforce strategy.

There is clearly a long way to go. The quality of information
upon which decisions are based will be crucial. Representation of
stakeholders on the ETCs, which has to include social services and
the independent sector, has to be determined, as does the modus
operandi. These will vary according to local circumstances and
local agendas. However this is done there will be implications
throughout the country for clinical support in a wide variety of circumstances and settings; this will inevitably be part of the dialogue
between clinicians and managers. For medicine, the introduction
of the Calman proposals along with developments in continuing
medical education will inevitably be influenced by the work and
initiatives coming from the ETCs. For the nursing profession there
is the added element that, from April of 1996, they have become
integrated with higher education.

Integration of nursing into higher education

Historically, nurses received their training in Schools of Nursing attached to hospitals with the effect that they tended to be isolated from other institutions of further and higher education. From the late 1980s onwards this isolation was ended by the formation of Colleges of Health/Nursing which established affiliation or association links with higher education. A small number became integrated into higher education, joining a modest number of university nursing departments that offered a joint degree and professional nursing qualification. In 1995 the NHS Executive announced that all colleges were to go out to tender for their full integration into higher education the following April.

How that integration has proceeded has depended very much on local circumstances, the size of the university, whether there was a medical faculty, and so on. Contract numbers for pre-registration training and continuing education have been negotiated between the former colleges, universities and Regional Offices. Arrangements have been made with Regional Offices to ensure that quality criteria are established and monitoring arrangements introduced. This development has meant that the ETCs have a crucial role in being the conduit between higher education and the wider commissioning process in the NHS. For the nursing profession the move into higher education has provided the opportunity to move towards an all-graduate profession. Such a possible development, however, serves to highlight the volatile and uncertain nature of higher education which is not, at present, a stable environment.

In the mid-1960s approximately 6% of 18 year olds entered higher education. Some 30 years on this proportion has increased to approximately one third. One effect has been to change the value of a degree. We are probably moving ever closer to the American situation where the bachelor's degree is a stepping stone to the masters programme, which is where academic weight and credibility is located. Lessons from the American experience are being considered in the major assessment of higher education at present being carried out by the Dearing Review. It would be ironic if, after many years of debate, nursing became an all-graduate profession only to find that the goal posts had moved. Whether this will prove to be the case remains to be seen.

Regardless of the recommendations it is clear that integration provides a different context in which reviews of, for example, Project 2000 will be interpreted and developed. Along with the introduction of the ETCs and continuing promotion of occupational standards as a common language and currency, the long-term direction of nurse training and education is probably less clear than it has been for some time. Added to this are the changes in the settings in which care is provided, especially with the promotion of a primary care led NHS.

Primary care led NHS

1996 saw the publication of three key documents in the ever increasing momentum towards a primary care led NHS. The first two, both published by the Audit Commission, outline a scenario in which resources move from the secondary to the primary sector and the difficulties associated with GP fundholding are identified in a way that enables local action plans to be drawn up to make fundholding more efficient and effective.

In the first document the Audit Commission reviews accident and emergency departments and a case is made for the contraction of facilities on a scale that could remove up to half the present available beds.[6] The implications of such a move upon the overall structure of health care are not explored in any detail but are likely to be considerable, not least for the infrastructure of secondary care locally where such facilities are removed and the increased demands placed upon local primary health care provision. It is for primary care that the second Audit Commission report on GP fundholding has a particular resonance.[7]

While the report does not question the principle and appropriateness of fundholding, it criticises the way that the scheme was introduced, in terms of both the speed of the changes associated with the initiative and the lack of preparation of GPs for their new roles and responsibilities. Particular emphasis is placed upon the lack of adequate piloting of the proposals, as with the introduction of Trusts, before they were adopted. This point has had a clear impact upon the third document, the government's White Paper on primary health care *Choice and Opportunity*.[8]

In the White Paper the government goes to great lengths to establish a framework that enables the proposals to be evaluated adequately before they are introduced. The proposals themselves centre around the rules and regulations of general practice and include consideration of: 'a salaried option for GPs, either within partnerships or with other bodies, such as NHS trusts ... practice based contracts ... a single budget for general medical services, other hospital and community health services, and prescribing with the practice responsible for purchasing or providing services within it'.[8]

Moreover, there is concern that there are 'disincentives for practices who want to replace a doctor with a nurse even where this might be more efficient and provide better patient services'.[8]

The implications of points such as these are considerable, not least for the impact upon professional relationships, both between and within professions. It is especially difficult, however, to begin to disentangle the complex strands in professional practice as it evolves in response to policy initiatives such as those outlined in this chapter.

Multi-disciplinary maze

The initiatives associated with occupational standards, ETCs, integration, and a primary care led NHS are very much the tip of the iceberg of activity in the NHS over the last 12 months. Nonetheless, together these initiatives outline what is increasingly becoming a complex multi-disciplinary mix where it is difficult for any one health care profession to ignore developments within the others.

When the NHS was created in 1948 it was possible for the medical profession, as the most powerful organised group in health care, largely to determine its own role within the new structures. Today it is still the most powerful group in health care but that power has begun to be curtailed. Patterns of demarcation are evolving and new rules are beginning to determine the contribution that any one profession can make to the design and delivery of health services. Former assumptions no longer apply. New alliances of cooperation need to be forged with the other health care professions; if they are not, there is a danger that the multi-disciplinary mix will become a multi-disciplinary maze where it is all too easy to lose direction.

REFERENCES

Harrison S, Pollitt C. Controlling health professionals: the future of work and organisation in the NHS. Buckingham: Open University Press, 1994.
NHS and Community Care Act, London: HMSO, 1990.
NHS Executive. Education and training planning guidance. EL(96)46. Leeds: NHSE, 1996: pp 6,7.
NHS Executive. Education and training in the new NHS. EL(95)27. Leeds: NHSE, 1995.
NHS Executive. Non-medical education and training — planning guidance for 1996/7 education commissioning. EL(95)96. Leeds: NHSE, 1995.
Audit Commission. By accident or design: improving A&E services in England and Wales. London: HMSO, 1996.

Audit Commission. What the doctor ordered: a study of GP fundholders in England and Wales. London: HMSO, 1996.

Department of Health. Choice and opportunity: primary care the future. London: HMSO, 1996: paras 2.4, 2.5.

2. Developments in commissioning and contracting in the NHS

Bob Hudson

Introduction: commissioning, contracting and the quasi-market

In the traditional organisation of the public sector, those who decided what was required were also responsible for running the organisations that provided it. It has been argued that this gave rise to two undesirable effects: firstly, a tendency for those responsible for the service to focus upon the organisation of provision rather than upon the needs to be met; secondly, a failure to specify the activities required of providers.

The emergence of 'government by contract'[1] is seen as a solution to these shortcomings. Work previously carried out directly by public sector organisations and controlled through organisational hierarchies is increasingly being carried out by contractors who are controlled through the terms of a contract. This is thought to imply a degree of separation between the parties to a contract — the 'purchaser-provider split'. In Britain, this represents an important extension of contracting — from relationships between private organisations and individuals, to relationships between public organisations and external contractors, and now to relationships between different parts of the same organisation. The application of this extension to the NHS has not been free of difficulty.

The early experience in health care

Much of the discussion on purchasing leverage is built upon the assumption that Health Commissions are the dominant purchasers of care. If they are not, then it is felt that their purchasing function will be weakened, for a single powerful purchaser is in a stronger position to negotiate better terms with suppliers and better able to plan future provision than would be the case with a diffuse set of buyers. In practice, the Health Commission purchasing role is not as dominant as the NHS White Paper seemed to assume. In particular, the role of GP fundholding has increased in both scale (by mid-1995, 41% of the population in England was served by a fundholding GP) and nature (with a choice of community, standard and total fundholding). Indeed, where 'total fundholding' has been established, covering the purchase of all secondary and community health care, the very continuation of Health Commissions may be called into question. Although supporters of fundholding such as Glennerster et al[2] argue that a multitude of rationing decisions made close to the user are a more accurate reflection of user preferences than 'some average arrived at in a district planner's office', this view is not universally held. Others point out that only Health Commissions undertake any kind of formal assessment of the needs of their catchment populations as a prior step to the negotiation of contracts with providers. Fundholders may still be inclined to base their purchasing decisions on historical patterns of demand combined with perceived efficiency savings. The truth, however, is probably that *all* purchasers of health care are still coming to terms with their new role. Most of the early emphasis was upon the providing role of self-governing Trusts, with purchasing wrongly seen as a relatively straightforward task. In reality, both purchasing and contracting are beset with a number of difficulties. The Audit Commission[3] identifies the following purchasing problems:

Inadequacy of epidemiological data. The most routinely available data relates to mortality rather than to the incidence of disease; for many common diseases, such as arthritis, mortality is not useful as an indicator of need. The use of data from GP practices can help, but systems are seldom compatible between practices, and those with good data tend not to be typical. Local surveys may be helpful, but will also be expensive.

Poor organisational integration. The Commission reported insufficient dialogue between those assessing needs and those with responsibility for actually implementing contracts with providers.

Inadequate measures of effectiveness. Conclusive evidence on the effectiveness of most services currently provided remains scarce; that which exists is often narrow in scope.

Variable spending levels. An early investigation by the Audit Commission found no model for the structure and staffing levels of purchasing bodies, and reported a variation between 0.5% and 2.0% in the costs devoted to the commissioning task.

As well as these general difficulties, a number of more specific problems with contracting have arisen; these are described below.

The amount of service required. Contracts have dealt with aggregate activity and have thereby been too blunt to obtain the changes needed, often simply rolling forward the previous year's figures.

Contract price. Pricing arrangements within some contracts have been single block payments which fail to reflect the wide range and unpredictable nature of work to be carried out. Such an arrangement may be convenient for cash-limited purchasers, but will not reflect the relationship between costs and activity levels facing providers.

Quality standards. To be effective, contracts have to specify quality as well as volume and costs, but quality remains difficult to define and measure.

Contract processes. Purchasers vary considerably in how much attention they pay to processes of negotiating and monitoring contracts. Timing may also be a problem. The Audit Commission suggests that a 'circle of uncertainty' can sometimes develop, with providers unwilling to quote prices until they know precisely what level of work to expect, and purchasers unable to commit themselves to a level of activity until they have prices from each provider to set against their available cash limit.

In addition to all of these obstacles to effective purchasing and contracting, there needs to be added the 'monopoly power' of most providers. This is partly a question of 'informational asymmetry', with providers possessing a much better knowledge of needs and clinical expertise than commissioners. More importantly, it is not normally possible for purchasers to encourage entry into the market. In particular, in markets for hospital services, the need for a minimum patient population size normally prevents hospitals locating in close proximity to each other, thereby leaving them relatively immune from competitive processes. In such circumstances, the purchaser-provider relationship needs to be based more upon trust and cooperation than competition.

New approaches to purchasing in the NHS

Although the purchasing role at Health Commission level has been relatively slow to develop, there have been innovations at a more devolved level associated with the fresh emphasis upon a primary care led NHS. For Higgins and Girling[4] these have provided an opportunity to shift the focus of strategic decision-making towards the notion of 'health gain' and towards greater accountability to local communities. They identify the following five broad approaches to a new form of 'locally sensitive purchasing'.

1. Locality-sensitive purchasing

In this approach, the purchasing decisions are retained by the central health commissioning agency, but geographical localities are used to sensitise the decisions by taking account of the views of those who live in or provide services to the locality. However, although intelligence gathering takes place at the local level, there is no devolution of budgets or purchasing power to these levels, and in this sense there is only a limited departure from the traditional centralist top-down culture.

2. Practice-sensitive purchasing

Here, the purchasing decisions are again retained at the health commissioning agency level, but are sensitised to the purchasing preferences of general practice, and may involve the setting up of notional practice-based budgets. In effect, practices indicate their service requirements and the health commissioning agencies act as purchasing brokers on their behalf. In this model, then, the locality plays a minor role, and the central relationship is between institutional purchasers and GPs.

3. Locality-based purchasing

In this model, purchasing decisions are taken at locality level. Higgins and Girling[4] identify two variants. In one, the purchasing decisions are made by locality purchasing managers deployed by the health commissioning agency working at geographical locality level. In the other, the purchasing decisions are made by a consortium of general practices, with the locality equating to the aggregate of the relevant practice populations.

4. Locality-based commissioning

This is a mixed model in which purchasing decisions taken at health commissioning agency level coexist with some commissioning activity undertaken at locality level. In particular, localities may take on a responsibility for service development and for developing community participation and self-help.

5. Practice-based purchasing

Finally there are those approaches in which purchasing decisions are taken at GP practice level — a model which encompasses GP fundholding in its current various formats. However, this approach entails a more strategic approach to needs identification and assessment than is usually the case with general practice, and also implies a greater degree of accountability than that currently in place.

Beyond the NHS: joint commissioning of health and social care

The links between health and social care are growing ever more tight and complex, with purchasing decisions taken by one agency typically having a knock-on effect on the other. However, the health and personal social services are seen as having major structural barriers rooted in history and bureaucratic politics, and as exhibiting different cultures and styles of management. The promise of joint commissioning is to offer several improvements upon this position: an avoidance of the wasteful use of resources; an end to arguments over service responsibility; and a means of curbing cost shunting between agencies. This is an agenda of high promise and ambition; despite the publication of practice guidance from the Department of Health in 1995, it is doubtful whether real progress has been made beyond a handful of enthusiasts.

The very nebulousness of joint commissioning means that it can operate at a range of different levels. Four distinct foci tend to be identified — user group, locality, issue-based, and individual.

User group focus

In user group commissioning, agencies commission a range of services for a particular user group. Typically this will cover some or all of the four traditional care groupings (learning disability, mental health, physical disability, old age), though there is growing recognition of other groups such as children with special needs, people with drug/alcohol problems and those with HIV/AIDS.

This reflects the organisation of traditional joint planning groups, which may well be used as the basis for a revised joint commissioning structure.

Locality focus

Joint commissioning with a locality focus would involve agencies commissioning specific services for a population within defined boundaries, typically based upon local electoral wards or GP surgeries. As with some of the NHS locality models, this is seen as more sensitive and responsive to the needs of local populations, though it may be difficult to apply in areas lacking natural communities with which people can identify.

Issue/service focus

In this model, authorities work together to commission a particular service which may then be used by more than one user group. Normally it would apply to services traditionally provided by a mixture of health and social services authorities such as day care, respite care, home care and equipment stores. Although this reflects main patterns of expenditure, it tends to be at odds with the current emphasis on a needs-based approach, as well as being limited in suitability for people requiring more than one service.

Individual focus

Individual-based commissioning requires authorities to commission a range of services for individuals through the care management system, with the possibility of pooled resources and joint purchasing arrangements for those users for whom there is a shared responsibility. In effect, this model constitutes a test of how well the new system of care management is working: if it is not effective on an intra-agency basis, then the likelihood of effective inter-agency care management is slight.

Evidence on the effectiveness of joint commissioning remains relatively scarce, but one early study by Hudson and Willis[5] identifies a number of general factors which were commonly influential in shaping the nature and extent of local joint commissioning activity:

Perceived significance of securing an impetus for change. In those authorities where significant progress had been secured, a number of factors seemed to have contributed towards the initial impetus for change. These included a shared vision on the part of senior management, a shared enthusiasm for operationalising the vision by second and third tier managers, coterminosity of health and local authority boundaries, and a willingness on the part of key stakeholders to adopt a medium-term perspective on likely benefits.

The centrality of trust. The concept of trust remains somewhat nebulous, but without it there can be no real impetus for change. Continuity of personnel was frequently mentioned as contributing towards the development of trust. Just as high trust is a precondition for successful joint commissioning, so joint commissioning cannot develop in a low-trust culture.

The significance of professional boundaries. In general, the more ambitious the joint commissioning remit, the greater the likelihood of a significant challenge to established boundaries. It is therefore important to see joint commissioning as being as much about how front-line providers relate to one another as about inter-organisational relationships between commissioners.

Impact of politics upon joint commissioning. The influence of politics is rarely explored in relation to joint commissioning, yet some models are tantamount to a major policy shift. Some localities seem to be unaffected by political intervention but, in others, joint commissioning has had to operate in a politically hostile climate.

The charging dilemma. The issue of charging was repeatedly raised, especially in those projects concerned with improving personal care at home. Various local devices were deployed to find a way round the problem, but the underlying dilemma of when to charge for a social care service and when to provide a service as free health care remains unresolved.

Engaging the interest of GPs. None of Hudson and Willis' fieldwork sites was able to report a sound relationship with GPs. Both fundholding and non-fundholding GPs are expected to play a much bigger role with the anticipated shift from secondary to primary care, but there was no clear way in which they collectively engaged in a dialogue with the other agencies who would need to be involved in this change.

The impact of external turbulence. A strong message coming from some localities was that joint commissioning had been hampered by external factors such as health service reorganisations, the restructuring of social services departments, the Local Government Review, and unpredictable annual changes to budgets.

External levers of change. There was a widespread view that joint commissioning had not been given sufficient weight by the Department of Health, and that greater encouragement could be given to enthusiasts and more sanctions applied to laggards. Among the suggestions were: greater flexibility on Section 28A transfers; ring-fenced money for joint commissioning; central resolution of the charging dilemma; and more robust monitoring of the use of the Department of Health Practical Guidance.

Conclusion

Although the 1990 NHS and Community Care Act critically depends upon different organisations working effectively together, the legislation also introduced new intersections between organisations which encourage competitive relationships. In particular, self-governing Trusts are free-standing bodies, and in a single locality may be separated into acute and community Trusts respectively; GP fundholders remain independent contractors who, while enjoying some control over health authority funds, are not adequately accountable to that authority for their use; and competition between providers from the statutory, voluntary and private sectors has been encouraged. In this turbulence, both health and social care purchasing agencies have found it difficult to step back and properly address a number of fundamental sequential questions about the commissioning task:

- *why* questions — why are commissioning (and joint commissioning) bodies in existence?
- *what* questions — what are the needs of the relevant population and what will be purchased?
- *how* questions — how will commissioning be operationalised and implemented?

The danger facing the commissioning role is that it focuses upon the third question without having addressed the first two. The next agenda is to shift the emphasis away from processes such as contracting and costing, and towards outcome-related commissioning.

REFERENCES

Stewart J. The limitations of government by contract. Public Money and Management 1993; July/September: 7–12.

Glennerster H, Matsaganis M, Owens P, Hancock S. Implementing GP fundholding: wild card or winning hand? Buckingham: Open University Press, 1994.

Audit Commission. Their health, your business: the new role of the District Health Authority. London: HMSO, 1992.

Higgins J, Girling J. Purchasing for health: the development of an idea. In: Harrison A, Bruscini S, eds. Health care UK 1993/4. London: King's Fund Institute, 1994.

Hudson B, Willis J. Analysis of joint commissioning developments in the Northern Region. Community Care Division, Nuffield Institute for Health, University of Leeds, 1995.

3. The need for evidence-based medicine

*David L. Sackett**

What is evidence-based medicine?

Evidence-based medicine (EBM), whose philosophical origins extend back to mid-nineteenth century Paris and earlier, is the conscientious, explicit and judicious use of current best evidence in making decisions about the care of individual patients.[1] The practice of evidence-based medicine means integrating individual clinical expertise with the best available external clinical evidence from systematic research. By individual clinical expertise we mean the proficiency and judgement that individual clinicians acquire through clinical experience and clinical practice. Increased expertise is reflected in many ways, but especially in more effective and efficient diagnosis and in the more thoughtful identification and compassionate use of individual patients' predicaments, rights, and preferences when making clinical decisions about their care. By best available external clinical evidence we mean clinically relevant research, often from the basic sciences of medicine, but especially from patient-centred clinical research into the accuracy and precision of diagnostic tests (including the clinical examination), the power of prognostic markers, and the efficacy and safety of therapeutic, rehabilitative, and preventive regimens. External clinical evidence both invalidates previously accepted diagnostic tests and treatments and replaces them with new ones that are more powerful, more accurate, more efficacious, and safer.

Good doctors use both individual clinical expertise and the best available external evidence; neither suffices on its own. Without clinical expertise, practice risks becoming tyrannised by evidence, for

* These ideas and suggestions have appeared in a number of other books and journals, among them the *Journal of the Royal Society of Medicine*, the *Journal of Public Health Medicine*, *Health Economics*, *Auditorium*, and several medical student journals.

23

even excellent external evidence may be inapplicable to or inappropriate for an individual patient. Without current best evidence, practice risks becoming rapidly out of date, to the detriment of patients.

The practice of EBM is a process of life-long, self-directed learning in which caring for our own patients creates the need for clinically important information about diagnosis, prognosis, therapy, and other clinical and health care issues, and in which we:

- convert these information needs into answerable questions
- track down, with maximum efficiency, the best evidence with which to answer them (whether from the clinical examination, the diagnostic laboratory, the published literature, or other sources)
- critically appraise that evidence for its validity (closeness to the truth) and usefulness (clinical applicability)
- apply the results of this appraisal in our clinical practice
- evaluate our performance.

What EBM is not

The above description of what evidence-based medicine is helps clarify what evidence-based medicine is not. Evidence-based medicine is neither old hat nor impossible to practise. The argument that 'everyone already is doing it' falls before evidence of striking variations in both the integration of patient values into our clinical behaviour[2] and in the rates with which clinicians provide interventions to their patients. The argument that evidence-based medicine can be conducted only from ivory towers and armchairs is refuted by audits in the front lines of clinical care where at least some inpatient clinical teams in general medicine,[3] psychiatry,[4] and surgery[5] have provided evidence-based care to the vast majority of their patients. Such studies show that busy clinicians who devote their scarce reading time to selective, efficient, patient-driven searching, appraisal and incorporation of the best available evidence can practise evidence-based medicine.

Evidence-based medicine is not 'cook-book' medicine; because it requires a bottom-up approach that integrates the best external evidence with individual clinical expertise and patient choice, it cannot result in slavish, cook-book approaches to individual patient care. External clinical evidence can inform, but never replace, individual clinical expertise, and it is this expertise that decides whether the external evidence applies to the individual patient at all and, if so, how it should be integrated into a clinical decision. Similarly, any external guideline must be integrated with individual clinical expertise in deciding how it matches the patient's clinical state, predicament, and preferences, and thus whether or not it should be applied. Clinicians who fear 'top-down cook-books' will find the advocates of evidence-based medicine joining them at the barricades.

Some fear that evidence-based medicine will be hijacked by purchasers and managers to cut the costs of health care. This would not only be a misuse of evidence-based medicine but suggests a fundamental misunderstanding of its financial consequences. Doctors practising evidence-based medicine will identify and apply the most efficacious interventions to maximise the quality and quantity of life for individual patients; this may raise rather than lower the cost of their care.

Evidence-based medicine is not restricted to randomised trials and meta-analyses. It involves tracking down the best external evidence with which to answer our clinical questions. To find out about the accuracy of a diagnostic test, we need to find proper cross-sectional studies of patients clinically suspected of harbouring the relevant disorder, not a randomised trial. For a question about prognosis, we need proper follow-up studies of patients assembled at a uniform, early point in the clinical course of their disease. Sometimes the evidence we need will come from the basic sciences such as genetics or immunology. It is when asking questions about therapy that we should try to avoid the non-experimental approaches, since these routinely lead to false-positive conclusions about efficacy. Because the randomised trial, and especially the systematic review of several randomised trials, is so much more likely to inform us and so much less likely to mislead us, it has become the 'gold standard' for judging whether a treatment does more good than harm. However, some questions about therapy do not require randomised trials (e.g. successful interventions for otherwise fatal conditions) or cannot wait for the trials to be conducted. If no randomised trial has been carried out for our patient's predicament, we follow the trail to the next best external evidence and work from there.

Why bother?

As physicians, whether serving individual patients or populations, we always have sought to base our decisions and actions on the best possible evidence; so why coin this phrase and push this terminology if there is nothing new here? There are five reasons:

- First, new types of evidence are now being generated which, when we know and understand them, effect frequent, major changes in the way that we care for our patients.
- Second, it is increasingly clear that, although we need (and our patients would benefit from) this new evidence daily, we usually fail to get it.
- Third, and as a result of the foregoing, both our up-to-date knowledge and our clinical performance deteriorate with time.
- Fourth, trying to overcome clinical entropy through traditional continuing medical education programmes does not improve our clinical performance.
- Fifth, a different approach to clinical learning has been shown to keep its practitioners up to date.

This different approach to clinical learning is called evidence-based medicine. However, before we go any further we want to stress that EBM builds on and reinforces, but never replaces, clinical skills, clinical judgement, and clinical experience. If you want to practise EBM, merge it with becoming the best history taker and clinical examiner you can be, incorporate it into becoming the most thoughtful diagnostician and therapist you can become, and consolidate it in your evolution into an effective, efficient, caring, and compassionate clinician.

A different approach to clinical learning has been shown to keep its practitioners up to date; recent developments and evaluations support the view that three EBM strategies can be successful in doing this. They consist of learning how to practise evidence-based medicine ourselves; seeking and applying evidence-based medical summaries produced by others; and accepting evidence-based practice protocols developed by our colleagues and augmented by strategies that help us improve our clinical performance.

Learning evidence-based medicine

The first effective strategy requires that we learn how to become life-long, self-directed learners of EBM as described above. Developed at McMaster University in Canada, and adopted and adapted at many other institutions around the world, this method of mastering life-long learning skills and habits has been evaluated in two sorts of ways. First, in a short-term trial among clinical clerks nearing graduation from medical school, clerks who received EBM-oriented clinical tutorials showed substantial improvements in their ability to generate and properly defend correct diagnostic and management decisions, while control clerks who received traditional clinical tutorials actually made worse clinical decisions after their clerkships than they did before (they had become less critical of advice provided by authorities).[6] Moreover, when McMaster graduates of the self-directed, problem-based EBM curriculum were compared with other Canadian medical graduates on their knowledge of clinically important advances in the detection, evaluation and management of hypertension, the latter group exhibited the usual, progressive deterioration in this measure of clinical competence, but the McMaster graduates remained at a high level and up to date, even 15 years after graduation.[7] Other programmes have shown that EBM skills can be mastered after several years out in practice (e.g. through journal clubs or less traditional, active programmes of continuing professional development).

Seeking and applying evidence-based medical summaries generated by others

The second effective strategy is incorporated by practitioners of the first, but also can be independently applied by those who, although unable to practise the full range of EBM themselves, desire to seek out and apply specific examples of EBM produced by others. In the past, this second group of clinicians was at the mercy of the throwaway journals, drug 'detailers', and traditional review articles, all of which have been discredited. For example, the traditional review article, in which an 'expert' states opinions about the proper evaluation and management of a condition, supporting key conclusions with selected references, has been shown to be both non-reproducible and, as a scientific exercise, of low mean scientific quality. One study showed that experts could not agree, even among themselves, about whether other experts who wrote review articles had:

a. conducted a competent search for relevant studies
b. generated a bias-free list of citations
c. appropriately judged the scientific quality of the cited articles
d. appropriately synthesised their conclusions.

Indeed, when these experts' own review articles were subjected to these same simple scientific principles, there was an inverse relationship between adherence to these standards and self-professed expertise (the correlation was –0.52 with an associated p-value of 0.004)![8]

Rather than relying on reviews of highly variable validity, clinicians seeking EBM now have two new information sources that are grappling with (and defeating) the problem of the sheer volume of clinical literature. The first is a new type of journal of secondary publication which originates with a team of librarians/ epidemiologists hand-searching dozens of clinical journals and selecting only those clinical articles (about diagnosis, prognosis, therapy, aetiology, prevention, quality improvement, continuing education, and economic analysis) that are scientifically sound and whose conclusions are likely to be valid. These articles are passed on to a panel of front-line physicians, who pick out those articles they judge to be clinically important. These rigorous scientific and clinical filters reject 98% of the clinical literature; it is the remaining 2% that appears in the form of structured abstracts, accompanied by commentaries from clinical experts that place them in their appropriate clinical context, and introduced by declarative titles that tell readers, up front, their clinical 'bottom lines'. The first of these publications, *ACP Journal Club* (*ACPJC*), is for general internists and began publication in 1991 from the American College of Physicians (ACP). A sibling publication, *Evidence-Based Medicine*, combines a subset of *ACPJC* abstracts with those derived from journals in general practice, surgery, obstetrics and gynaecology, paediatrics, and psychiatry. Begun in 1995, *EBM* is a joint venture of the British Medical Journal Publications Group and the ACP.

The second new information source for clinicians seeking EBM is even more systematic. It is an outgrowth of the scientific methods developed to combine (into overviews or 'meta-analyses') the growing numbers of randomised trials of the same or similar treatments for the same health condition. When properly carried out on as high a proportion as possible of all relevant trials (since *MEDLINE* misses about half the published trials,[9] detailed journal searching, often by hand, is required to avoid bias) these systematic reviews provide the most accurate and authoritative guides to therapy. The performance of systematic reviews of therapy is so logical a step in progress towards evidence-based health care that it has become the focus of a rapidly growing international group of clinicians, methodologists, and consumers who have formed the Cochrane Collaboration. The systematic reviews that are beginning to flow from this unselfish collaboration form the *Cochrane Database of Systematic Reviews (CDSR)*. The *CDSR* is updated each time an important new trial is reported, and the reviews are providing the highest levels of evidence ever achieved on the efficacy of preventive, therapeutic, and rehabilitative regimens. They are published on computer diskette and compact disk, on the Internet, and in a variety of other forms (including the *EBM* journals of secondary publication).[10] A related set of systematic reviews are prepared by the NHS Centre for Reviews and Dissemination at the University of York in England, and these, along with two other databases, are published alongside the *CDSR*. Further information about these four databases, which together comprise the *Cochrane Library*, is provided in the Appendix (pp. 30–31).

Thus, busy clinicians seeking clinical 'bottom lines' will increasingly be able to eschew non-expert 'expert' reviews and self-serving commercial sources and find brief but valid summaries of best evidence on a growing array of clinical topics, appraised according to uniform scientific principles.

Accepting evidence-based practice protocols developed by colleagues

Regardless of whether clinicians practise or seek out EBM, they can still practise up-to-date medicine by adopting evidence-based practice protocols and submitting themselves to strategies that have been proven (in randomised trials, of course!) to alter clinical practice for the better[11], by:

1. receiving individualised audit and feedback about what we are doing right and wrong (the growing use of computers in clinical practice enhances the potential effectiveness of this strategy[12])
2. receiving advice from a respected teacher (who has learned EBM)
3. being visited by a non-commercial 'detailer' (who is informing and encouraging us about specific evidence-based ways of caring for patients rather than exhorting us to prescribe specific drugs)
4. taking a 'mini-sabbatical' or preceptorship in a place where EBM is practised.

These strategies have been shown to be effective in helping us overcome at least some of the barriers imposed by both the lack of clinically important information and the social and professional context within which we practise medicine, and can help us move from opinion-based practice towards evidence-based medicine.

REFERENCES

Sackett DL, Richardson WS, Rosenberg W, Haynes RB. Evidence-based medicine: how to practice and teach. Evidence-Based Medicine 1996.

Weatherall DJ. The inhumanity of medicine. British Medical Journal 1994; 308: 1671–1672.

Ellis J, Mulligan I, Rowe J, Sackett DL. Inpatient general medicine is evidence based. Lancet 1995; 346: 407–410.

Geddes JR, Game D, Jenkins NE, Peterson LA, Pottinger GR, Sackett DL. Inpatient psychiatric care is evidence-based. Proceedings of the Royal College of Psychiatrists' Winter Meeting. Stratford, UK. January 23–25, 1996.

McCulloch P. Personal communication, 1995.

Bennett KJ, Sackett DL, Haynes RB, Neufeld VR. A controlled trial of teaching critical appraisal of the clinical literature to medical students. Journal of the American Medical Association 1987; 257: 2451–2454.

Shin JH, Haynes RB, Johnston ME. Effect of problem-based, self-directed undergraduate education on life-long learning. Canadian Medical Association Journal 1993; 148: 969–976.

Oxman A, Guyatt GH. The science of reviewing research. Annals of the New York Academy of Science 1993; 703: 125–134.

Dickersin K, Sherer R, Lefebvre C. Identifying relevant studies for systematic reviews. British Medical Journal 1994; 309: 1286–1291.

Fullerton-Smith I. How members of the Cochrane Collaboration prepare and maintain systematic reviews of the effects of health care. Evidence-Based Medicine 1995; 1: 7–8.

Davis DA, Thomson MA, Oxman AD, Haynes RB. Evidence for the effectiveness of CME. A review of 50 randomized controlled trials. Journal of the American Medical Association 1992; 268: 1111–1117.

Johnston ME, Langton KB, Haynes RB. Effects of computer-based clinical decision support systems on clinician performance and patient outcome. A critical appraisal of research. Annals of International Medicine 1994; 120: 135–142.

APPENDIX — THE COCHRANE LIBRARY

The *Cochrane Library* is a regularly updated electronic library designed to provide users with the evidence needed for informed decision making. Launched in April 1995 under the name the *Cochrane Database of Systematic Reviews*, it has now been renamed to reflect the inclusion of further related databases, making it the most comprehensive source of evidence for all those with an interest in evidence-based health care.

The *Cochrane Library* now contains four databases:

- the *Cochrane Database of Systematic Reviews (CDSR)*
- the *York Database of Abstracts of Reviews of Effectiveness (DARE)*
- the *Cochrane Controlled Trials Register (CCTR)*
- the *Cochrane Review Methodology Database (CRMD)*.

A new simplified interface has made the *Cochrane Library* more user friendly by allowing users to enter a search term and with one key stroke retrieve all reviews on that topic, together with the most complete list of trials available on any database. The *Cochrane Library* is available in CD ROM for Windows and in 3.5 inch disk for Windows.

For further information about the Library's four databases and its annual subscription rates, please contact the BMJ Publishing Group, PO Box 295, London WC1H 9TE; tel: 0171 383 6185/6245; fax: 0171 383 6662.

4. Recent developments in resource allocation and budget setting in the NHS

Stuart Peacock

Introduction

In 1995 the NHS Executive implemented modifications to the way in which funds for Hospital and Community Health Services are distributed in England.[1] Hospital and Community Health Services (HCHS) accounts for about 77% of total NHS expenditure in England (£21.4 billion in 1992/93). Since 1976 funds have been allocated according to a weighted capitation formula designed to distribute resources on the basis of the health needs of the population, and this principle of a weighted capitation formula has remained intact since then. A major contribution to the most recent review of the weighted capitation formula was some technical work commissioned by the Executive from a team of health economists and statisticians at the University of York.[2]

Principles of resource allocation in the NHS

In all aspects of the provision of health care services there is a need for central budget holding bodies to allocate resources on a rational basis. Some form of equity judgement, whether implicit or explicit, is always present in the allocation process. The founding principles of the National Health Service included the notion of equality of access for those with equal need. This equity judgement has remained pivotal in recent resource allocation mechanisms.

In the formative years of the health service much of the health and social services budget was distributed to areas on the basis of incremental adjustments on past expenditure. This system tended to reward areas with already high availability of health care services, and created perverse incentives to inflate expenditure levels to attract larger budget allocations. This resulted in perceived inequalities in the provision of health care and led to the establishment of a system of allocating resources through weighted capitation formulae. Such formulae indicate how much an area would spend if it were to provide some standard level of health care with a standard level of efficiency, whilst taking into account the area's demographic and social characteristics.

The first formula was developed by the Resource Allocation Working Party (RAWP) in the early 1970s and covered the HCHS sector. The remit was to correct existing inequalities in the pattern of resource distribution, and to construct an allocation mechanism which was responsive to populations' health needs. The conclusions of the RAWP group were that resources should be allocated to Regional Health Authorities on the basis of population weighted (or adjusted) for three factors:

1. differences in the *age/sex structure* between areas
2. differences in the *need* for health care between areas
3. unavoidable *geographical* differences in the costs of providing services.

The RAWP group recommended weighting for morbidity using condition-specific Standardised Mortality Ratios (SMRs) as a proxy for differential health needs of populations.[3] The formula assumed that the need for health care had a one-to-one relationship with SMR in the absence of empirical evidence to suggest otherwise. The allocations based on the final formula were used as targets, on which regions would converge over a number of years.

In 1985 the government announced a review of RAWP to 'fine tune' the formula to be more responsive to needs,[4,5] and it was on the basis of this review that a new formula was introduced in 1990 and remained in force until 1994. The review was conducted by constructing an empirically based model to analyse the determinants of hospital utilisation in small areas (electoral wards).[6] By explaining variations in utilisation patterns across England the authors sought to find the underlying health needs which drive the use of health care services. The review of RAWP recommended that the new formula should use all-cause SMR as a measure of needs, that the weight on SMR should be reduced, and that the formula should also include the Jarman index of social deprivation. The government chose to implement these recommendations only partially, omitting the Jarman index and changing the weight on SMR. Under the formula regions were given discretion as to how revenue allocations were made to DHAs. A range of sub-regional allocation mechanisms has resulted. A fuller review of resource allocation methods has been given by Mays and Bevan.[7]

The review of RAWP came under fierce criticism, resulting in a further revision of the national formula. The health needs component of the new formula is based on the empirical analysis at York. The new weighted capitation formula consists of four elements:

- population
- an age adjustment
- a needs adjustment
- a cost adjustment (or market forces factor).

The formula can be expressed simply in terms of the calculation of the weighted population of each area in the allocation mechanism. If the weighted population is termed WP then the formula can be written:

$$WP = POP \times (1+a) \times (1+n) \times (1+c)$$

where:

POP = the population of the area
a = the adjustment for age structure
n = the adjustment for needs
c = the cost adjustment.

The national average values for a, n, and c are zero. Each area therefore has a measure of its weighted population for health care relative to its actual population. The HCHS budget is then divided according to the weighted populations of all areas.

A major point to note about the weighted capitation formula is that each of the three adjustments is treated independently. An area may have a relatively young population, leading to a negative value of a. At the same time, the area may also experience high morbidity, leading to a positive value of n. Finally, depending on local labour and capital costs, the area may have either a negative or a positive cost adjustment factor c. Any one authority may therefore have some parts of the formula working to increase its revenue share, while other parts serve to reduce it.

For example, consider a health authority with a relatively young population, for which per capita health care needs are estimated to be 4% below the national average. This leads to an age weighting of 0.96. However, given its age structure, the authority has a relatively needy population, with morbidity 11% above the national average.

This leads to a needs weighting of 1.11. Finally, the authority is in a part of the country where the cost of purchasing a given package of health care is estimated to be 15% above the national average. This leads to a cost weighting of 1.15. The approximate net effect of these three considerations is to give each person in the authority a *weighting* of:

$$0.96 \times 1.11 \times 1.15 = 1.225$$

That is, for every person in the population, the authority will receive about 22.5% more than the national average per capita allocation. Hence the expression *weighted capitation*.

It is important to keep in mind that the weighted populations only indicate targets on which revenue shares might be expected to converge over the years. Actual allocations will move towards targets at a speed determined by the government.

Under the new formula the age and cost adjustments have been developed by the Department of Health. The age adjustment is based on an age/cost curve which estimates the relationship between age and resource use by individuals using broad age group bands. The cost adjustment has been termed the consolidated market forces factor, and accounts for geographical differences in the cost of labour and capital. The most important part of the weighting mechanism, however, is the needs adjustment. The remainder of this chapter focuses on this element of the formula.

The York Study

The work undertaken at the University of York was commissioned to address several methodological and statistical shortcomings identified in earlier formulae.[8, 9] It also allowed the study group to make use of up-to-date information from the 1991 census which was previously unavailable.

The empirical study was based on the notion of identifying a national 'average' response (in terms of inpatient utilisation) to variations in health care needs. Two types of determinant of demand were considered important in causing utilisation: the health care needs of the population, and the supply of health care facilities. The need for health care is an elusive concept which cannot be measured directly. However, it is possible to construct a wide range of potential indicators of need, including indirect social determinants of demand for health care as well as direct measures of health status. The consideration of supply reflects the widely held belief that the availability of health care services affects demand for those services. Potentially this occurs in two ways: firstly, in situations of excess demand utilisation may be suppressed due to constraints in supply; secondly, there is evidence which suggests that the supply of physicians can induce demand.[10] The intention was therefore to construct a statistical model relating utilisation to indicators of health care needs and supply. A full description of the modelling techniques employed is given elsewhere.[2,11] The theoretical model employed is shown in Figure 4.1.

The model suggests that the level of utilisation in an area is determined by the availability of health care to that area, and the health care needs of the population. The supply of health care to an area is determined by needs and utilisation (since earlier allocation mechanisms distributed funds on the basis of needs and utilisation), and by other socioeconomic characteristics of that area which may shape the pattern of health care provision. The study recognized that health needs influence utilisation both directly (arrow a), and indirectly (arrow c), and allowed for the full effects of needs to be captured in modelling. The analysis produced a new formula based on two separate elements: the acute model and the psychiatric model. Each contains SMR and a cluster of census-based needs variables which were found to be most important in the empirical analysis. Tables 4.1 and 4.2 show the health and social variables used in the York formulae.

The most noteworthy features of the models are the strong

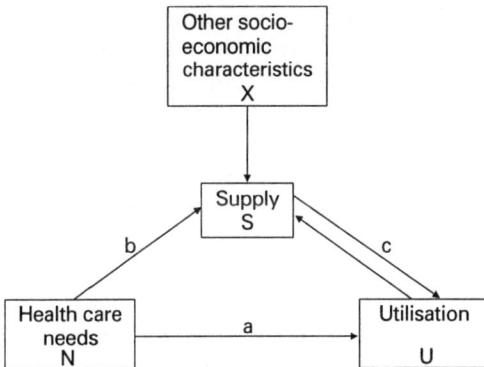

Fig. 4.1 The demand for health care,

Table 4.1 Acute model

Variable
• Standardised Mortality Ratio (under 75)
• Standardised limiting longstanding illness (under 75)
• Proportion of pensionable age living alone
• Proportion of dependants in single carer households
• Proportion of economically active who are unemployed

Table 4.2 Psychiatric model

Variable
• Standardised Mortality Ratio (under 75)
• Proportion of persons in lone parent families
• Proportion born in New Commonwealth
• Proportion of adult population permanently sick
• Proportion of dependants with no carer
• Proportion of pensionable age living alone

impact of self-reported illness amongst those aged under 75 in the acute model, and the continued presence of the under-75 SMR in both models.[12] The proportion of elderly people living alone was also found to be a strong determinant of utilisation and appears in both models.

The analysis considered many alternative measures of health status and social conditions. It is important to recognise that just because a specific variable is not explicitly included in the models does not mean that it is ignored. It is likely that a specific variable will be correlated with the chosen factors to a greater or lesser extent, and so its impact may well be accounted for in the models. For example, although substandard housing conditions do not appear in either model, these might be highly correlated with, for instance, the 'proportion of pensionable age living alone' variable, and so their impact will (to the extent of that correlation) be captured in the models. In practice, it can be considered unlikely that the models fail to capture any major dimension of needs.

The York work was based on utilisation of NHS inpatient facilities, which comprise about 45% of the HCHS. In implementing the work, the Department of Health had to decide which needs model to apply to the various other programmes which make up the remainder of the HCHS, such as outpatient and day case services, mental handicap services, community services and maternity services.

The Department has chosen to split total HCHS activity into three categories:

1. an *acute* sector, which includes acute inpatients and outpatients, geriatrics, ambulance services and maternity, and represents 64% of expenditure
2. a *psychiatric* sector (including psychiatric inpatients and outpatients and community services) which represents 12% of expenditure
3. an *other* sector, representing 24% of expenditure.

The acute model is used to distribute the acute block of funds and the psychiatric model is used to distribute the psychiatric block of funds. The Department has chosen to apply no needs weighting at all to the 'other' block, which comprises mental handicap, general community services, other hospital and administrative services, and a miscellany of smaller items. The details of the three blocks are shown elsewhere.[1] The decision to disaggregate the HCHS budget in this way should be seen in the light of the previous system, in which the 'square root of under-75 SMR' was applied to the entire HCHS budget.

Implications of the new formula

Assessment of the impact on District allocations of the new needs indices is complicated by two factors. Firstly, the previous system allocated funds to Regions which adopted a variety of methods for allocating to Districts. Secondly, Districts' allocations may have been different to the targets implied by the Regional allocation formulae.

For simplicity, the comparison presented below ignores the Regional tier by comparing the impact of the new arrangements with the use of the square root of SMR (under 75) applied to Districts directly. There is no suggestion that previous allocations were in accordance with this use of the SMR; the comparisons are intended simply to highlight the geographical implications of the new formula compared to the old, without considering actual allocations.

In order to illustrate the implications of the York models, and policy choices concerning the construction of the national formula, analysis is presented for a sample of six Districts (boundaries as at April 1992). Table 4.3 shows data for Liverpool, Central Manchester, and City and Hackney, three of the poorest inner city

Table 4.3   Needs as a percentage of national average in six Districts

	Old formula (square root of SMR index)	York acute index	York psychiatric index	DoH formula (24% no weight)	Full needs formula (24% acute weight)
Liverpool Central	114.7	121.8	146.0	119.5	124.7
Manchester	122.7	129.7	208.1	132.0	139.1
City & Hackney	112.5	121.0	181.3	123.2	128.2
Huntingdon	89.0	86.7	63.4	87.1	83.9
Mid Surrey	89.9	82.2	73.6	85.4	81.2
Tunbridge Wells	91.1	86.3	69.0	87.5	84.2

areas; and Huntingdon, Mid Surrey, and Tunbridge Wells, three affluent Districts. Full results for all Districts have been published elsewhere.[13]

The impact of the various needs indices is shown as a percentage of the national average per capita. Thus the national per capita average is 100, and the figure of 122.7 under the old square root of SMR formula for Central Manchester implies that the District would get 22.7% per capita more than the national average. The York acute model is slightly more redistributive than the old formula, giving Central Manchester an index of 129.7. In general, the new acute index results in modest swings in allocation from low needs to high needs areas. In contrast the psychiatric model is strongly redistributive, drawing a very sharp distinction between areas with high needs (predominantly inner cities) and the shire areas.[13] Central Manchester has more than double the national average level of psychiatric need with an index of 208.1, three times that of Huntingdon.

As noted above, in implementing the York indices, the Department of Health has chosen to apply a weight of 0.64 to the acute index, 0.12 to the psychiatric index, and 0.24 to the no needs index (effectively an index of 100 for every District in England). For example, in Central Manchester, the Department formula results in a combined index of:

$$(129.7 \times 0.64) + (208.1 \times 0.12) + (100.0 \times 0.24) = 132.0$$

Most interest in the NHS has centred around the gainers and losers relative to the previous square root of SMR-based index. Table 4.3 confirms that use of the new formula results in substantial gains for inner city areas at the expense of shire areas. Loosely speaking, gaining areas experience an SMR which is low relative to its health care needs, whilst losing areas experience an SMR which overstates their health care needs.

The decision by the Department of Health to apply no needs weighting to 24% of HCHS expenditure is likely to be a controversial feature of the new formula. For example, it can be argued that the 'community', 'other hospital' and 'administrative' categories of expenditure are likely to be proportional to hospital use, as indicated by the York needs indices, rather than proportional to crude population. In the absence of any more persuasive evidence, it can be argued that use of one or both of the York needs indices may be preferable to using no needs weighting for these categories. Similarly, although there is no evidence that the prevalence of mental handicap is associated with social conditions, it is plausible to suggest that the resource implications of mental handicap for the NHS are highest in areas with high levels of poverty; for example, carers in more affluent areas may make greater use of private provision.

Clearly there is room for debate about how to weight the 24% (and indeed about how to weight services such as geriatrics and maternity which are currently given the acute weight). In order to illustrate the importance of this issue, Table 4.3 presents results where the Department of Health formula has been amended so that the 24% of expenditure allocated with no needs weighting is instead weighted by the York acute index. That is, 88% of HCHS expenditure is allocated according to the York acute model and 12% according to the psychiatric model. This has been called the 'full' needs formula. To return to the previous example, the Central Manchester needs index becomes:

$$(129.7 \times 0.88) + (208.1 \times 0.12) = 139.1$$

This calculation allows estimation of the impact of the policy decision to apply zero needs weighting to 24% of expenditure. The Department of Health index gives a needs score of 132.0 to Central Manchester, 5.1% lower than the full needs index. Conversely, Mid Surrey gains 5.2% compared to the full needs index.

Conclusions

This chapter has sought to explain the principles of macro level resource allocation in the NHS and to shed light on the redistributive effects of the new formula for distributing HCHS funds to health authorities. Under the new Department of Health formula a large volume of HCHS funds will be redistributed between health authorities. The York team have estimated that £776m of the £21 000m allocated under the new formula will be redistributed from low to high needs areas on the basis of the new needs indices. This represents a swing of £261m from the old square root of SMR formula, illustrating the extent to which funds would have been inequitably distributed under the old system.

The decision of the Department of Health to apply a zero needs weight to 24% of expenditure considerably dilutes the redistributive impact of the new formula. The treatment of this 'other' block of services is therefore of crucial importance. It is not suggested that use of the acute model to allocate the problematic 24% is necessarily appropriate; for example, some of the services may be better allocated using the psychiatric model, which would result in even larger swings than those shown in Table 4.3. The zero weighting may indeed be more suitable for some services. However, the large swings shown in the table do highlight the sensitivity of allocations to how the 24% is treated. There is an urgent need for research on determinants of need in this large block of services. To this end, the implementation of the new formula has come under close scrutiny from the House of Commons Select Committee on Health, and the Department of Health has recently expressed its intention to review the allocation of the currently unweighted 24%.

The analysis presented above refers to targets on which Districts will be expected to converge over a number of years. Much depends on the speed at which Ministers choose to phase in the new formula. In fact, they can hardly be said to be implementing the new arrangements zealously. The 1995/96 Regional allocations were simply a 3.55% cash increase on the previous year's, and therefore make no acknowledgement of the new formula.[14] At the subregional level, however, the new Regions do appear to be adopting the new needs formula. Widespread evidence of Districts using the needs indices to allocate funds to localities and fundholding practices is also emerging. With the need for locality budgeting rising as Districts merge, and the advent of total fundholding, it appears that weighted capitation will have an increasingly significant role in subdistrict budget setting. Moreover, whilst initial attempts to derive a satisfactory national formula for fundholders failed,[15] the York study team has recently been able to confirm that the use of the acute index is indeed appropriate for allocations to fundholders.

It must be recognised that the resource allocation process is ultimately highly political. What matters is that the basis of the political choices is completely understood so that it can be debated in an informed manner. The resource allocation issue is highly important to the NHS for several reasons. The most obvious is simply that a good mechanism will secure a fair allocation of resources, which should follow the founding principles of the NHS. Aside from equity arguments, it is also inefficient to misdirect resources towards areas that can make less good use of the funds than areas deprived of funds. It is also important for the NHS as a whole that all areas suffer equal pain from cash limits applied to the service. This helps to ensure that all Members of Parliament can expect to get their fair share of complaints from constituents, and the government of the day may therefore receive accurate messages about the electorate's preferred level of overall funding for the NHS.

REFERENCES

NHS Executive. HCHS Revenue Resource Allocation. Weighted Capitation Formula. NHS Executive, 1994.

Carr-Hill RA, Hardman G, Martin S, Peacock S, Sheldon TA, Smith P. A formula for distributing NHS revenues based on small areas use of hospital beds. Centre for Health Economics, Occasional Paper. York: University of York, 1994.

Department of Health and Social Security. Sharing resources for health in England. Report of the Resource Allocation Working Party. London: HMSO, 1976.

Department of Health and Social Security. Review of the Resource Allocation Working Party Formula: interim report by the NHS Management Board. London: DHSS, 1986.

Department of Health and Social Security. Review of the Resource Allocation Working Party Formula: final report by the NHS Management Board. London: DHSS, 1988.

Coopers and Lybrand. Integrated analysis for the Review of RAWP. London: Coopers and Lybrand, 1988.

Mays N, Bevan G. Resource allocation in the Health Service. Occasional Paper in Social Administration 81. London: Bedford Square Press, 1987.

Mays N. NHS resource allocation after the 1989 White Paper: a critique of the research for the RAWP review. Community Medicine 1989; 11: 173–186.

Sheldon TA, Carr-Hill RA. Resource allocation by regression in the NHS: a statistical critique of the RAWP review. Journal of the Royal Statistical Society (A) 1992; 155: 403–420.

Cromwell J, Mitchell JB. Physician-induced demand for surgery. Journal of Health Economics 1986; 5: 293–313.

Carr-Hill RA, Sheldon TA, Smith P, Martin S, Peacock S, Hardman G. Allocating resources to Health Authorities: development of method for small area analysis of use of inpatient services. British Medical Journal 1994; 309: 1046–1049.

Smith P, Sheldon TA, Carr-Hill RA, Martin S, Peacock S, Hardman G. Allocating resources to Health Authorities: results and policy implications of small area analysis of use of inpatient services. British Medical Journal 1994; 309: 1050–1054.

Peacock S, Smith P. The resource allocation consequences of the new NHS needs formula. Centre for Health Economics, Discussion Paper 134. York: University of York, 1995.

NHS Executive. 1995–96 cash limits exposition booklet. NHS Executive, 1994.

Sheldon TA, Smith P, Borowitz M, Martin S, Carr-Hill RA. Attempt at deriving a capitation formula for setting general practitioner fundholding budgets. British Medical Journal 1994; 309: 1059–1064.

5. Capital investment in the NHS

Diana Sanderson

Introduction

Recent years have seen considerable changes to the nature and funding of capital developments in the NHS. Historically, the NHS has placed considerable emphasis on the acquisition of capital assets. Until 1991, when capital charges were introduced, capital was effectively a 'free good', and the NHS had an excess of buildings and much surplus land. Furthermore, many hospital buildings were old — some even having been built as workhouses in the Victorian era — and in poor condition. Money for capital developments was allocated to Regions, and was bid for by health authorities via Approval in Principle documents. Developments generally took many years to reach fruition, and many fell by the wayside.

Two significant changes have occurred during the 1990s: the requirement to develop business cases in order to gain approval for capital developments, and the need to explore private finance opportunities. This chapter describes the changes that have taken place recently with regard to capital investment in the NHS. In order to prepare a sound business case, it is essential for managers and doctors to work closely together, especially for certain parts of the process.

The pre-1991 system and its shortcomings

Prior to 1991, capital development monies were allocated to Regions on a weighted population basis. Districts (which were responsible for their Directly Managed (hospital) Units) would bid for these monies by preparing an Approval in Principle document. This required an option appraisal to be undertaken to identify the most appropriate development. Option appraisal was formally introduced into the NHS in 1981 to try to ensure that careful consideration was given to capital requirements before building started, and that the 'costs' and 'benefits' had been assessed and the risks identified. The 1970s had seen many hospital building projects run into financial problems of varying degrees of severity, those encountered by the Liverpool Teaching Hospital project being particularly significant.

The Regions inevitably received requests for far more capital developments than they could fund with their limited allocations, and so many bids were unsuccessful. The Regions rarely seemed to make their choices about which schemes to fund in an explicit manner, the allocation of funds resembling something of a lottery, at least to those whose bids were regularly unsuccessful. In some Regions, an informal 'queuing' system emerged, with Districts knowing that it would be their 'turn' for a major slice of the budget in a particular year. Alternatively, large schemes were sub-divided into 'phases', so that everybody, in theory, could regularly receive a small slice of the cake. In practice, however, many of the latter phases did not receive any funding, resulting in 'dozens of hospitals ... (being) ... frozen in some "interim phase"',[1] which made them impossible to run efficiently. This process meant that schemes were often out of date if and when they were finished, and indeed in many cases they were out of date by the time approval to start was granted. Furthermore, capital, once acquired, was effectively a 'free good', which enhanced its attractiveness. There were no incentives to use capital efficiently and effectively.

Although 'private finance' is a term that has only recently entered the day-to-day vocabulary of the NHS, it is interesting to note that partnerships between health authorities and the private sector were first advocated by Kenneth Clarke when he was health minister in 1985, when such ventures were reckoned to have a potential value of £400m. Then, in 1989, the White Paper *Working for Patients*[2] — the document that heralded so many fundamental changes to the NHS — made this desire more explicit by emphasising the government's desire to encourage partnerships involving the private sector:

As health authorities become more business-like in their approach to the provision of services, and to the use of the resources at their disposal, they are increasingly looking at the scope for involving the private sector. Examples include joint ventures where the NHS provides land and a developer puts up a building, or where a major service is contracted out to the private sector. There may also be opportunities for an authority to work with a private developer to achieve a net saving. The Government is determined to encourage these schemes whenever they are consistent with value for money and the proper control of public expenditure.

In recognition 'that a degree of misunderstanding has existed in the NHS over the earlier guidance', the Department of Health published EL(89)MB142, *Use of Private Sector Capital in the NHS (unconventional finance)* in October 1989.[3] The term 'unconventional finance' was applied 'to any means of obtaining the ownership and/or use of capital assets other than by direct purchase financed from allocations, receipts or donations'. The two key concerns were 'value for money' and 'proper control of public expenditure'. The importance of 'value for money' was stressed, for, given that the government is usually able to borrow at lower interest rates than the private sector, other benefits would be needed to offset the extra financial cost if such a scheme were to be cost-effective for the NHS.

Retaining control of public expenditure was also seen to be vital, and the government was keen to ensure that 'unconventional finance cannot be used as a means of circumventing Government decisions on the rate of capital formation in the public sector'. The guidance therefore stated that, if a health authority acquired an asset through unconventional finance arrangements that it would otherwise have purchased using conventional finance, the Department of Health might offset the capital allocation to the Regional Health Authority concerned 'to reflect the fact that private finance obviates the need for a capital payment'.[3] Given that the demand for new capital developments always far outstripped the Regional allocations, these two requirements led to anomalous situations. For example, a health authority could clearly demonstrate that a particular development employing unconventional finance delivered excellent value for money, but be opposed by the Regional Health Authority. The RHA might agree that the proposed development was indeed desirable, but oppose because the resulting reduction in their capital allocation would prevent them from funding one of their preferred developments.

Initially, the post-White Paper era, with its emphasis on competition, choice and the efficient use of resources, seemed to provide considerable scope for joint ventures between the NHS and the private and/or voluntary sectors. Exploring the possibilities for joint ventures for the care of elderly people was particularly popular (especially given the poor quality of much NHS estate being used to provide long-term care at the time), but overall progress was slower than had been expected and hoped, with negotiations requiring considerable amounts of hard work, commitment and perseverance. Furthermore, in some cases, concerns were raised about conflicts between public accountability and commercial confidentiality — not disclosing contract details could lead to accusations of secrecy and lowering standards of care. Above all, however, considerable confusion seemed to exist in the Department of Health itself about unconventional finance, which probably explains why so few joint ventures came to fruition at this time. Schemes attempting to respond to the challenges of *Working for Patients* appeared to be being strangled at birth by 'parental' red tape and bureaucracy.

Capital charges

During this period another significant development was in its formative stage. The concept of capital charges was introduced to the NHS during 1989, and implemented on 1 April 1991. In the time between their conception and birth, a comprehensive exercise was undertaken across the country to collate an equipment assets register for each health authority (remember, we are still in the pre-Trust era where hospitals are Directly Managed Units — DMUs). These asset registers covered equipment or 'groups of equipment', valued at £1000 or more, used for the provision of health care — there were some interesting discussions about the grouping of items such as tables and chairs at the time! They were then coupled with land, building and engineering services valuations provided by the District Valuer's office for each health service site to give the total asset value on which capital charges were to be made.

Capital charges were introduced partly to make NHS overheads more comparable with those in the private health care sector, and thus 'level the playing field' with regard to unconventional finance. More importantly, perhaps, they were also intended to impose real financial incentives to use NHS capital more efficiently and effectively — the days of capital as a gift from the state were over. Capital charges, which currently amount to around £2.3 billion,[4] are essentially a circular flow around the system. The Trusts, having raised them through their charges to their purchasers, have to pay them to the Treasury, who in turn allocate resources to the health authorities. Nevertheless, despite being 'nominal' rather than 'real' payments, their introduction has forced Trusts to reassess their capital assets and requirements. Large new capital developments may initially seem very attractive, especially given the NHS's 'obsession with investing in bricks, mortar and equipment',[1] but will not remain so if they raise prices so high that the

Trust becomes uncompetitive. Beliefs and behaviour regarding capital investments have undoubtedly changed as a consequence of the introduction of capital charges.

The Capital Investment Manual

The publication of the long-awaited *Capital Investment Manual* (CIM)[5] in June 1994 was the next major milestone during the 1990s. This manual comprises an overview and seven separate, though inter-related, guides to practitioners, entitled:

- *Project Organisation*
- *Private Finance Guide*
- *Business Case Guide*
- *Management of Construction Projects*
- *IM&T Guidance*
- *Commissioning a Health Care Facility*
- *Post-project Evaluation.*

Some highly publicised examples during the early 1990s of total failure to adequately monitor and control the delivery of some major capital schemes, especially those involving major IT systems, were partly responsible for causing the amendment and replacement of the earlier guidance. In addition, the creation of the internal market had given Trusts the responsibility for managing their own capital development schemes, with chief executives being responsible for the management of capital schemes from their inception to the post-project evaluation. According to the overview:

The *Capital Investment Manual* seeks to reflect and reinforce the important changes that have taken place over recent years, both with the introduction of the NHS reforms and with the changing patterns of health care delivery. In doing so, it aims to ensure that local expectations of health care provision are not raised beyond what is realistic within the context of the service as a whole and to bring the demand for NHS capital more into equilibrium with its supply. The new process is intended to reduce unnecessary and often expensive planning work which subsequently proves to be abortive.

The last sentence is likely to bring a wry smile to the faces of many of those who have been involved in the preparation of business cases, for this is generally a very time-consuming process.

If a Trust wishes to receive external funding for a capital development project, it must first prepare an Outline Business Case

(OBC). Although option appraisal remains a core activity, the new guidance stresses the importance of establishing the strategic context before starting to identify and appraise the costs and benefits of the various possibilities. In order to establish the strategic context it is necessary:

- to consider the current service and facilities and their shortcomings
- to identify future demand for the service
- to demonstrate an understanding of the competitive forces in the market served by the Trust
- to establish a case for change.

Once a case for change has been made, option appraisal techniques are used to identify the preferred option. It is essential to demonstrate clearly that this is not only superior to doing nothing, but is also affordable for the Trust. In addition, the impact of the preferred option on prices must be identified and purchaser agreement obtained — an OBC without purchaser support will be rejected by the Regional Office to which it is submitted. Ideally, purchasers should work closely with the Trust, or at least be regularly informed of progress, so that they are not suddenly faced with a request to express their support for a development about which they know nothing. Purchasers face many competing demands on their scarce resources, and although they may agree that a particular service is in need of development, it may not be one of their immediate priorities for additional expenditure. The 'discipline' of the market should therefore work to ensure that unnecessarily 'grandiose' schemes are not recommended, and that any increases in costs due to increased capital charges on a new facility are (more than) offset by revenue savings.

The preparation of an OBC provides many opportunities for managers and clinicians to work closely together. For example, although managers or external consultants will generally be responsible for preparing the actual submission, input from clinicians is essential, especially when establishing the strategic context, identifying the long and short lists of options, and determining the weighted benefit scores for each of the short-listed options. Given that managers and clinicians tend to approach such issues from very different perspectives (as explored in some of the chapters in Section 3), it is important that everyone is clear about the process and its rationale at the outset. Clinicians may have a vision of their 'ideal' service and the developments needed to achieve this utopia, but if the purchasers (even after considerable persuasion) are not prepared to support such developments, due to their impact on prices, then such options are non-starters. Idealism needs to be tempered with realism, but this does not mean that innovative schemes cannot succeed. Indeed, the enforced discipline of preparing and gaining purchaser support for an OBC can lead to the development of innovative schemes that are both affordable and beneficial.

Once a scheme has been approved at the outline stage, the Trust is allowed to proceed to the development of the Full Business Case (FBC) document. Although the guidance states that private finance possibilities should be considered as part of the OBC, it is at the FBC stage that private finance moves from the wings to centre stage. The next section focuses on the private finance initiative (PFI).

The Private Finance Initiative

The PFI has gradually gained momentum across the whole of the public sector, including the NHS, during the 1990s. As Appleby states:[4] 'In 1992 the Chancellor announced a radical change in the government's attitude to the involvement of private finance in the provision of public services. Many of the restrictions on private funding were removed and in 1993 the NHS, along with other public services, was encouraged to seek collaborative private funding for public works through the private finance initiative'.

Furthermore, it was agreed that privately financed schemes could provide funding over and above that approved by the Department of Health, although it should be noted that 'despite honeyed assurances that the PFI would increase capital spending, the NHS capital budget is to be cut by nearly £400m in the next three years in the expectation that the private sector will plug most of the gap'.[6] Progress to date has undoubtedly been slow, and much time and money has been spent (or earned) as Trusts, their advisers and other 'partner' organisations have grappled with the PFI process. Although the CIM included a *Private Finance Guide*, its limitations were soon exposed as the NHS tried to get to grips with the PFI in practice.

A variety of general guides to the PFI in the public sector have been published by the Treasury and/or the Private Finance Panel during the 1990s. For example, *Private Opportunity, Public Benefit: progressing the private finance initiative* was published by the

Treasury and the Private Finance Panel in November 1995.[7] This introduced a fundamental change to the PFI process. Prior to its publication, every PFI proposal had to be tested against the preferred public sector option (e.g. as identified in the OBC) to demonstrate value for money. However, as a consequence of the new guidance, the public sector comparator should only need to be used 'where one is realistically available in a similar timescale'.[7] The NHS Private Finance Unit, however, decided to adopt a more cautious line, still requiring Trusts to work up the publicly funded preferred option in detail as part of the FBC.

Two key NHS Executive publications — HSG(95)15: *Private Finance and Capital Investment Projects*[8] and HSG(95)48: *Information Management and Technology (IM&T) Procurement and Private Finance*[9] — appeared in March and November of 1995 respectively. The original CIM guidance on the PFI and HSG(95)15 were replaced in July 1996 by a new CIM document — *The Private Finance Initiative in the National Health Service: a guide to processes and legal requirements*.[10] This new guidance, which recognises that PFI 'has become a key policy for delivering improvements to the quality and cost-effectiveness of public services', has been prepared by the Private Finance Unit.[10] It is based on the experience gained by those Trusts that have already made progress in the use of the PFI, highlighting the main issues and procedures involved. It also includes several checklists. It will be welcomed with open arms by everyone actively involved in, or considering, a PFI project.

Progress to date with PFI

As stated above, progress with PFI has generally been limited to date, tending to be restricted to relatively small schemes (i.e. below £15m). For example, in 1992/93 around £34m of private capital was used in England under the PFI, and £42m was involved in 1993/94. However, 32% of the funding over these two years was for clinical waste incineration schemes, and 55% for the lease of staff or office accommodation.[4] The Department of Health predicts that private finance will increase from £47m in 1995/96 to £165m in 1996/97, and to around £200m each year to 1998/99. At these levels it would account for around 13% of the government's capital input, which, according to Appleby,[4] was reduced by nearly £300m in 1996/97.

For these predictions to be realised, considerable progress will have to be made on large PFI building schemes, and this is where things seem to have ground to a (temporary?) halt. Several high profile developments have hit the headlines, and indeed some Trusts have received approval for their major capital developments. The problem seems to be signing the actual contract with the development and financial consortia. A new build and refurbish scheme at South Buckinghamshire Trust worth £35m was approved in November 1995, and in January 1996 John Horam, Parliamentary Secretary at the Department of Health, revealed details of a new £50m project at St James's University Hospital, Leeds, which includes a new 166-bed paediatric wing and an 80-bed patient hotel. He hailed this latter deal as meaning: 'that patients at St James's will be cared for in a superb state-of-the-art hospital wing. This is precisely what the PFI is about — better NHS care, better buildings, and better value for the country's investment in the health service'.[11]

April 1996 saw Stephen Dorrell, the Secretary of State for Health, giving the go-ahead for the first major hospital to be built on a greenfield site under the PFI. The 'Norfolk and Norwich 2000' development would provide a new hospital of about 700 beds at a cost of £170m, and replace two existing hospitals. He also announced that Swindon's Princess Margaret Hospital would be rebuilt to provide a new 250-bedded hospital under a £90m privately funded scheme.[12] One of the biggest problems seems to be getting agreement with regard to the affordability of these large schemes. Although they may be affordable and provide good value for money over a lifetime of, say, 60 years, the funding arrangements may require very high lease/rental payments in the first few years. The knock-on effect on prices is likely to be unacceptable to purchasers, who are unable to commit the sums of money required by the developers and their financiers in the early years. Pokora and Roberts[13] provide an interesting account of Swindon's experience, which highlights some of the problems encountered in the Trust's 'search for the holy grail'.

The time and resource requirements associated with the PFI process are another serious concern, with some Trusts 'expecting to shell out as much as £2m on consultancy fees on the larger schemes'.[6] Even testing for the PFI for relatively modest developments may cost a Trust over £100 000, and if the bid is unsuccessful the money has to come from somewhere in the NHS, leading to concerns that patient services will suffer. The new guidance, and an accumulating pool of skilled organisations, may help to reduce Trusts' consultancy costs in the future, but the whole process is nevertheless very time-consuming. Furthermore, there are grave doubts that schemes that cannot attract private finance (e.g. due to being located in deprived areas with little opportunity for other income-generating developments) will not be funded from NHS capital either, which could lead to some areas losing out while more prosperous ones flourish.

Conclusions

So, what does the future hold with regard to capital developments in the NHS? There is no doubt that the requirements imposed, initially by the options appraisal process and, latterly, by the *Capital Investment Manual*, have had a significant impact upon the nature and scale of such developments. Following the processes described in these documents has imposed a discipline upon the NHS which helps to ensure that capital developments and investments both meet local needs and offer value for money to the taxpayer. The OBC/FBC split ensures that potential schemes must have been appraised in some detail, gained purchaser support and been approved by their Regional Office before proceeding to explore the PFI possibilities in depth.

The Conservative government is undoubtedly strongly committed to the continued use of the PFI throughout the public sector. For example, Chancellor Kenneth Clarke, speaking to the CBI PFI conference in July 1996, said that: 'the public ... decide a business is good by the service provided and the same should apply to government'.[14]

With £5.5 billion of deals agreed across the spectrum of the public sector, and many others in the pipeline, the PFI seems to be gathering momentum nationally, albeit somewhat slowly in the NHS. Experience to date suggests that further changes to the requirements will be needed for many significant capital developments to proceed from the drawing board onto greenfield or existing hospital sites. Many people associated with the NHS are sceptical about the PFI, but others have embraced it as a way forward, especially for large schemes, from the deadlock of relying on bids for regional allocations.

Will a change of government make a difference? There are significant problems associated with a return to using public funding for all capital developments (either in the NHS alone or in the public sector as a whole) due to the likely impact on taxation. Although the electorate may desire the benefits of such developments, it may be unwilling to pay for them through higher taxes on an ongoing basis. However, it should be noted that revenue requirements for the NHS are likely to rise under the 'PFI scenario' as it is rolled out, because lease and rental payments will replace capital charges in the prices set by Trusts. With capital charges, the money stayed within the system, whereas with leases and rents it leaks out of the NHS. For a PFI scheme to be approved, the FBC has to demonstrate that a considerable amount of risk is transferred from the NHS to the private sector. If the private sector is to accept this, it needs to be confident that it can earn an acceptable return on its investment (e.g. through running parallel income generating schemes) within what it believes to be a reasonable time scale.

The NHS seems to be at a crossroads with regard to financing capital developments. Will it go further down the PFI route, or will it return to relying solely on public sector funding? To facilitate the former, the government needs to intervene to ensure that its 'flagship' schemes do indeed proceed, to show that the PFI does indeed deliver on big schemes as well as small ones. A return to the latter form of funding may result in much less new investment in the NHS. Given the longevity of many buildings currently being used by the NHS, the next few years promise to be crucial in determining the type of capital assets that will be used to deliver health care (and, indeed, all public sector services) well into, and possibly beyond, the next century.

REFERENCES

Black A. Make PFI a capital idea. The Health Service Journal (1996); 19 September.
Department of Health/Secretaries of State for Health, Wales, Northern Ireland and Scotland. Working for patients. London: HMSO, 1989.
Department of Health. Use of private sector capital in the NHS (unconventional finance), EL(89)MB142. London: Department of Health, 1989.
Appleby J. Financing the NHS. In: NAHAT NHS Handbook 1996/97. Tunbridge Wells: JMH Publishing, 1996.
NHS Executive. Capital investment manual. London: HMSO, 1994.
Dix A. Capital games. The Health Service Journal 1996; 15 February.
HM Treasury/Private Finance Panel. Private opportunity, public benefit: progressing the private finance initiative. London: Private Finance Panel, 1995.
NHS Executive. Private finance and capital investment projects, HSG(95)15.
NHS Executive. Information management and technology (IM&T) procurement and private finance, HSG(95)48.
NHS Executive. The private finance initiative in the National Health Service: a guide to processes and legal requirements, draft version (final version, for insertion into the Capital Investment Manual, due in early 1997).
HMG. Government opportunities (A monthly publication which details information on the procurement of Central Government services through open competition.) London: Information Publications, March 1996.

HMG. Government opportunities. London: Information Publications, May 1996.

Pokora D, Roberts D. In search of the Holy Grail. The Health Service Journal 1996; 15 February.

HMG. Government opportunities. London: Information Publications, August 1996.

Appleby J. Financing the NHS. In: NAHAT NHS Handbook 1993/94. Tunbridge Wells: JMH Publishing, 1993.

Lyall J. Taking the initiative. The Health Service Journal 1994; 15 September.

Issues in clinical practice

INTRODUCTION

Peter Moore   Lorraine Foster

This section of *Managing Medicine* ranges widely across issues that directly affect doctors in the health service.

In Chapter 6, **Sheila Williams** looks at support for clinicians in management, and gives advice on how medical managers can make the best of their secretaries, human resource department, financial assistant, and business manager.

In the present and future health service it is becoming increasingly important that doctors keep up to date. **Pauline Fryer** examines this in Chapter 7, looking not just at continuing medical education, but rather at a more rounded approach to continual professional development as a vehicle for positive change.

The next three chapters look at the changing interface between doctors and other health care professionals, particularly nurses. **Peter Moore** and **Lorraine Foster** describe a multi-disciplinary approach to paediatric collaborative care planning in a surgical unit, and the development of a single document which covers all aspects of a patient's care from the outpatient clinic through to the ward and operating theatres, and finally to discharge.

The evolving role of the nurse practitioner in two different clinical environments — surgery and endoscopy — is described in the following two chapters. **Lorraine Foster** and **Peter Moore** are joined by **Amanda Flood** and **Surrinder Kaur** in a comprehensive examination of these new and exciting roles for nurses.

Nowadays the public, politicians, and other parties such as health insurers, want consultants to be accredited specialists. In Chapter 11 **Alastair McGowan** looks at how specialists and their institution achieve this, using trauma services as an example.

In Chapter 12, **Charles Collins** examines workloads for consultants in the light of a variety of changes that are taking place around the traditional consultant job. The impact of these changes — such as the reduction of junior doctors' hours, and a suggested specimen job description for the future consultant — is debated.

Finally, in these days of purchasers and providers, there is a need to link doctors into contracting. **Paul Smith** gives an overview of this in Chapter 13.

This is a time of great change for doctors and nurses, and we hope that this section begins to answer some questions, stimulates thought, and also suggests other areas which need exploring in the future.

6. Support for clinicians in management

Sheila Williams

Introduction

One of the key features of the National Health Service is the diversity which exists within it: diversity of organisations and how they are structured; diversity of roles; and diversity of professional groups and the relationships, both formal and informal, between groups. Underpinning all of these is a diversity of values — that collection of beliefs and attitudes which influences all our activity.

NHS staff develop their values from different sources:

- personal values relating to an individual's identity
- professional values deriving from the purpose, education and training of the profession to which they belong
- organisational values born from the identity, culture, role and driving forces of a health care organisation.

Such diversity provides a richness of ideas, experience and valid different viewpoints; it can also produce tension, misunderstanding and confusion. Through constructive management and extensive, open debate, however, such negative aspects can be channelled into a process of quality decision making. This is particularly useful in situations where there is no one clear choice to be made.

A health care manager's focus is on the needs of different groups (e.g. the elderly, children, or those with learning difficulties) and the resource implications and needs for those groups. He or she is concerned with the following types of questions: what financial resources are required and what are available; what are the employment, deployment and skill requirements for staff working with such groups? However, most clinicians (and other health care professionals) focus on the individual patient and the best possible package of care for that individual. When a clinician moves into management on a wider scale than that of managing self, his/her practice and junior staff, it is because of that primary focus and its underlying values that difficulties and tensions arise. The patient appears to retreat whilst the trappings of management — business plans, policies, budgets, meetings, information, paperwork — become constraints.

What is required is a way of working which acknowledges and respects the contributions of all individuals. A high value must be placed on participation, commitment and collaboration, and conflict has to be managed openly, constructively and in a non-punitive fashion.

Such an approach necessitates:

- that individuals, particularly clinicians and managers, understand the purpose and scope of each others' roles in order to empathise with differing viewpoints
- willingness and ability to contribute to organisational activity and understand priority organisational issues
- creating a climate where organisational expectations of standards and behaviour are honestly discussed, clarified and are given commitment
- supporting individuals to help them to let go of outmoded/unwanted practices/behaviours and to develop their understanding of and commitment to the paradigm shift taking place
- working across organisational and professional boundaries.

All staff in a health care organisation have the potential to be a resource and a supportive colleague, but there are some whom a clinician in management should particularly seek out and strive to develop effective working relationships with. They exist to provide their own specialist input which, when intelligently combined with the clinician's unique viewpoint, can develop into a powerful vehicle for improvement, change and innovation. They can also save a clinician-manager considerable time, effort and energy!

Such specialist contributors include finance managers, information analysts, human resource (or personnel) specialists, business managers, medical secretaries, and personal assistants. To understand a little about the purpose, scope and background of such people is to understand how to make the best use of their skills for mutual benefit.

Where to start

The starting point is to know who these people are and where they are located. Differing organisational structures within the NHS can sometimes make them a little troublesome to find. For example:

- In a clinical directorate structure, finance and business managers may be appointed to each directorate or shared between smaller ones.
- Human Resources may exist as a separate directorate; generalist human resource managers may be allocated to provide a total service to other directorates or the total service may be provided centrally with different people providing different aspects across the whole range of human resources services.
- Finance and Information can often live within one directorate, as can Finance and Contracting.

The key to understanding this is to obtain a copy of the organisation's management structure, study it, ask questions about it, and put names to job titles. The person at the top is often unlikely to be the one who can provide the most direct *operational* help. It saves time, effort and temper to seek out the specialist managers who are responsible for providing their service to you and your specialty. Typically, these will be the 'middle managers' within an organisation.

Trust, openness and understanding are at the heart of effective working relationships. Very often, apparently conflicting priorities are in reality different facets of the same coin. If clinicians and managers can develop a shared 'comfort zone' or areas of agreement, then they can be encouraged to venture beyond their perceived boundaries to explore different, innovative ways of working. If they get into difficulties they can re-visit their mutual comfort zone to reaffirm shared understanding and look again for alternative approaches.

There is one issue in establishing effective working relationships which can be very frustrating for a clinician — the job mobility of career managers. In the early stages of a clinician's career there is considerable mobility through short-tenure appointments. When a clinician becomes a consultant a relative degree of permanency is attached to the post. This is quite different from the situation of career managers: there is an expectation that career managers will move on regularly; they are often subject to short fixed-term or rolling contracts; they are unable to progress far within one organisation because of 'down-sizing' or reduction in management tiers.

This often gives rise to feelings of fragmentation and lack of management continuity. It is now more likely that consultants will provide the continuity and stability within the organisation and it is from their relative permanency of position and greater historical perspective of the organisation that consultants derive a proportion of their influence. New managers need to be able to access that perspective, whilst consultants need to access the experience and knowledge imported into the organisation. The purpose and scope of the various specialist roles are explored in the following sections.

Human resource managers

Scope

The role and focus of Human Resources (also often referred to as HR) is changing, with increasing emphasis on the importance of becoming a 'corporate player'. This requires contributing to the general management and performance of the organisation as a whole, advising on strategy, becoming more customer-focused and responsive to 'business' needs, and providing support to managers to enable them to own and deliver for themselves human resource systems such as recruitment, discipline and grievance procedures. This latter point may be summed up as the view that people are best managed by their line manager with specialist support when necessary.

Most human resources departments will cover:

- recruitment and selection
- employee relations
- pay/rewards and job evaluation
- workforce planning
- performance management
- industrial relations
- employment services
- training and development.

Human resource managers should be able to offer advice, guidance and support across the whole range of services, but areas particularly helpful to a clinician in management are shown in Box 6.1.

Box 6.1   Areas where human resource managers can help clinicians

- Legal and effective recruitment — ensuring recruitment takes place within organisational policy (e.g. equal opportunities, job share schemes) and legal requirements (e.g. Race Relations Act, Sex Discrimination Act); extensive

employment legislation now exists and is very comprehensive in terms of its applicability to jobs
- Employee relations — advising and supporting in handling grievance and disciplinary issues, including dismissal
- Employment services — contracts and contractual matters such as terms and conditions of service
- Health and Safety — policy and procedures regarding aspects such as safe working practices and hazards/accidents (particularly important now that the NHS is no longer covered by Crown Immunity)
- Performance Management — aspects such as managing sickness/absence, performance reviews/appraisals, and managing poor performers
- Training and Development (T&D) — e.g. the availability of internal and external T&D activity, arrangements for study leave, and budgets and resources for T&D.

Background

Human Resources managers are recruited from varied backgrounds: some may have worked their way up through personnel administration, others may be direct graduate recruits with a little experience, whilst others may be recruited from outside the NHS with considerable experience in other areas. All will possess or should be working towards their professional qualification as a member of the Institute of Personnel and Development. This qualification entails formal study of general and specialist aspects of human resource management and general management.

Current issues

Human Resources managers are currently concerned about a variety of issues, including:

- the role, contribution and organisation of the Human Resources function
- strategy, policy, change management and organisation development
- pay/rewards — local pay bargaining, local terms and conditions of service
- performance management
- Human Resources implications/aspects of changes such as contracting-out and redeployment.

Currently, Human Resources in the NHS has a massive agenda and there is genuine concern that the skills do not exist or that there are not sufficient people with them to tackle some of the 'new' issues.

Information analysts

Scope

Since the days of the Resource Management Initiative in the NHS, Information and Information Technology services have proliferated. The NHS reforms have underscored the need for health care organisations to produce quality information and to institute the systems which will make such information accessible. Apart from clinical information, NHS Information Departments need to collect information to support business planning, contracting and quality monitoring. Within Information Departments, specialists can be found whose role it is to analyse information users' requirements and to capture, collate, interpret and present information in a relevant, meaningful way so that it is of use and value to non-specialists.

Information analysts should be able to offer advice and help in the areas of interest to clinician-managers shown in Box 6.2.

Box 6.2   Areas where information analysts can help clinicians

- Advising what information is available; from which sources/systems; how accessible it is; how it can be presented
- Working with clinician-managers to determine their regular information requirements
- Knowledge of local systems and standard software and assistance with the design of small PC-based systems
- Provision of statistical information/returns
- Identifying other local systems, not within the remit of the Information Directorate, whose outputs would be of value (e.g. finance systems for financial management activity).

Background

Analysts are drawn from both NHS and non-NHS backgrounds, and have differing qualifications and educational achievements. There is no one overall qualification; analysts may have qualifications, for example, in computing, informatics (the science of information) or information management and technology.

Considerable work is going on through the activity of the

Information Management Group, the Institute for Health and Care Development, and Regional IM&T Training Advisors to specify the competencies required by Information Management and Technology staff in the NHS. This has led to a new qualification for such professionals which is aimed at developing the skills required in the NHS. It is competence-based, which means that candidates taking the qualification must demonstrate their ability in a particular skill *in the workplace* and not just by means of an examination paper.

Current issues

Information analysts are currently concerned about a variety of issues, including:

- implementing the extensive National Information Management and Technology Strategy
- getting information from systems not originally designed to collect and yield it
- managing the explosion of information needs arising from the NHS reforms without swamping themselves and users in unwanted paperwork.

Finance managers/management accountants

Scope

Finance managers operate at two distinct levels:

1. the strategic level — dealing with financial policy, planning and resourcing
2. the operational level — dealing with finance and budget systems and information, financial planning and forecasting for service developments, and costing/pricing.

Finance managers will be able to offer assistance and support in the areas shown in Box 6.3.

Box 6.3   Areas where finance managers can help clinicians

- Budget setting, management and control
- Financial planning for business cases or service developments
- Costings, cost comparisons, cost-benefits, option appraisal
- Financial information (e.g. forecasts for managers)
- Interpretation and application of financial policy/probity issues (e.g. sponsorship, hospitality).

Background

Finance managers come from both NHS and non-NHS backgrounds. There appears to be a tendency to try to recruit from non-NHS backgrounds in order to ensure that the type and levels of skills now required in the NHS are drawn in. Finance managers are expected to possess one of the professional accountancy qualifications (e.g. CIPFA, CCAB), and higher-level posts are generally not available to the unqualified.

Current issues

Finance managers are currently facing a variety of issues, including:

- financial planning
- Private Finance Initiative
- meeting their Trust's set financial targets
- providing meaningful and accurate costings
- developing skills of non-finance managers.

Business managers/service managers

Scope

Where these roles exist, they can be very varied in content. Fundamentally, it is a co-ordinating role, bringing together the ideas and views of all the different contributors to directorate, departmental or specialty activity and building them into a cohesive business or service development plan.

They may be involved in activities as diverse as:

- co-ordinating business planning
- review and development of services
- capital programme planning
- market research
- complaints
- contracting
- income generation.

This varied role is often shared between specialties. The value for a clinician-manager is in:

- helping to translate clinical thinking and planning into business plans
- co-ordinating intra-specialty plans/developments.

Background

Business managers are recruited from both NHS and non-NHS backgrounds. The business manager post has, of late, become attractive to nurse managers seeking career moves into general management. There are no specific qualifications for an NHS business manager. They are often members of the Institute of Health Service Management, and may possess a management or business management qualification (from Certificate to MBA level). Some recruiters of business managers are specifying accountancy qualifications, and many ask for graduate or graduate-level education.

Medical secretary/personal assistant

Scope

This must be by far the most familiar non-medical role to clinicians and as such it is not intended to dwell on its scope, since most clinicians adapt the role of the medical secretary to suit their own needs, preferences and systems.

There are, however, issues arising out of this individualisation of the role which are worth discussing, since an appreciation of them will help clinicians to work more effectively with their medical secretaries.

Line management responsibility or direct reporting?

Arrangements for the management of medical secretaries vary. A secretary may report directly to a supervisor of secretaries or to an individual clinician(s), or he/she might have a dual responsibility to both a supervisor and clinician(s). All of these reporting relationships have their merits, but they can also produce tension and confusion for the individual secretary. A supervisor is concerned with the effective deployment and performance of the secretarial resource as a whole, whereas a clinician is more concerned about obtaining a reliable, quality performance from his/her 'own' secretary. Good communication and cooperation between all three parties is essential if the secretary is not to feel manipulated and have divided loyalties.

Clarity of objectives and priorities

Since the vast majority of the work of a medical secretary is generated by the clinician(s), it is important that she/he knows what to concentrate on and when and where the limits to his/her ability to act independently lie.

Rewards and career prospects

Career prospects for medical secretaries are relatively limited within the NHS, but could include upgrading or promotion to personal assistant or supervisor posts, or sideways movement to non-medical secretarial posts and into administration/junior management. There is currently little scope for financial rewards for good performance, although as the move to local pay and conditions gathers momentum, health care organisations are looking at different types of reward packages. Upgrading is often tried as a means of rewarding performance, but this may be difficult. For example, increased scope or amount of responsibility is usually the main criterion for upgrading, not increased workload. Furthermore, it is a post which is upgraded, not a particular individual. Upgrading entails an ongoing recurring financial commitment, for the increased salary has to be found year on year. Where a post can be upgraded and the funding is available, it would generally not be automatically offered to the current post-holder. An equal opportunities employer would make it available to at least internal competition, which can be upsetting for the current post-holder. Where upgrading is being considered, clinicians should draw on the advice and expertise of the human resource manager.

Other types of reward for performance should be considered. Examples include:

- support for personal or professional development (time off, fees/expenses, books/other resources)
- formal and public recognition of performance (local award, Employee of the Month/Year, national award, such as Secretary of the Year).

Background

Medical secretaries come from a variety of backgrounds and have differing educational attainments. Traditionally, shorthand and typing (especially audio) have been their core skills, but increasingly information technology skills are taking precedence, including word processing and use of databases, spreadsheets, graphics, presentation software, and desk-top publishing. There are specific training courses provided by colleges for medical secretaries and a professional association — AMSPAR. For experienced non-medical secretaries there are a number of training resources available to assist with medical terminology which may be available in Training or Information Management and Technology Departments.

Conclusions

The NHS is no stranger to change — in virtually every decade since its inception there has been at least one major change. What is perhaps different about the recent reforms is that they have occurred during a period of rapid, major changes in the nature, structure and continuity of work worldwide, the full impact of which has yet to be seen. Whilst such change will bring its 'winners' and 'losers', it also provides new opportunities to reshape and redefine health care provision and services to meet the needs of local communities through to the next century. This may involve forming and participating in difficult and uncomfortable decisions as well as envisaging and describing innovative development. From their unique position in the NHS, clinicians should be at the forefront of developing these opportunities and leading the debate in conjunction with their managers and other professional colleagues.

FURTHER READING

Handy C. The empty raincoat. London: Arrow, 1994.
IHSM. Future health care options. IHSM paper. IHSM, 1993.
Moore W. Is doctors' power shrinking? Health Service Journal 1995; 9 November: 24–27.

7. Continuing medical and professional development for consultants: a vehicle for positive change

Pauline Fryer

Introduction

This chapter describes initiatives within Scunthorpe and Goole Hospitals NHS Trust, a third wave Trust, to develop a positive, healthy culture of learning, particularly focusing on the development of consultant medical staff. The Trust employs 2200 people and provides mainly secondary hospital and community-based services to a largely rural population of around 200 000 in North Lincolnshire. It has an income of £50 million and employs about 200 medical personnel, including 48 consultants. In common with the rest of the National Health Service and other modern organisations, the Trust operates in an environment of constant turbulence and rapid change. The need for continuous, regenerative and focused learning has never been greater.

As part of its organisational development agenda, the Trust needs to develop into a more viable, dynamic corporate organisation which nurtures professional excellence and energy balanced with organisational commitment and focus. Promoting the sharing of personal and professional learning within and between multidisciplinary teams can be a powerful vehicle for such positive change, as we discovered within the Trust.

Background

In the spring of 1994, Continuing Medical Education (CME) and Continuing Professional Development (CPD) were relatively new concepts in their present form. The requirement for continued development of clinical knowledge and practice has always been part of the individual medical professional's philosophy. However, the traditional approaches to clinical learning have been challenged by rising public expectations and pressures for national standards of patient care, combined with rapidly changing service delivery patterns and advancing health care technologies. In response, the Royal Colleges started in 1993/94 to develop forms of accreditation for CME activity, and to seek evidence of the professional updating of fully qualified professionals in order to retain their right to continue in professional practice (e.g. the Royal College of Obstetricians and Gynaecologists CME recommendations and arrangements).

The reaction within the Trust to this trend was varied. The views of doctors ranged from:

- What is CME; is it anything different?
- Will I have the time and resources to do it?
- What will it mean for my clinical practice?
- What will happen if I do not meet the standards?

Managers also had concerns, including:

- How can the Trust help doctors to continue to develop professional practice and excellence within the framework of the organisation's Strategic Direction?
- How can we ensure that effective learning actually occurs (rather than just 'time spent' on educational activities) and becomes a normal part of the way we work in the Trust?
- How can the Trust help doctors (and others) develop new approaches to learning to meet the demands of the radically new ways of working required, now and in the future?
- How can we ensure that training and education resources and clinical time are effectively deployed?
- How do we encourage the minority of clinicians who do not participate in clinical and personal development?

A small steering group of individuals, including the Director of Human Resources, the Director of Post-Graduate Medical Education and the Medical Director, decided to use the issues around CME to engage consultants in new ways of thinking about, and undertaking, professional development. The aim was to use the energy and interest of most doctors in self-development as a lever for business-enhancing change to develop the Trust's learning culture.

In order to be successful, to survive, but more importantly, to thrive in the modern environment of 'disorder and unpredictability', as described by Durcan,[1] everyone in a Trust like ours needs to be working in a common direction, guided by clear, shared values, objectives and understanding. Durcan recognised that in the modern environment of radical change 'the future is unknowable' and 'change cannot be managed', rather it has to be 'created'. Continuously changing circumstances and increasing customer needs in the NHS, therefore, demand a working environment of continuous learning and improvement, genuine staff participation and involvement, and increased responsiveness and flexibility.

The necessity is to become a 'learning organisation' which 'facilitates the learning of all its members and continuously transforms itself'.[2] Without this continuous learning the organisation will be unable to change quickly and radically enough to survive, let alone to thrive.

A shared understanding of the Trust's aims and values and the development of a culture of continuous learning and improvement are central to the Trust's Human Resources Strategy to develop organisational capacity and capability to stay ahead of change. Set within the context of the external environment of rapid 'unknowable' change, Figure 7.1 highlights the inter-relationship of these and other elements within the Trust's Human Resources Strategy.

As Revans[3] proposed, organisations cannot flourish 'unless the rate of learning is equal to or greater than the rate of change'. In this environment of uncertainty the 'process of learning to learn, that takes place on the journey',[1] or of 'double loop learning', as Argyris[4] called it, may actually be far more important than the final destination. The development of 'double loop learning' and a true learning culture empowers people to see change as an opportunity to learn, understand and let go of old ideas and assumptions, rather than to resist change or see it as something to be managed or overcome.

Historical ways of CME learning no longer suffice. Professional and personal learning and development need to be integrated with management and organisational development. This is particularly the case for consultants, as they all have to lead and manage their own practices, irrespective of whether they have additional managerial roles. Most consultants also have responsibilities for training and developing doctors in training or other non-training grade doctors, and can be powerful role models and leaders across the range of professions. Development of this key group of individuals can therefore contribute significantly to the development of supporting staff and the organisation as a whole.

A greater emphasis was required on self-managed development

'First class, first choice' health services

A workforce which is flexible, patient-centred and effective

Employee and industrial relations

Management development

Training and development

Trust aims and values

Flexible workforce resourcing and deployment

Organisational development — continuous learning and improving

Pay and rewards

Performance management

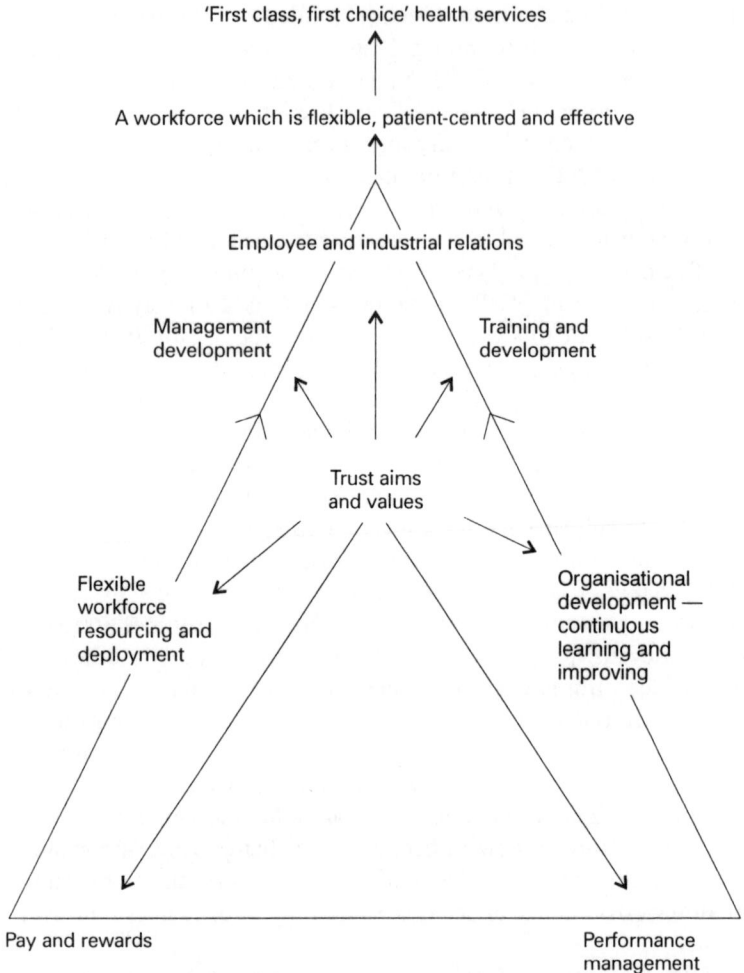

Fig. 7.1   Human resources strategy — 'towards improved performance'

and structured, focused training and education activities. It was also crucial to ensure that learning was transferred into changed practice, and from one sphere of activity and one profession to another. The skills of team working, cross-functional/organisational working, and project working needed to be developed. Individuals and the Trust needed help to move from responding and coping with change to developing a capacity to thrive on, and actively promote, change.

Locating the energy and vehicles for change

Having decided to use the interest in CME as a focus for positive change, numerous 'one-to-one' and group discussions were held with lead consultants from the major specialties across the Trust. Loosely using Egan's model[5] for initiating and managing change, consultants were asked to identify the current position of personal and professional learning in their specialty, their ideal vision for the future, and possible strategies for achieving the vision. These discussions helped to develop understanding of the issue and to promote and encourage many examples of good learning practice already in existence. Two common themes emerged:

1. A range of concerns and issues about the implications of the developing Royal Colleges' requirements for CME (e.g. those of the Royal College of Physicians). This was particularly the case where the Colleges had not yet provided any CME guidelines.
2. The need for improved physical facilities on site to facilitate education, learning, training and development activities for doctors. The pre-existing facilities were clearly felt to inhibit effective learning, acting as a barrier in part to the realisation of some individuals' 'preferred scenario'.

These two areas of consultant interest and energy became the main focus for what Egan[5] calls 'business-enhancing change' — practical initiatives within the Trust to improve the learning environment and culture for consultants (and others).

Developing understanding and a local approach to CME and CPD

The first major vehicle for change was the concerns and issues relating to CME. The local steering group sought to use these concerns and issues to initiate dialogue within the consultant group and raise awareness of effective learning approaches. The aim was to develop a local approach to CME and CPD which had the support of consultants and was consistent with the Trust's aims and values. The steering group identified three requirements:

1. the need to develop the capacity of individual consultants to manage their own *total* development (both clinical and non-clinical) continuously
2. the need for a more structured, team-based, flexible but focused approach to CPD

3. the identification and planning of learning and development needs, integrated with the Trust's strategic direction and business needs.

At the start of the initiative there was considerable confusion and concern about the new CME requirements and their implications. This was used as an entry point for discussion with individual consultants and/or specialties to:

- open up the prospect of wider learning needs and other ways of learning
- focus on the particular learning and education issues and problems in each specialty
- build understanding of the developing national CME scene
- share/encourage ideas about possible different approaches/best practice from elsewhere and from other specialties
- raise awareness and emphasise the relevance of effective learning to their work and that of the Trust
- start to close the gaps and create links between the consultants' individual motivation, the needs of the Trust, and new ways of working, behaving and learning.

The publication of the excellent CPD paper by the Standing Committee on Post Graduate Medical and Dental Education[6] was timely and helpful in legitimising and supporting much of the local debate. Other Trust multi-professional management and organisational opportunities and activities were also used to explore views and values, and to develop a common understanding and ideas about what effective CPD really meant and how it could best be pursued within the Trust. Gradually a new perspective of a more dynamic and integrated approach to CPD started to emerge.

A consultation paper on CPD was produced, reflecting the views of doctors and raising a number of controversial policy issues and options for wide debate. It deliberately sought to challenge historical ways of thinking about CME and CPD. From this further debate was encouraged in a number of forums. The feedback provided direction for the subsequent development of a local policy approach to CPD and CME within the Trust, with clear policy standards and examples of good practice. The policy approach was endorsed by the Hospitals Consultants Committee in 1995 and is being used within the Trust to promote and further develop good practice in CPD.

The development of a viable business case for a multi-purpose training and education centre

The second vehicle for change was the concern about training and education facilities. It was clear from the outset of the project that political and financial support would not be available internally or externally for the development of improved educational and training facilities solely for medical staff. It was also apparent that an emphasis on developing facilities for the exclusive use of one group would run counter to the Trust's approach to organisational development. In the modern complex market environment of the NHS, effective multi-disciplinary and cross-functional team working was becoming essential for the Trust's survival and growth — the integration of learning and development activity across all staff groups was needed, both to reflect that reality and to promote and support it.

A multi-professional project group was established with the remit of testing whether a viable business case could be made for the development of a multi-purpose, multi-professional training and education centre within the Trust, which had the support and commitment of the key stakeholders, particularly consultants. It was hoped that the project group, and the establishment of such a centre, would help to promote collaborative and effective multi-professional team working, understanding and learning, and increase opportunities for consultants (and others) to engage in local multi-professional team learning and development activities.

The style and manner of working within the project team was itself a lever for change and innovation, bringing together a range of disparate views and functions (including the local College of Health, Medical, Finance, Paramedical, Nursing and Human Resource functions), and building a collaborative shared vision of integrated personal, multi-professional and organisational learning. At the outset strong tribal, functional and historical interests were evident, particularly amongst some doctors and some other professionals who were concerned about sharing/losing resources and control, and who, in some cases, were also concerned about identity and status issues. The group was encouraged to explore current and future trends in training and education in the light of aspects such as changing health care, demography, and technology, and to consider their implications for the role of training, education and learning within the Trust and for training and library facilities.

This work led to the identification by the group of common goals and values and a recognition of the value and appropriateness of multi-purpose learning facilities and activities. Detailed research was then carried out by group members into the type and level of interest internally and externally in such a facility, promoting the vision of integrated learning in the process. The results established a justifiable basis of need for a multi-purpose centre which would have the support of a wide range of users, in partnership with the College of Health. A detailed business case was developed with input from all the professional groups and subsequently approved by the Trust Board. The new centre was completed in February 1996 and symbolises an important stepping stone in the direction of travel towards a genuine learning culture with the Trust.

The outcomes of change

So what has changed? The new multi-purpose training and education centre and a written CPD policy and standards of good practice are only the outward signs of change. What is far more important is the variety of positive and observable behavioural and attitudinal changes derived from a willingness and ability to 'see' and experience the world in a different way. The steering group and the various organisational development initiatives did not create that change, rather they helped to provide new insights, to challenge old ways of thinking, and to liberate a capacity to respond effectively to the changing environment so that, in 'seeing differently', new realities and innovations started to become both possible and desirable. New insights are an essential part of cultural change. As Egan states, 'the key to change is awareness'.[5] Kinston[7] believes that 'the crucial element of change is understanding ... without a cultural shift you cannot get an action shift'.

Some specific examples of change are described below.

a. Multi-professional and team learning activity is on the increase and is seen in a more favourable light, not as the only means of learning, but as a valuable contribution to improved team working and quality of care to patients and in breaking down unhelpful and unnecessary barriers. Examples include shared audit learning and activity between the professions, particularly medical and nursing, and multi-disciplinary learning on communicating with patients and relatives.

b. An increased capacity to innovate and experiment with new ways of working and learning.

c. Active involvement of consultants in a range of organisational and management development activities.

d. Improved identification of holistic development needs (i.e. personal and professional).

e. A clear recognition by the majority of consultants that CME is part of the total, life-long development of the individual embraced within CPD, which itself is set within the context of wider environmental change and the Trust's business needs of providing first choice, first class services to patients, GPs and others.

f. A more explicit recognition of the need for and desirability of balancing personal, professional and organisational development needs, exemplified by specialty dialogue regarding development priorities derived from the specialty business plan and strategic objectives.

g. Increased use of alternative forms of learning to meet individual development needs (moving away from over-emphasis on a 'conference attendance' approach to CPD).

h. An increased recognition of the importance of translating learning into improved practice as the best measure of effective CME/CPD, rather than the 'time spent' credit-based approach of some Royal Colleges. Multi-professional audit has been particularly helpful in highlighting the benefits of applying learning to improve practice.

The culture change involved in developing a learning culture does not happen overnight — it takes time, energy, extensive dialogue, and numerous vehicles for change to establish new ways of working. However, significant first steps have been made within Scunthorpe and Goole Hospitals NHS Trust in a crucial area with a key group of people. This will promote our continuing aim to become 'First class, first choice for health care for local people'.

ACKNOWLEDGEMENTS

I am grateful for the assistance of Dr Gorajarla Vijayasimhulu, MBBS, DMRD, FRCR, Director of Post-Graduate Medical Education and Consultant Radiologist, and Mr Stuart Tindall, ChMFRCS, Medical Director and Consultant Surgeon at Scunthorpe and Goole Hospitals NHS Trust.

REFERENCES

Durcan J, Kirkbride P, Obeng E. The revolutionary reality of change. Directions. The Ashridge Journal, Ashridge Management College, September 1993: 4–9.

Pedler M, Boydell T, Burgoyne J. The learning company: a strategy for sustainable development. London: McGraw Hill, 1993.

Revans R. The ABC of action learning. Bromley, Kent: Chartwell-Bratt, 1993.

Argyris C. Overcoming organisational defences. Boston: Allyn & Bacon, 1990.

Egan G. Adding value — a systematic guide to business driven management and leadership. San Francisco: Jossey-Bass, 1993.

Standing Committee on Post-Graduate Medical and Dental Education. Consultant paper. A working paper on continuing professional development for doctors and dentists. London: HMSO, 1994.

Kinston W. Personal communication, 1995.

8. Collaborative care planning

Peter Moore   Lorraine Foster

Introduction

In 1993, Virginia Bottomley, then Secretary of State for Health, stated that treatments that hospitals should provide must prove their worth in three different ways:

1. they must meet the needs of the patients
2. they must be clinically effective
3. they must represent value for money.[1]

In addition, a professional body — the Royal College of Surgeons — has suggested that up to 40% of elective procedures should be performed as day cases. Such changes in health care policy, together with demands from purchasers, will lead to Trusts having to assess how they deliver their services in order to meet these criteria.[2]

One area of development is that of collaborative care planning; this is used as a base to set objectives to analyse the quality of care delivered. When a patient attends hospital for an elective procedure, he or she is referred by the GP with documentation outlining the problem. On arrival in clinic the same documentation is repeated and confirmed by the specialist, who then lists the patient on a waiting list. On arrival at the hospital, the data is collected for a third time by the admitting nurse into the nursing notes a short time later. The same data is collected for a fourth time by the house surgeon for the medical notes just before the patient goes to theatre. The same data is collected again by the anaesthetist and recorded in the anaesthetic notes. It would seem that there is a strong case for a single multi-disciplinary document containing all the required clinical and legal information which would map the patient's passage from the GP to the outpatient department, through hospital stay until discharge back to the care of the GP.

81

One area of general surgery was examined to see whether this concept of a single multi-disciplinary document was feasible. It was decided to look at low risk simple surgery, which would have defined outcomes. Looking at the surgical workload, the area most suited was routine paediatric general surgery within a District General Hospital setting. The documentation developed was described as a Paediatric General Surgical Collaborative Care Plan, and the process of its implementation and the analysis of its use forms the substance of this chapter.

Collaborative care planning

'Collaborative care planning', 'critical pathways' and 'case management' are all terms used to describe the process of planning care through a multi-disciplinary approach which enables more patient-centred care to take place and also provides documentation that will enable cost savings and evaluation of care to be monitored and improved. Ideally, collaborative care planning allows care to be focused around the patient without disrupting the structure of the hospital and produces a single document that follows the patient in a systematic way through an episode of care.

If properly constructed, the document should be accurate, reduce duplication of documentation, and should also be user-friendly. Hewitson[3] outlines three types of benefits, described below.

1. Direct benefits to the patients

To implement the Collaborative Care Plan, an analysis of current practice would need to be undertaken. The development of collaboration with the patient at the outset ensures that he or she is informed of all interventions that are intended in the predetermined care plan. Delays should be eliminated by improving continuity of care and facilitating discharge planning, whereby the patient returns to the care of the family and GP as quickly as possible.

2. Benefits to the multi-disciplinary team

The Collaborative Care Plan is a dynamic forum for multi-disciplinary discussion which results in improved communication, clarification of roles, and a deeper understanding of each other's contributions to create a united rather than an isolated sense of purpose. Development needs of staff can be identified because ownership arises from the formulation of a unique plan with defined professional responsibility, allowing devolved decision making and better use of resources. The above factors should contribute to the potential improved job satisfaction.

3. Benefits to the organisation

Contract specification can be enhanced by having the agreed key interventions throughout a health care episode. This information will assist in identifying cost per case or cost per care group. Ongoing multi-disciplinary clinical audit will be facilitated, allowing potential improvements in the quality of care. Both retrospective and prospective audits can be undertaken, and analysis of the data should provide better utilisation of available beds.

Development of the Paediatric Day Care Collaborative Care Plan

The standards defined for the patients using the Care Plan were derived from *A guide for purchasers of paediatric services* (1994) from the British Association of Paediatric Surgeons,[4] the Trust's *Patient Charter Standards*,[5] and the Audit Commission's *Paediatric Gold Standards*.[6] These were circulated to interested parties who potentially would be involved in the care of paediatric day care surgical patients, as shown in Figure 8.1.

The various professionals involved were contacted individually and their requirements for the Collaborative Care Plan were ascertained. When all these had been pooled, a working party was set up with a nucleus of a consultant surgeon, a consultant paediatrician, a clinical nurse specialist in paediatrics, a consultant anaesthetist, and the research co-ordinator. They developed a prototype of the Care Plan. Other members of staff — such as outpatients staff, theatre and recovery staff, pharmacy staff, and general management — were co-opted when each section of the plan was being formulated. This was time consuming, but it was important that each group was involved and informed so that they became enthusiastic in supporting the plan and receptive to the changes involved.

The prototype document was brought to a collective meeting of all interested parties for further discussions. Modifications were made and the document was agreed at a second meeting, where arrangements were made for a six-month pilot study to determine

Fig. 8.1 Collaborative care planning approach to patient-centred care

any operational problems with its use. Before the pilot study could commence certain changes needed to be introduced. At that time it was routine for children to be seen as outpatients at a normal general surgical clinic, but this was not acceptable from the standards that had been established. A dedicated paediatric general surgical clinic was therefore introduced on a fortnightly basis, with patients being referred to one general surgeon who agreed to undertake all the basic paediatric general surgical elective work. There were some cases that were more suitable to be seen by a surgeon with a urological interest, and so a further paediatric surgical clinic was created for this sub-specialty. In order to meet the standards, the general surgical operating lists had to be adjusted so that one list per fortnight could be dedicated to elective paediatric surgery only. This coincided with an adjustment in the paediatric general surgical bed booking so that blocks of beds could be reserved for the specific paediatric surgical list. Coupled with this, charitable donations to the hospital allowed modification of the methods for transferring patients from the ward to the operating theatre. This involved decorating a theatre trolley to look like Thomas the Tank Engine for children under the age of three, and the provision of two electric jeeps instead of a theatre trolley so that children could drive themselves to theatre from the ward. Once these arrangements were made, it was elected to institute the pilot project using the collaborative care document.

The document is an eight-page booklet. The first page contains basic patient information (e.g. age, name, date of birth, next of kin) plus Patients Charter data including date of referral, date and time arrived and seen in clinic, the history and examination and a plan of action. If the patient is added to the waiting list, the consent form is signed at that time. The part of the document concerning the outpatient visit is signed and photocopied and a copy sent to the GP, replacing the routine outpatient letter.

The rest of the document follows the patient through the hospital admission. The second page contains the pre-registration houseman's pre-op clerking, followed by the anaesthetic assessment, the pre-medication and the pre-operative nursing checklist. The page is completed by the operation notes. On the opposite side of the open page is the intra-operative record of the anaesthetist and the safety check from the nursing staff in theatre. The next page is used by the nurse in the recovery ward and it then follows on to the post-operative checks that take place on return to the paediatric ward. There is a section for complications and medical and nursing evaluation.

At each point as the patient moves through the hospital and the Care Plan moves from one professional to another the document is signed by the appropriate member of staff and then passed on to the next stage. The back page of the document constitutes the discharge letter, which is filled in by the doctor and the nurse before the patient leaves the hospital. There is also a section for a discharge prescription of medication (e.g. analgesia antibiotics). This page is photocopied and sent to the GP, and a copy is also given to the patient to take home. Thus there is no need for a separate discharge letter, as both the GP and the patient are in possession of the discharge data immediately on the patient's return to primary care.

Implementation

After the Collaborative Care Plan had been created, it was implemented and audited on a prospective basis. There were certain teething troubles — for example, the print room at the hospital had to make several attempts to construct the Care Plan exactly as designed. Once the Plan had been printed, it was introduced in the outpatient department. Because of the movement from a general surgical to a paediatric clinic, there was a change in outpatient staff, and they were introduced to the Care Plan at the same time as it was introduced to the hospital. This required some additional input from the consultant surgeon and the research department, but it was nevertheless quite a smooth process. Once the patients were admitted to hospital for their surgery, the Care Plan was enthusiastically adopted by the ward staff. Although there were slight problems when it was transferred to theatre, these concerns and difficulties were quickly smoothed out after a simple explanation at the beginning of the theatre list to various members of staff.

After the Plan had been in use for six months, an audit took place which showed that, although initially the defined standards were not met, the nominated standards were being achieved by the end of the six-month period. These included standards such as:

- All children should be under a named paediatrician (100% compliance).
- All entries should be legible (all Collaborative Care Plans were legible).
- All Collaborative Care Plans must be fully completed. Initially, only 13% of the Care Plans were completed, due to the change in outpatient staff, but by the end of the pilot all Care Plans were fully completed.
- At least 75% of children are to be seen by the consultant within 30 minutes of arriving at the Clinic (80% of children were seen within 30 minutes).

Although standards were being achieved, it was felt that the Plan needed modification in the way some of the sections were structured in order to improve the user-friendliness. This is not surprising, as it was considered unlikely that the first draft that was implemented would be perfect.

Research findings

It was the intention of the research study to test the hypothesis that collaborative care planning does actually have benefits to the Trust, the patients and their carers, and staff. Collaborative care planning had already been introduced at Scunthorpe for elective day case paediatric surgery and had been audited. It was necessary to test the Collaborative Care Plan on staff who had not used it before. For this reason Goole, our sister hospital which also undertakes paediatric surgery, was the ideal choice. Questionnaires were distributed before and after the Collaborative Care Plan's implementation to all staff who would use the document. These were then used to compare the quality and effectiveness of the document. The study looked at both qualitative and quantitative issues which impact on the document.

Discussion on responses to qualitative issues

Questions were based around how easy or difficult it was to extract information from the Care Plan compared to the old-style documentation. The results reflected how the compact manner of the document supported ease of access to information. Bearing in mind how difficult it was to access information within the old-style documentation, the next question dealt with how easy or difficult it was to show a plan of the patient's expected route through the system. Staff responses showed conclusively that they felt the documentation improved the ability to identify a pathway of planned care, which could be used to explain their episode of care to the patients. The staff also reinforced the view that it was an ideal document to use as an educational tool for patients, carers and trainees. Staff were asked to comment on the quality of the patient's written records compared with the old documentation. Although the responses showed that quality was better with the Collaborative Care Plan, there was still room for improvement. Staff found that the Collaborative Care Plan was easier to read and gave a more comprehensive view of the patient's care.

Discussion on responses to quantitative issues

One of the primary objectives was to reduce the number of times information had to be written on a Care Plan. This was dramatically reduced in all aspects of the Care Plan, from an average of four times down to twice, as shown in Table 8.1.

The second question dealt with the average amount of time that staff spent recording all the information. Once again there was a vast difference, with a higher percentage of staff spending less time documenting care, as shown in Table 8.2.

Other quantitative questions were based on whether or not staff had seen or used a Collaborative Care Plan. This would give an indication of who would need to be targeted for education in the use of Collaborative Care Plans.

Table 8.1 Number of times information is given

	Using the old documentation	Using the Collaborative Care Plan
Operation details	6	4
Unit number	10	6
Ward	10	7
Name	11	6
Observations	11	6
Consultant	9	5

The study proved that less time was spent on documenting patient care and that duplication and repetition were reduced. Information was captured more effectively and used both as an educational tool and for audit purposes. Staff involved in putting together the document agreed that they developed an increased awareness of other's roles in the total episode of the patient's care. Collaborative care planning in paediatric surgery is being introduced in the awareness that the benefits are worth striving for, and further work is continuing in implementing this type of documentation for other specialties.[7]

Future plans

As intimated earlier, the initial draft of the Collaborative Care Plan has been further developed to increase its user-friendliness. It has also been made more generalised, so that it may be adapted for other areas of general surgical day case care. It is still necessary to have a separate paediatric document, but the adult day case document is being developed along similar lines.

The enthusiasm with which the Collaborative Care Plan was adopted has led to an increase in the profile of paediatric surgery within the hospital. From the outpatient department, through the

Table 8.2 Amount of time spent recording information

	Using the old documentation	Using the Collaborative Care Plan
Less than 15 minutes	40%	42%
16–30 minutes	32%	20%
31–45 minutes	23%	5%

ward and the operating theatre, great strides have been made in accommodating children in a more sensitive environment. The paediatric general surgical clinic now takes place in the paediatric department, with dedicated paediatric nurses. Information sheets have been developed for children and for their parents. Before the children are admitted to hospital for their operation they receive an invitation to the 'Saturday Club', where they and all the other children having surgery that week meet for a party on the ward. The party is hosted by the nurse who saw them in clinic (who will also look after them on the ward) and the nurse who is running the theatre list for that week, thus providing continuity and familiar faces. The children are introduced to the ward and invited to go along to the operating theatre to have a look round. They also have the opportunity to play on the jeep and sit a mock driving test which allows them to drive the jeep up to theatre on the day of their operation.

The anaesthetic room has been decorated with cartoon figures, and a television set with a video machine has been installed so that after the children have been driven up to theatre in the jeep they can then watch their favourite video whilst they are being prepared to be put to sleep.

Pre-medication has been modified so that the dose given is enough to relieve anxiety but not to sedate, so the children are still aware and cooperative when they come up to theatre, rather than confused. This has been of great benefit in the smoothness of anaesthesia and lack of distress for the children. Various post-operative methods of pain relief have been adopted before the child leaves theatre (e.g. regional blocks with long-acting local anaesthesia, long-acting analgesic suppositories, local anaesthetic cream) which can be used according to the site and type of operation. An area of the recovery ward has been decorated specifically for children, but it is policy to return them to the paediatric surgical ward as soon as possible, allowing them to recover in their own bed with their parents at their side.

The combination of pre-operative education of children and their parents together with the modifications to their treatment in hospital has improved the speed of recovery of the children. It is very uncommon that any of them need to stay overnight post-operatively, so they return as soon as possible to their home surroundings where they can relax and recover in familiar circumstances.

As mentioned earlier, following the success of the Paediatric Collaborative Care Plan, the Plan for Adult Day Case Surgery has evolved and is being implemented. The issues concerning the management of change of working into a new area of the Trust have been very interesting, and responses have varied. Goole Hospital has embraced the Plan enthusiastically and been positive in its modification. Its staff have already introduced pre-operative assessment as part of their routine planning for day case patients, with very few teething or operational problems. At Scunthorpe Hospital, in contrast, the concept of pre-operative assessment associated with the introduction of a Collaborative Care Plan has created considerable anxiety. As is nearly always the case in these circumstances, it is a matter of education and communication. The problems have been addressed and are in the process of being devolved to the users of the document. In this way they can gain ownership of the document and implement changes, which is crucial if they are to become comfortable with the new requirements. Not all reaction is negative, however; other specialties are now approaching the research department, including ENT, Urology, Ophthalmology and Maxillofacial Surgery, where plans for further collaborative care documents are well underway.

The ultimate challenge — collaborative care for inpatients — still remains. With the complexity of major surgery there is more likelihood of deviation from the Collaborative Care Plan (e.g. the risks of complications are higher, the recovery time is longer). Even if total implementation of collaborative care planning cannot take place, the examination of the flow of patients through a complex inpatient procedure, and the ways in which different patients deviate from an 'ideal' pathway, would allow contracts to be negotiated to accommodate the more complex patient who develops a problem. In addition, the demand upon beds, theatre time, ancillary services such as physiotherapy, rehabilitation, and social services would be highlighted, so that future contracts may be negotiated from a sounder base.

This chapter has shown that collaborative care planning is a dynamic method of approaching patient care in the present health care climate. It is an area that will be given further consideration and, if the initial success continues, will be implemented throughout the Trust.

REFERENCES

Johnson S. Pathway to the heart of care quality. Nursing Management 1995; 1, (8).

Royal College of Surgeons. Guidelines for day case surgery. London: Royal College of Surgeons, 1995.

Hewitson P. Collaborative care planning. A team approach to care. International Journal of Health Care and Quality Assurance 1992; 5, (2): 12–16.

British Association of Paediatric Surgeons. A guide for purchasers of paediatric surgical services 1994. London: The British Association of Paediatric Surgeons, 1994.

Scunthorpe and Goole Hospitals NHS Trust. Patient charter standards. Scunthorpe and Goole Hospitals NHS Trust, 1993.

Audit Commission. Recommendations for children's services — gold standards paediatric care. London: Audit Commission, 1994.

Foster L, Maloney L. Paediatric day surgery collaborative care planning. Northern Day Surgery Bulletin 1995; 7.

9. The evolving role of the surgical nurse practitioner in the acute setting

Lorraine Foster   Amanda Flood   Peter Moore

Introduction

The launch of the United Kingdom Central Council's *The Scope of Professional Practice*,[1] together with measures to reduce junior doctors' working hours,[2] has resulted in changes in the boundaries between the clinical work of nurses and junior doctors. Other factors, such as a decline in the number of surgical/medical staff, consumer demands, and radical reforms of nurse education, have brought about the evolution of the nurse practitioner. The so-called 'Heathrow Debate'[3] brought together professional leaders to discuss the challenges facing nursing and midwifery in the twenty-first century. Their discussion on how the role of the nurse would evolve by the year 2010 brought more debate and raised questions such as:

- How will substitution impact on the role of nursing?
- What will be the context in which nurses work?
- How will the public react to the changing role of nursing?
- How will accountability, authority and responsibility be altered?
- What are the implications for initial training, education, retraining and continuous training?

The debate did produce a consensus about what nursing constants there would be:[3]

the work of the nurse, whatever the setting, draws upon a tradition of caring, based around both skills and values and includes:

- a co-ordinating function;
- a teaching function, for carers, patients and professions;
- developing and maintaining programmes of care;
- technical expertise, exercised personally or through others;
- concern for the ill but also for those currently well;
- a special responsibility for the frail and vulnerable.

An agenda was proposed for consideration based on the five themes shown in Box 9.1.

Box 9.1 Five themes for nurse development

- Models and settings: the continuum of care from hospital to community; possibilities of nurse provider units; nurses as technicians; nurses with greater autonomy
- The task and the knowledge base: the core activities of nursing, training for these, and research into their effectiveness
- Resources: recruitment and funding
- Education: for the new nursing roles, and to spread the Project 2000 philosophy amongst nurses already trained
- Leadership: responsive to changing needs.

All these items have relevance to the changing role of the nurse. For many nurses and clinicians, the development of the nurse practitioner role, with its advanced skills and increased levels of autonomy, seems to be the way forward. There has already been a significant increase in nurse practitioners employed in the UK, with the majority working in primary care.[4]

An exploratory study was carried out in 1993 to identify the professional, educational and management issues that the changes in these roles would raise.[5] There were benefits and problems for patients, junior doctors and nurses, mainly relating to how the new roles for nurses were valued and the amount of autonomy the post holder would be allowed, depending on previous education. The researchers suggested that the substitution of nurses to undertake large parts of junior doctors' clinical work is neither a cheap nor an easy solution to the long-standing problems of junior doctors' hours. The research implied that where a role had been expanded over a longer period of time, there were benefits for the Trust, patients and staff, in terms of improving quality of patient care and the reduction of junior doctors' hours.

Definition of a nurse practitioner

The role of a nurse practitioner must not be confused with that of a nurse specialist. The nurse specialist role draws on the 'expansion' of nursing skills, having responsibility for direct patient care, whereas the nurse practitioner takes on skills that are essentially medical and where nursing is not a prerequisite.[6] The role has been defined as: 'one not included in nurse training and comprising tasks normally undertaken by a doctor but which may be delegated to a nurse who had received appropriate training'.[7] Nurse practitioners have diagnostic and prescribing powers, the authority for referral, and have a particular interest in counselling and health education. The UKCC states:[8]

specialist practitioners will exercise higher levels of judgement, discretion and clinical decision making. They will be able to monitor and improve standards through supervision of practice, clinical audit, provision of skilled professional leadership and the development of practice through research, teaching and support of professional colleagues.

The UKCC[8] recommend that specialist practitioners functioning at this level within a specialty should be educated to first degree level, therefore becoming experts in clinical practice. The advanced practitioner level, according to the UKCC,[8] 'is not an additional layer of practice to be added to specialist practice. It is an important field of professional practice concerned with the continuing development of professionals in the interest of patients, clients and the health services'. The UKCC go on to state:

Advanced nursing practice is concerned with:
- adjusting the boundaries for the development of future practice;
- pioneering and developing new roles which are responsive to changing needs;
- advancing clinical practice, research and education to enrich nursing practice as a whole;
- contributing to health policy and management and the determination of health needs;
- continuing the development of the professions in the interests of patients, clients and the health services.
This advanced practice will lead to:
- innovations in practice;
- an increase in nursing research and research-based practice;
- the provision of expert professionals who will have a consultancy role;
- high level professional leadership;
- increased political and professional influence in respect of nursing and health services;
- expert resources for education, supervision and management.
Practitioners acquiring these advanced skills will be at Masters and PhD level.

The duties of a surgical nurse practitioner will vary from Trust to Trust, depending on the specific specialist surgery and whether the Trust already has nurse practitioners in post. It is important when developing this role to co-opt senior members of nursing and medical staff and other professionals from within the organisation in order to define the boundaries of the post and to give support for the post. The nurse practitioner will be a first level registered nurse who will have a minimum of 5 years post-registration in a general surgical area and has an in-depth knowledge of general nursing. The nurse practitioner will function independently, or within a team of doctors, or alongside a single medical practitioner, within agreed protocols. In addition, the nurse practitioner will demonstrate competence in a wide range of skills that will complement the doctor in the delivery of health care in primary and acute care areas.

The possible duties of a surgical nurse practitioner are described below.

Management of pre-admission clinics

This enables the nurse practitioner to counsel her/his patients if appropriate, and provides an opportunity to determine the patient's fitness for surgery/anaesthesia. Any social problems can be picked up at pre-admission, reducing the possibility of delayed discharge. Advice and education can be given to patients and their carers regarding surgery and convalescence. Close liaison with both medical and nursing staff at this stage can highlight any problems that may occur during the patient's inpatient stay. The nurse practitioner may take the patient's history (protocol-based) and prepare patients' documentation and discharge letters. Protocols can be used at this stage to determine the specific tests and investigations to be carried out.

Intravascular activities

Nurse practitioners will perform venepuncture, initiate treatment, write up i.v. fluids (protocol-based), and insert i.v. cannulae. If it is part of the specific role, the nurse practitioner will also give cytotoxic treatments (which will also be protocol-based), along with prophylactic antibiotics and anticoagulants.

Liaison with other professionals

The nurse practitioner will liaise with other professionals, such as:

- anaesthetists — to discuss issues relating to operating lists and other associated problems
- physiotherapists — to discuss the continuing care of patients post-operatively
- occupational therapists — to facilitate rehabilitation
- pharmacists — to discuss the formulation and development of specific protocols in analgesia, antibiotic treatment and thrombolytic therapy
- general practitioners — in order to continue care into the primary setting.

The Greenhalgh Report,[9] which was commissioned by the Department of Health, researched into the activities which junior doctors and nurses both practised. The report concluded that 11–16% of junior doctors' time was taken up with:

- patient history-taking
- cannulation
- phlebotomy
- administration of i.v. drugs
- referring for investigations
- writing discharge letters.

The report also concluded that when nurses undertook these activities there was no difference in quality. The report recommended that these activities should be shared, along with other activities. This was not welcomed by some of the nursing profession, as it was seen as a 'task-oriented' approach to care and was yet another activity to be taken on by nurses who were already feeling the pressure of increased workloads due to the loss of student nurses for Project 2000.

Assisting in the operating theatre

One of the developing roles of the nurse practitioner in surgery is that of surgical assistant. The National Association of Theatre Nurses (NATN) in their publication *The Nurse as Surgeon's Assistant*[10] state:

The term 'Surgeon's Assistant' refers to the role undertaken by a registered nurse providing skilled assistance and some surgical intervention under the supervision of a surgeon. This role must not be confused with the role of 'First Assistant', which refers to the registered nurse providing skilled assistance to the surgeon on an ad hoc basis. The term 'surgical intervention' is the important difference, and more training and education are required to accomplish this role. This role also includes the use of flexible cystoscopes in urology and sigmoidoscopes in gastro-intestinal surgery.

Accountability

Clause IV in *The Scope of Professional Practice*[1] states: 'the practitioner should acknowledge his or her limitations, not undertake anything he or she has not been trained to do and if any adjustments are made to professional practice, the practitioner is accountable if anything goes wrong'.

The nurse is now professionally accountable for her or his own actions at all times, and this requires her or him to be competent, knowledgeable and skilled. The UKCC also states that 'the practitioner shall acknowledge any limitations of competence and refuse in such cases to accept delegated functions without first having received instructions in regard to those functions and having been assessed as competent'. Therefore it must first be established what is acceptable for the nurse to undertake and for what the nurse is prepared to be accountable.

Professionally, there are no limits to what nurses can do, as long as their employer is aware that they are doing it, they approve of it, that it is safe, and that it enhances the quality of patient care. *The Scope of Professional Practice*[1] brings to an end the requirement that nurses, midwives and health visitors gain extended role certificates to carry out extra duties. It places responsibility for competence firmly on the individual nurse's shoulders. The code explicitly warns nurses to 'honestly acknowledge any limitations of knowledge and skill and take steps to remedy them'. Thus, it is clearly left to the individual nurse to decide how much she/he will do. This could prove difficult if the pressure is on and the 'questionable' jobs are waiting to be done. For example, a particular nurse may not be happy, or feel competent, to carry out a particular duty, but she/he may be told that the nurse on the previous duty was happy to carry out that duty, and therefore feels pressured to do the same. The onus is now on the practitioner as to whether he/she expands his or her role. The problem here is that there is no uniformity across the country and training for practitioner roles may vary quite considerably from one Trust to another.

Problems of expanding practice

There is no clear indication on which way the role of the nurse should take. The UKCC clearly states that the 'extended roles' (in their old definition) are no longer suitable, as the concept is task-oriented and detracts from the holistic approach to health care. However, since the 'extended roles' have been discontinued, there are no clear guidelines as to how the 'expanded' practice is to be monitored. The decision to adjust practice is left to the individual practitioner. Nurses are now under pressure to update and expand their practice; if they do not, they may see technicians and other professions take on these roles. This will benefit the doctors by reducing their working hours, but will fragment the holistic care which nurses are able to give. Both the nurse practitioner and managers need to know the boundaries of the role, otherwise confusion and lack of clarity will prevail. The nurse must be able to refuse to take on new tasks that may compromise the standard of care.

The role of the nurse practitioner may still be viewed as that of the nurse becoming the doctor's handmaiden, or it may be interpreted as cheap labour, for nurses are cheaper to train and cost less to employ than doctors or technicians. There is an underlying fear that the evolving role of the nurse practitioner is a response to the needs of medicine — the clinician is dictating practice, assuming responsibility for supervising practice, and then incorporating this in the nursing role.

Diamond[11] states that 'there are still some employers that are unaware of their employee's expanded roles and so fail to carry out competency checks'. The nurse practitioner would be defenceless under the umbrella of vicarious liability. The employer must be informed of the practitioner's expanded role, in order to accept liability. Read[12] states that 'some hospitals have found that by introducing practitioner roles for part of the time, expectations have been raised, these cannot be met when the post holder is not present. Others have found that the post holder extends quality of service, no-one else's work has been reduced'.

Some clinical assistant grades of medical staff feel threatened by the developing nurse-led roles and fear they may lose their jobs.[12] There may also be resistance from junior doctors, for the report from the Trent Scheme[13] found that a few doctors complained that their training was restricted due to the appointment of an advanced practitioner.

Benefits of the nurse practitioner role

The role of the nurse practitioner in surgery has many benefits for medical and nursing staff and patients. Quality of patient care is improved through the continuity of patient care. The nurse practitioner is able to follow the patient from the outpatient department through to discharge into primary care. Job satisfaction is improved, although research has suggested that nurse practitioners are more satisfied with intrinsic work factors such as achievement and responsibility and less satisfied with extrinsic factors such as salary and supervision.[14] Multi-professional relationships are improved, and mutual respect for each member's individual profession is enhanced. The nurse practitioner provides an effective channel of communication and continual support to both patient and clinician.

Training programmes

There must be a structured training and assessment programme. Nurses are now taking on roles in endoscopic and urodynamic studies, and it is therefore critical that they are trained and assessed in the use of new equipment, and have the ability to identify problems such as equipment malfunction. Training must be individualised, although there is a common core of skills and knowledge required for most nurse practitioner roles. The programme should be built on the competencies and experience of each practitioner, and must provide training and assessment in all the new areas of practice which the nurse will be required to undertake. As well as providing training for clinical skills, wider educational needs should be considered, not just in areas such as anatomy and physiology, but also skills in management, negotiating and audit.

Thought must be given to the preparation of appropriate trainers. There must be clear roles and responsibilities for trainers of these specialist practitioners, and commitment of time and resources from all appointed trainers. Each trainer must have a clear statement of what is expected and must be aware of the training needs of each individual nurse practitioner.

Training must be provided in collaboration with the specific clinician and the other members of that clinical team. Because of vicarious liability, all adjustments to the scope of professional practice should first be accepted by the Trust Board and other medical and nursing forums as appropriate. There must also be an ongoing review of the nurse's competence; any new task being performed should be reviewed at regular intervals and performed at regular intervals to ensure a maintenance of skill levels. Assessment will be performed by the appropriate consultant, who will have worked with members of the nursing and anaesthetic staff to compile the necessary standards of competence and outcomes. Documentation of achievement will follow the same format as that used in *The Scope of Professional Practice*.[1] There must also be a format that considers non-achievement.

At present, nurse practitioners cannot legally:

- certify death
- establish a diagnosis
- prescribe drugs to take home
- initiate prescriptions
- initiate radio-diagnostic tests.

Conclusion

As yet, there is no literature addressing the cost-effectiveness of the nurse practitioner in the acute setting, and efforts to calculate cost-effectiveness have hitherto been focused on primary care. Financial gains from employing nurse practitioners in the acute setting will be an area of potential future research, and will give more information on the efficacy of the nurse practitioner role. There still seems to be considerable conflict over the definitions of expanded roles, in spite of *The Scope of Professional Practice*[1] and the *Code of Professional Conduct*.[15] There are still problems concerning the preparation and protection of nurse practitioners' roles and responsibilities. Support must be given even to the most experienced nurse, as role ambiguity and isolation can put the development at risk. The emergence of these new health care practitioners should not mean that nurses replace doctors and create another hierarchical layer of nursing, but that they provide a better quality service and a wider choice of care.

REFERENCES

United Kingdom Central Council for Nursing, Midwifery and Health Visiting. The scope of professional practice. London: UKCC, 1992.
NHS Management Executive. Junior doctors. The new deal. London: NHS Management Executive, 1991.
Department of Health. The challenges for nursing and midwifery in the 21st century. London: Department of Health, 1994.
South East Thames Regional Health Authority. Nursing in South East Thames: nurse practitioner projects 1992–1994. London: SETRHA, 1992.

Dowling S, Barrett S, West R. With nurse practitioners, who needs house officers? British Medical Journal 1995; 3: (11).

Maguire J. The expanded role of the nurse. London: King's Fund, 1980.

Molde S, Diers D. Nurse practitioner research. Nursing Research 1985; 34: (6) 362–367.

United Kingdom Central Council for Nursing, Midwifery and Health Visiting. PREP and You. London: UKCC, 1995.

Greenhalgh and Company Limited. The interface between junior doctors and nurses — a research study for the Department of Health. Macclesfield: Greenhalgh, 1994.

National Association of Theatre Nurses. The nurse as surgeon's assistant. London: NATN, 1994.

Diamond B. Legal aspects of nursing. London: Prentice Hall, 1990.

Read S. Catching the tide: new voyages in nursing? Sheffield: Sheffield Centre for Health and Related Research, 1995.

Read S, Graves K. Reduction of junior doctors hours in Trent Region: the nursing contribution. Sheffield: Trent RHA/NHS Executive Trent, 1994.

Satreit BJ. Health care dollars and regulatory sense — the role of the advanced practice nursing. Yale Journal on Regulation 1992; 9: (2) 417–488.

United Kingdom Central Council for Nursing, Midwifery and Health Visiting. Code of Professional Conduct. London: UKCC, 1991.

10. The evolving role of the nurse practitioner in endoscopy

Surrinder Kaur

Introduction and background

The role of a flexible sigmoidoscopist/counsellor was developed by East Yorkshire Hospitals NHS Trust in conjunction with the Surgical Academic Unit (Postgraduate Medical School, University of Hull). Subsequently, the first English National Board (ENB) 9N81 Colorectal Screening Course for Nurse Practitioners was developed. The experience provided a template for the development and validation of the ENB A87 Nurse Practitioner in Upper Gastro-Intestinal Endoscopy Course. The purpose of this chapter is to share the experiences gained principally in the role and in the development of a course related to flexible sigmoidoscope screening. Factors which need to be considered when developing nurse practitioner roles in endoscopy are put forward as checklists.

The need for nurse practitioners to evolve in endoscopy is related to health needs and to service quality initiatives. A greater number of investigative, screening and therapeutic procedures can be performed in open access clinics. This in turn impacts on the role of the nurse and nursing practice. The nurse can contribute to the provision of continuity of care and the reduction of patient waiting times. Participation in screening programmes enables nurses to contribute to the ethos of the *Health of the Nation* targets[1] and the improvement in the health status of the population. It also adds a new dimension to the role and contribution of nurses to public health.[2] Endoscopy clinics which separated investigative work from therapeutic work would enable medical consultants to utilise their skills more effectively, especially if nurse practitioners undertook the screening and the consultant undertook the diagnosis and therapeutic aspects.

It is envisaged that more and more people will use endoscopy services due to the knowledge that may be gained to enable conditions to be identified and treated early. For example, *Helicobactor pylori* is a common cause of ulcers and gastric problems. The presence of the bacterium prevents ulcers from healing; the longer the bacterium is present in the stomach, the greater the risk of stomach cancer. The chances of a person having this bacterium increase with age. Upper gastro-intestinal endoscopy can now be used to investigate this condition so that it can be treated.

Colorectal cancer has been reported to be a health problem second only to lung cancer.[3] In the United Kingdom there are almost 31 000 new cases of colorectal cancer annually, leading to approximately 20 000 deaths.[4] The prognosis correlates to the stage of the disease. If screening programmes detect localised pre-symptomatic cancers and pre-cancerous polyps, preventive measures can then be instigated by removing adenomatous polyps prior to their malignant transformation.

The American Cancer Society and the American College of Physicians recommend that asymptomatic adults older than 50 years of age should undergo screening by sigmoidoscopy.[3] In Britain, there is no national screening programme, despite the fact that the annual death toll exceeds that of breast and cervical cancer.[5] The impediments to screening programmes relate to the lack of availability of screening services, the expense of the examination, and the lack of qualified practitioners. Cost reduction and an increase in qualified practitioners could be achieved by nurse practitioners.

Role development

The Professor of Surgery and the Senior Lecturer/Consultant in the Surgical Academic Unit have a specialist interest in colorectal screening and research. The Unit is involved in a Medical Research Council (MRC) colorectal screening project using flexible sigmoidoscopy. This necessitated additional qualified practitioners; consequently discussion arose about developing a flexible sigmoidoscopist/counsellor nurse practitioner role.

The development of a nurse practitioner role in endoscopy and supporting educational courses was a multi-disciplinary effort — a crucial factor in its successful implementation. Management, educational and clinical practice issues had to be considered; those involved therefore included the Professor of Surgery, the Senior Lecturer/Consultant Surgeon, the Nursing Director, the Professional Development Nurse, Nurse Managers, the Principal

Lecturer from the Humberside College of Health, the Nurse Practitioner (designate), and the Endoscopy Unit Manager. External advice was obtained from a clinical nurse specialist from another Trust who is a member of the British Society of Gastroenterology.

In considering the role and course development, the following checklist of questions was used:

- What supporting literature is available?
- Why is there a need for a nurse practitioner role in endoscopy?
- What is the definition of the role?
- Should the role be specific to lower or upper endoscopy?
- How will the role contribute to the enhancement of the care and quality of the service provided in the endoscopy unit?
- Who should be trained to undertake the role?
- What would be the training requirements?
- What would the effect of the nurse practitioner role be on the boundaries of other nurses' and doctors' roles?
- How would the development of the role affect the training and experience of doctors?
- Could a business case be established for such a role?

The literature review identified nurse practitioner roles in endoscopy that have been developed in America and an evaluation of the training undertaken. Correspondence with the Cleveland Clinic in Florida[6] revealed that they had nurse-led colorectal clinics. The role of the nurse was to undertake a detailed nursing and medical history to assess whether the patient required anorectal examination or flexible sigmoidoscopy, and to assist with specialised anorectal physiological studies. The Cleveland Clinic also have colorectal nurse clinicians, who appear to have further expanded their skills. They evaluate the health status of selected patients and perform investigations according to accepted protocols prescribed by medical physicians. In addition, they order investigations, have prescribing rights, participate in ward rounds, write nursing and medical orders, and provide counselling and health education to patients and their families. Finally, they participate in research and evaluation of care.

The British Society of Gastroenterology (BSG) Working Party produced the *Nurse Endoscopist* report.[7] It supported the proposition that suitably trained and supervised nurses should be able to carry out diagnostic oesophago-gastro-duodenoscopy and sigmoidoscopy. Training should follow the same schedule recommended for medical endoscopy, including attendance at a recognised course. The report made recommendations for practice which influenced role and course development.

The successful development and evolution of a nurse practitioner role is dependent upon the endoscopy staff and users having a common vision and philosophy about the way in which an endoscopy service is provided. The vision[8] was to develop a multi-professional endoscopy service, which recognises skill sets that will be shared by doctors and nurse practitioners. The aim is to work towards ensuring that equitable standards for endoscopy techniques and training are maintained by nurses and doctors in the Trust. In doing so, the Endoscopy Unit would be able to offer 'one stop open access clinics' (e.g. a one stop colorectal clinic, a rectal bleeding service clinic). This would enable direct referral by GPs, with the patient undergoing assessment, investigations, diagnosis, health education and counselling in one visit. Family counselling would also be developed, due to the familial and genetic links of cancer.

It was recognised that a nurse practitioner role was preferable to a technician role. A technician role in the Endoscopy Unit, in which a nurse merely carried out lower or upper endoscopies, would be task-oriented and would not necessarily contribute to a better service to patients, who are already exposed to numerous personnel on hospital visits. Nor would a technician approach give job satisfaction to the post holder. A technician role in endoscopy would also give rise to the question of whether or not a nurse was needed. In Japan, upper gastro-intestinal endoscopy for stomach cancer is reportedly undertaken by non-nursing/medical staff.

The job description that was devised for the nurse practitioner sigmoidoscopist/counsellor is shown in Box 10.1.

Box 10.1 East Yorkshire Hospitals NHS Trust job description for the Nurse Practitioner Sigmoidoscopist/Counsellor

---

Title: Nurse Practitioner Sigmoidoscopist/Counsellor
Grade: G/H (dependent upon experience)
Managerially responsible to: Nurse Manager
Clinically responsible to: Nurse Manager/Professor of Surgery

Role:
The nurse practitioner will be expected to develop specific skills in the area of sigmoidoscopy, colorectal ultrasound, health education and patient counselling. The practitioner will carry a case

load. The practitioner will undertake screening on behalf of the consultant surgeon and participate in research.

Aims of the role
- To improve and maintain quality of care for patients undergoing investigative flexible sigmoidoscopy.
- To develop a counselling service for a specific client group.
- To participate in the development of protocols of care.
- To provide advice to patients and nursing staff on healthy lifestyles and lead health promotion activities related to this clinical field.

Summary of duties and responsibilities

Endoscopy
- Participate in the development of protocols of clinical management.
- Undertake clinical assessment within agreed protocols.
- Undertake flexible sigmoidoscopy with due regard to patient safety, and safe use of equipment.
- Identify abnormalities and act according to protocols.
- Maintain a case load of patients, organise systems and records to ensure appropriate follow-up.
- Participate in case review and ward rounds.
- Participate in teaching/training of nursing staff and other disciplines.
- Provide advice to other health care professionals.
- Provide advice to patients and promote lifestyle changes.
- Establish an effective communication network and liaise with all relevant health care disciplines.

Counselling
- Provide a counselling service for patients with colorectal disease referred by consultant.
- Work within British Association of Counselling Code of Practice and agreed hospital protocols.
- Provide information on appropriate associations, help and guidance centres.

Clinical/professional
- Undertake education and training and successfully meet assessment criteria to undertake all aspects of the Nurse Practitioner role.
- Ensure views of consumers are effectively sought, channeled

and acted upon, including the efficient actioning of
complaints in accordance with Trust policy.
- Participate in the development of information systems and
audit.
- Manage resources within established parameters.
- Demonstrate clinical leadership by initiating change and
evaluating outcomes to improve client care.
- Promote professional practice and ensure compliance of
relevant legislation, UKCC codes of practice, Scope of
Professional Practice and guidelines, Trust and Unit policies.
- Advise Nurse Managers on issues concerning professional
practice.

The job description will be subject to review with the Nursing
Director, and other responsibilities will be included to meet the
service needs following discussion with the post holder.

The Trust management team and Board approved the role and
course development. The legal and insurance aspects were discussed with the Trust lawyers and insurers. In giving approval for
the employment of the nurse practitioner, the Trust would be providing vicarious liability; it was therefore important that the practitioner was prepared and was competent to undertake the role.

Following the advertisement and recruitment process, a nurse
was appointed with a background in surgery on a 'G' grade, which
was changed to 'H' grade following completion of training. A
detailed induction package was implemented. The next stage was
to implement a comprehensive training plan involving personal
tuition by the Academic Unit staff (e.g. anatomy and physiology,
colorectal diseases and management, flexible sigmoidoscopy techniques). Clinical supervision and training was provided by the
Senior Lecturer/Consultant in the Endoscopy Unit. The practitioner undertook the ENB 906 Endoscopy nursing course. The
Professional Development Nurse provided advice relating to
courses the nurse could access within and outside the Trust and
provided nursing professional support as required. Formal support
was given once a month. The nurse practitioner maintained a professional profile and attended clinical supervision workshops, a
counselling course and relevant conferences.

The record of practical training for flexible sigmoidoscopy was
kept by the practitioner in a log book; this was useful for reflecting

upon experience. The practical training consisted of 35 observations of the technique, 35 withdrawals of the scope, and 35 supervised full procedures. Evaluation of sigmoidoscopy training for nurses and residents has been undertaken by a number of American clinicians. Disario and Sanowski[9] found that nurses and physicians gained proficiency in this technique at a mean of 20 procedures, although one nurse did not achieve proficiency until after 35 procedures. The conclusions drawn indicated that nurses could perform screening sigmoidoscopy in as safe and effective a manner as doctors. Rosevelt and Frankle[10] and Maule[11] describe the training of nurse practitioners in colorectal cancer screening using a 60 cm flexible fibreoptic sigmoidoscope. Both papers endorse the view that nurses can perform the procedure competently. Schroy[3] advocated the use of video endoscopy by nurse practitioners and its review by a physician endoscopist as a feasible approach to ensure quality control and to extend the available resources for performance of the examination. Video taping was adopted in the Trust and a protocol drawn up for the review process.

ENB 9N81 Colorectal Screening Course for Nurse Practitioners

Clinical protocols were developed to support the nurse practitioner role. These, together with the success of the training programme, encouraged the idea of developing an approved course. The consultants expressed a desire for a course which was approved by the nursing professional body, the English National Board (ENB), rather than merely attaining University academic validation. The reasons for this are shown in Box 10.2.

Box 10.2   Reasons for preferring ENB approval

- A national outline curriculum would be set.
- Educational and professional standards would be adhered to.
- The nursing aspects of the role would be identifiable and at a specialist level.
- The course would be a module of the ENB Advanced Award pathway leading to graduate status.
- The course would have a Credit Accumulation Transfer (CAT) rating of 24 points at academic level three; it would also be part of the College of Health degree pathway.
- The course would carry a professional kite mark.

The ENB 9N81 Colorectal Screening Course[12] was spread over a 14-week period, which included 11 study days. The course focused on the themes shown in Box 10.3.

Box 10.3   The themes in the ENB 9N81 Colorectal Screening Course

- Autonomous nursing practice
- Colorectal screening and flexible sigmoidoscopy techniques
- Counselling skills
- Health promotion
- Normal and disordered anatomy and physiology
- Legal, moral and ethical issues
- Clinical decision making
- Developing evidence-based nursing practice.

Course selection was based on the requisites shown in Box 10.4.

Box 10.4   Course selection requisites

- A first level general nurse
- A minimum of 6 months' endoscopy experience
- Evidence of ongoing education and development
- Awareness of current professional issues (e.g. Scope of Practice, clinical supervision, developments in endoscopy, BSG recommendations and guidelines)
- Support of the Trust, consultant endoscopist and nurse manager
- Availability of clinical experience and quality of clinical supervision in the nurse's own unit.

Whilst applications were received from 'E' grade staff nurses, only 'F' grades and above were selected for the course. Learning was also facilitated by the use of open learning packs related to record keeping, and a study guide related to anatomy and physiology was designed by the Trust Nurse Practitioner. The assignment work consisted of developing, maintaining and auditing records and presenting patient care studies. The last assignment related to the presentation and development of a practice development plan. This was a practical plan that the nurse practitioner would use in the 12–18 months following the course to develop the role and practice. The plan was expected to have been negotiated with the nurse's clinical supervisor and nurse manager and to have involved the endoscopy team. For the plan to be successful, it needed to address the elements shown in Box 10.5.

Box 10.5   Elements needed in a successful practice development plan

- A clear vision for the direction of the nurse practitioner role within the context of the endoscopy business plan
- A philosophy for practice
- A conceptual framework for patient-centred care delivery
- A plan to audit and evaluate the role and care delivery
- Priorities for practice development with clear objectives and an action plan
- A marketing plan for the role
- A plan for the dissemination of the role and clinical initiatives in the organisation and nationally
- Evidence of protocols and guidance for practice.

Preparation for the role of nurse practitioner draws upon a wide knowledge base consisting of nursing, psychology, sociology, medicine, research, and law. The components are integrated into clinical practice and decision making. It is the knowledge required to analyse critically and apply clinical judgement which constitutes the distinction between training someone to do a task and educating someone to practise in an accountable and autonomous manner.

A semi-structured reflective journal was kept by the participants to record critical incidents, and to reflect upon the development of skills in assessment, counselling, health education and technique of flexible sigmoidoscopy. A log of 35 observations, 35 withdrawals and 35 full procedures was also kept. It was acknowledged that whilst clinical learning outcomes related to the technique could be reached with fewer procedures, some cases might take longer. The purpose of stipulating numbers was to ensure that the participant was exposed to a range of experiences and observations of the colo-rectum. Endoscopy video taping and photographs were undertaken as part of the case review process in discussion with clinical supervisors.

Participants undertook their clinical practice in their own organisations. Clinical supervision was provided by their own consultant endoscopist. They, together with the participants' nurse managers, were invited to the course briefing day, the presentation of practice development plans and the course evaluation.

Professional supervision was provided within their own organisation. The consultant and professional development nurse provided tutorial support and supervision as required.

Participants completing the course gave an excellent written and group evaluation, stating that the integration of theory and practice had been achieved to assist their role development and that the assignments were of practical value. By-products of the course included the nurse practitioners developing a group clinical supervision model for themselves. This was seen as vital for ongoing development, as well as playing a part in the risk management element of the role. Three nurse practitioners became ENB specialist registry members, and they also became involved in writing for publication and influencing policy-making bodies in their own Trusts and the BSG group.

Financially, the course was supported by the Trust, and fees of external participants covered the course costs. Participants' salaries were paid for by their Trusts. Following training, some participants were upgraded to 'H' grade.

Most new initiatives encounter difficulties or resistance to the change. This development was an exception to the rule, primarily because a team approach was taken and each individual contributed his or her skills and knowledge to 'make things happen', both for the role and course development. Role development took six months from planning to implementation. The course was written and validated in six weeks.

Evaluation of the role will take place as a formal part of the MRC research project in the Surgical Academic Unit. The intention is to seek research funding to evaluate the role development of a cohort of nurse practitioners who have completed the course.

The future

At present there are very few nurse practitioners in endoscopy who have undergone a recognised educational programme, although there are nurses who are undertaking flexible sigmoidoscopy with local training. This could lead to variable standards of preparation and practice. A professionally approved course ensures that practitioners who have achieved the learning outcomes are safe to practise. The experience has been used to develop the ENB A87 Nurse Practitioner course for Upper Gastro-Intestinal Endoscopy, which requires longer preparation due to the variety of abnormalities of structure and function of the upper gastro-intestinal tract. A nurse will undertake the course before being appointed to the role in the Trust. When standards for nurses are being established, it gives rise to the question whether doctors should be prepared to the same standard. Senior house officers in the Trust will undertake shared learning on both courses; this ensures that skills are being shared and not transferred to nurses. The intention in future is to identify ways of gaining conjoint approval from the Royal College of Physicians and the Royal College of Surgeons for the ENB courses, or at least to lobby for standards of doctors' preparation being no less than those of nurses.

In conclusion, the evolving role of the nurse practitioner is dependent upon the collaboration and team work of consultants, managers, nurses and educationalists. It requires detailed planning, and the Trust must fully support such roles and ensure that adequate lead-in time for development is given.

ACKNOWLEDGEMENTS

To the team members involved at East Yorkshire NHS Hospitals Trust: Graeme Duthie; Mark Hughs; June Bedford; Rachael Hodgson; Professor Monson; Kevin Wedgwood; and Carol Ringrow.

REFERENCES

Department of Health. The health of the nation. London: Department of Health, 1993.

Standing Nursing and Midwifery Advisory Committee. Making it happen – nurses, midwives and health visitors contribution to public health. London: DoH, 1995.

Schroy PC, Wiggins ST, Winawer SJ, Diaz B, Lightdale CJ. Video endoscopy by nurse practitioners; a model for colorectal screening. Gastro-intestinal Endoscopy 1988; 24(5): 390–394.

Austoker J. Screening for colorectal cancer. British Medical Journal 1994; 309: 382–386.

Atkin WS, Cuzick J, Northover JMA, Wheynes DK. Prevention of colorectal cancer by once only sigmoidoscopy. Lancet 1993; 341: 736–739.

West S. Personal communication, 1995.

British Society of Gastroenterology Working Party. The nurse endoscopist. London: British Society of Gastroenterology, 1994.

Hodgson R. Endoscopy practice development plan. Personal communication, 1995.

Disario JA, Sanowski R. A sigmoidoscopy training for nurses and resident physicians. Gastrointestinal Endoscopy 1993; 39: 29–32.

Rosevelt J, Frankle H. Colorectal cancer screening by nurse practitioner using 60 cm flexible fiberoptic sigmoidoscope. Digestive Diseases and Sciences 1984; 29(2): 161–163.

Maule WF. Screening for colorectal cancer by nurse endoscopist. The New England Journal of Medicine 1994; 330(3): 183–187.

East Yorkshire NHS Hospitals, Humberside College of Health, Hull University. English National Board 9N81 Course Submission Document, 1995.

11. The provision of trauma services and the development of accreditation

Alastair McGowan

Introduction and background

Development of the first part of the implementation of a regional major trauma system is outlined in this chapter. Key background information is presented, followed by a description of the process of design and implementation.

Injury is the leading cause of death in the first four decades of life. It accounts for more years of life lost than cancer and heart disease combined. For every one patient who dies from injury, there are three more who are rendered permanently disabled. The economic consequences are difficult to assess, but it has been estimated that accidents 'cost' the equivalent of 1% of the gross national product and that road traffic accidents cost the exchequer £2.8 billion in 1985.

In 1988, a Working Party of the Royal College of Surgeons of England under the chairmanship of Professor Miles Irving published a landmark report on the *Management of Patients With Major Injuries*.[1] In this report, 1000 consecutive deaths from injury were reviewed. The case notes were scrutinised by a panel of four assessors who asked themselves the question: 'If this patient had been admitted to a fully staffed and equipped American-style trauma centre, might death have been prevented?'

The assessors concluded that 20% of the deaths in hospital might have been prevented if the above criteria had been met. The Working Party recommended:

- greater consultant involvement in the early management of injury
- the establishment of trauma centres to which the most seriously injured could be transferred from District General Hospitals
- a team approach to the management of injury
- an expansion of Advanced Trauma Life Support (ATLS) courses

115

- monitoring of standards via a national audit scheme such as the Major Trauma Outcome Study (MTOS)
- encouragement of research into trauma.

Not surprisingly, the report attracted headlines and widespread attention. Much of the attention focused on the more glamorous of the recommendations, and trauma centres became the focus of subsequent discussion. As a consequence of this attention, a prospective comparative trial was established between the City General Hospital in Stoke, which was designated as a trauma centre and given extra resources and staffing, and two large District General Hospitals in Hull and Preston. The results of this study are awaited (and are overdue), but no-one seems optimistic that the results will achieve significance.

I am one of a group of practitioners in the field who welcomed the report and its recommendations, but who had some concerns about their interpretation and the emphasis which was subsequently placed on them. Our position is best encapsulated in the concern that the wrong question was asked of the assessors. It was our hypothesis that the question should have been: 'If this patient had been admitted to a fully staffed and equipped and properly organised District General Hospital, might death have been prevented?'

We think that the same 20% of deaths would have been preventable under such a system. We further hypothesised that early consultant involvement, a team approach to injury, and widespread propagation of the ATLS course might allow the framework for the necessary organisation of a District General Hospital to receive major trauma and to prevent avoidable deaths.

The Advanced Trauma Life Support course

The Advanced Trauma Life Support (ATLS) course is a carefully designed and monitored two-day course for doctors, which has been developed by the American College of Surgeons since 1979.[2] It is run in the UK under the control of the Royal College of Surgeons. Instructors for the course are selected from senior doctors who are themselves successful students of the course. They are subsequently taught in educational techniques and supervised as they first apply them.

The course content is under continual review, and addresses itself to the priorities of management in the first hour after injury.

A comprehensive manual (which is read before the course), lectures, workshops and skill stations are used to demonstrate safe techniques for some life-saving surgical interventions, to impart a necessary core knowledge, and, most importantly, to reinforce a systematised approach to the patient so that the greatest threat to life is sought first and, if present, dealt with first.

The course started in the UK in 1988 and has spread throughout the country. Standards are rigorously maintained by the Royal College of Surgeons. The courses evaluate extremely positively; I reviewed 650 consecutive participants and found that 96% had actively recommended the course to others, and that 97% had altered their practice in at least one way as a consequence of attendance. Given that 30% of the participants were consultants with established patterns of practice, the change in their behaviour, which they themselves report, is indicative of the powerful learning package which ATLS has become.

The Major Trauma Outcome Study

The Major Trauma Outcome Study (MTOS)[3] is a retrospective descriptive study of injury severity and outcome, initially organised by the American College of Surgeons Committee on Trauma; it is now collecting data from the USA, Canada, Australia and the UK. UK results are co-ordinated by the University of Manchester. Data are currently held on more than 120 000 trauma patients. The data are analysed periodically and the results sent in confidence to the participating institutions to support local audit activity. The collection of data for MTOS makes use of scores of anatomical injury and the patient's physiological response to that injury.

All patients with injury admitted to hospital for more than three days, or who require intensive care facilities, or who are transferred for specialist care, or who die in hospital, are entered into the MTOS statistics. Pre-hospitalisation information is also collated, as well as details of the seniority of the doctors attending a patient in hospital and the times of their involvement. Timings and nature of surgery are also recorded. The 'outcome' referred to in the study's title relates to whether or not the patient is alive or dead on the 90th day after injury. No measure of disability is included. Using the scores of injury severity and a physiological response, a probability of survival can be worked out, and this is used to identify those patients who are unexpected survivors or who die an unexpected death. This information is useful for local case review.

Given the large numbers of returns which have now been sent to the UK database, a hospital's overall performance can be judged against the UK performance, provided certain case-mix characteristics are sufficiently matched. Performance in my own hospital is such that in our most recent returns, which are based on all our trauma cases since 1991, we have three excess survivors per 100 patients treated when compared to what would be predicted.

The process of accreditation

Within the old regional framework, there was a Regional Medical Advisory Group in Yorkshire. In 1990 this group considered the best way to provide services for the seriously injured in Yorkshire, and there was widespread consensus that the type of model referred to above and based on District General Hospitals would be a suitable starting point for such a regional system. Subsequent developments of trauma centres would further strengthen the regional system, but it was felt that the necessary initial building block should be based around the receiving District General Hospital.

A working party of this group — consisting of an accident and emergency consultant, an orthopaedic surgeon, an anaesthetist, a hospital manager, a purchaser, and a consultant in public health medicine — drafted a set of standards which could be applied to a District General Hospital that would allow it to be designated as a major trauma receiving hospital. These standards required that the site had: the necessary facilities, such as an operating theatre available for 24 hours a day; an adequately staffed and sized intensive care unit; and requisite radiology, pathology and blood transfusion services. However, the core requirement of the standards was the existence of a pre-arranged, multi-disciplinary response to the arrival of a patient with major injuries, including the involvement of consultants and junior doctors who had undergone ATLS training. The standards are shown in Appendix 1 (p. 123).

A copy of the proposed standards, with the suggestion that hospitals could volunteer themselves for an accreditation system (wherein they would be visited by external assessors to judge whether or not the standards were met), was distributed widely to every interest group that could be identified in the Yorkshire region. All purchasing authorities, provider units, community health councils, patient organisations, and professional organisations were contacted, and the working group waited, in some apprehension, for their responses. The suggestions attracted many and varied comments. What was surprising, however, was that the comments that were made addressed themselves to the details of the standards rather than to the underlying principle and philosophy that hospitals could volunteer themselves to take part in an accreditation process. No-one indicated by any means, formal or informal, that they held any reservations about such a suggestion.

Surprised but encouraged, the working party sought to develop an accreditation process by which hospitals could be judged. The King's Fund Organisational Audit Department was invited to assist the working party with the development of the system, and their experience in the field has been the key to the development of the system thus far.

The process of accreditation

The process was designed on the precepts that the accreditation had to be visible, understood, and valued by all parties concerned. The personnel involved, and the methods which they used, had to be seen to be credible and objective. It was agreed that the system would be built around:

- the supply of documentary evidence prior to an assessment visit
- an assessment visit
- a review of collected information by an accreditation board which would be quite distinct from the assessors who performed the visit.

Documentation

Each of the standards which had been set was reviewed with the King's Fund Organisational Audit Department. Documentary evidence that could be supplied by a hospital was identified for each standard. A list of the necessary documentation is shown in Appendix 2 (p. 124). This documentation had to be provided to the assessors four weeks before the assessment visit. It was accompanied by a self-assessment proforma filled in by staff of the hospital, in which they judged their own performance against the standards which had been set.

The assessment visit

It was planned that the assessment visit would last for one day and would be carried out by two assessors and a team leader. The aim of the visit would be to test objectively whether the criteria for dealing with patients with major injury were being met by the hospital. The assessment visit was a form of peer review conducted by a senior consultant and a senior nurse, both of whom had to be experienced in dealing with major injury and had to be practising health care professionals from another District. The team leader acted as a link between the assessment team and the hospital. He or she did not participate in the interview sessions, but aimed to facilitate subsequent discussions. Four weeks before the visit each assessor was sent a self-assessment form by the hospital, necessary requested documentation, and a timetable of the interviews that each assessor would undertake.

The assessment visit was obviously complex, and therefore a specific training package was designed for all those who were to be involved in assessment visits so that they could develop the necessary skills. A one-and-a-half day package was put together with the help of the King's Fund, covering interviewing skills, listening skills, observational skills, time-keeping skills, note-keeping skills, and report writing. Workshops and role play allowed the handling of anticipated problems to be practised.

All the assessors were thoroughly briefed on the background to the scheme, the purpose of the scheme in the long term, and the purpose of the assessment visit in the short term. During the visit, the assessment team reviewed among themselves any problems identified by the hospital self-assessment and agreed areas and responsibilities for eliciting further information. At the end of each day, the visiting hospital would receive oral feedback on the visit, and the assessment report had to be written and agreed by the assessors within 48 hours.

The Accreditation Board

The report to the Accreditation Board addressed each of the standards, answered whether or not the standard was being achieved, and allowed comments when necessary. The Accreditation Board comprised the Regional Chief Executive; a senior clinician; and the Chairman of a Purchasing Authority.

The following paragraphs illustrate part of the process. A key component of the assessment was the availability of ATLS-trained doctors. The documentary evidence to be supplied before the visit would include the rotas for ATLS providers for the month of the visit and the preceding two months (or agreed alternative). In practice this would mean that a rota would be supplied to the visitors for the middle grade cover in the orthopaedic department, the general surgical department, the anaesthetic department, and accident and emergency department; these would have to be cross-checked against a list of ATLS providers from the hospital to ensure that one was always on duty within the hospital.

During the visit itself key areas that had been identified from examination of the documentation could be explored, but in addition it was agreed that the visitors would, at a minimum, check:

- arrangements for ensuring that there is an ATLS provider available to the A&E Department
- the extent to which the ATLS provider is given the necessary authority to lead the trauma team, which may include more senior medical staff, effectively
- the practicalities of access to the emergency theatre
- the response of consultant staff to being called to a major trauma victim
- availability of blood transfusion products.

The pilot scheme

Three hospitals in Humberside were identified for a first attempt at the accreditation process. The process of the supply of documentation, its scrutiny by assessors, the visit by assessors, the writing and submission of the report, and the supply of feedback to the hospital have been evaluated by all parties concerned. Some minor modifications to the standards themselves have ensued, but the process has not been altered as a consequence of its first field trial.

Of the three hospitals assessed, one received unconditional accreditation, another received provisional accreditation, as one standard had only been partially fulfilled, and the third hospital had accreditation withheld because several key standards had not been achieved.

Conclusions to date

The initial premise that this process could be used to improve standards in hospitals seems to be borne out. Necessary organisational changes to facilitate the delivery of care for injured patients have been implemented. Involvement in the Major Trauma Outcome Study has been improved. Every hospital in Yorkshire is currently submitting data to the national database.

The hospital which failed to achieve accreditation at its initial visit was not penalised in any way. If the system were to be applied, then hospitals which do not obtain necessary minimal standards would not receive major trauma patients. Ambulances carrying patients who are thought to have sustained major injury would be driven past such hospitals and go to the nearest accredited hospital. This would be a significant change in practice, and in some areas would be especially difficult because of geographical considerations. The initial standards which have been set, however, are attainable by every District General Hospital in Yorkshire. The scheme has never had the closure of DGHs to emergency admissions as an objective, but this issue would need to be addressed if the scheme were to spread further, for this would be the likely consequence of failure to achieve accreditation.

The standards are under annual review, so that they can reflect the evolution of best practice in the field. Various pressures, principal among them manpower issues, may work towards reducing the 24-hour availability of all emergency services in all DGHs. The process of accreditation could facilitate this if it were to become a reality.

Postscript

Peter Burdett-Smith et al recently published an article in *Injury*[4] showing a statistically significant improvement in outcome from major injury in Leeds following the introduction of ATLS training and a team approach to trauma.

At a re-visit six months after the first visit, the hospital which failed to achieve accreditation received unconditional accreditation. No new facilities had been required. The visiting assessors commented on the 'profound change of attitude' and that 'ownership of the problems surrounding major injury was evident'. All three hospitals who subjected themselves to the accreditation process report the experience to have been beneficial.

REFERENCES

Royal College of Surgeons of England Working Party. Management of patients with major injury. 1988.
American College of Surgeons. Advanced trauma life support manual, 5th edn. 1993.
Yates DW, Woodford M, Hollis S. Preliminary analysis of the care of injured patients in 33 British hospitals: first report of the United Kingdom major trauma outcome study. British Medical Journal 1992; 305: 737–740.
Burdett-Smith P, Airey M, Franks A. Improvements in trauma survival in Leeds. Injury 1995; 26(7): 455–458.

APPENDIX 1 — THE REQUIRED STANDARDS

Criteria	Comments	Achieved
1. There must be an ATLS provider (a doctor who has successfully completed the Royal College of Surgeons of England Advanced Trauma Life Support course) in the hospital and available to the A&E Department at all times.		YES/NO
2. There is an emergency operating theatre available 24 hours per day (i.e. a theatre able and ready to receive a major trauma patient within 30 minutes of notification by the ATLS provider).		YES/NO
3. Consultant staff are available via a 24-hour on call system for orthopaedics, anaesthetics, general surgery and radiology, and will respond to the arrival of a major trauma patient within 30 minutes.		YES/NO
4. A 24-hour CT scan service is available, with staff available within 10 miles or 30 minutes.		YES/NO
5. There is a fully staffed intensive care service, as specified in *Principles for Emergency and Urgent Care in Yorkshire*, produced by Yorkshire RHA in March 1992.		YES/NO
6. There is a 24-hour pathology service which includes blood gas analysis, full haematology service, chemical pathology, blood transfusion services and bacteriology.		YES/NO
7. There are agreed and up-to-date policies for tertiary referrals when an appropriate specialty is not provided on site. Services that should be covered are cardiothoracic surgery, orthopaedic surgery, maxillofacial surgery, neurosurgery, paediatric surgery, spinal injuries, plastic surgery, microvascular surgery, and burns services.		YES/NO
8. There is a written and up-to-date policy for requesting donor organs and/or tissue for transplantation.		YES/NO

APPENDIX 2 — DOCUMENTATION REQUIRED PRIOR TO THE ACCREDITATION VISIT

Prior to the assessment visit, the following documentation will be submitted to Northern and Yorkshire Region. This will be photocopied and sent out to the assessment team four weeks before the visit is scheduled to take place.

1. Policy for the response to the arrival of a major trauma victim
2. Deputising details for the lead specialist in accident and emergency
3. Junior medical staff rotas for the accident and emergency department for the month of the visit and the two preceding months (or agreed alternative)
4. Procedures for checking the registration status of junior medical staff in the accident and emergency department
5. On call rota for the accident and emergency consultant and appropriate deputy for the month of the visit and the two preceding months (or agreed alternative)
6. Nursing rotas for the month of the visit and the two preceding months
7. The Majax plan
8. Plans of the hospital grounds showing access and egress routes for emergency ambulances
9. Rotas for ATLS providers for the month of the visit and the preceding two months (or agreed alternative)
10. Lists of theatre activities
11. Bed availability and staff profiling of the intensive care unit
12. Policies for tertiary referrals
13. Policy for requesting donor organs and/or tissue for transplantation.

12. Consultant workloads in the post-Calman era

Charles Collins

Introduction

The 'Calman Report' of the Working Group on Specialist Medical Training was published in early 1993.[1] The key ingredients are the 'move towards more Consultant-based hospital services with the clear advantage to patients' and the development of a 'set of principles that govern the relationship between service and training' with 'progressive assessment of trainee's competence and a shorter more concentrated training'. This policy document, taken in conjunction with *Achieving a Balance*[2] and *Hours of Work of Doctors in Training: The New Deal*,[3] requires a radical change from traditional consultant-led practice. Consultant-based practice can be distinguished from a consultant-provided one by not carrying with it the expectation that consultants would have to sleep in hospital whilst on call. Nevertheless, there is an implication that consultants will be involved in almost all decision making and interventional procedures carried out on patients, even if often in conjunction with their trainees. In other words, consultants will have to devote more of their time and energy to active training and teaching than has hitherto been usual, in addition to taking on a closer involvement in every patient episode. It is hardly surprising that consultants feel apprehensive, not to say exhausted, at the prospect of these changes, particularly when they are already subject to growing pressure to increase their service activity to meet the contracts and other obligations of their Trusts.

However 'Calman' is being put into practice, it should not jeopardise the strength of medical education in this country — its integration of service and training. Service-based learning implies that trainees should be exposed to that service which is necessary for their training; they should not provide the backbone of the Health Service, but should still have sufficient freedom to make decisions and carry out operations, not always with a senior immediately at hand, in order to expand their clinical skills and gain self-confidence. There is therefore a need to strike the correct balance between service and training for both the trainers and the individual trainees.

In the past, consultant surgeons have tried to cope with increasing workload demands by working harder and longer themselves; pressurising their trainee surgeons to increase service activity, whether emergency or elective; taking on clinical assistants; or employing staff grade or associate specialist help. Some surgeons have been able to maintain standards of personal commitment far in excess of that reflected by their contracts of employment, others have compromised their quality of care that they have offered to their patients, and most have allowed or encouraged clinical service work to be undertaken by others who may or may not be adequately trained and supervised. These compromises do not measure up to the expectations or requirements of the individual patient, the public, the referring practitioners, the purchasers, or the politicians. Nor are they acceptable for trainees in the future. What is required is a workload which will enable the consultant to provide the high quality patient care he would like, using evidence-based techniques of management by which he is enabled to keep up-to-date. He needs time for this, in addition to time to talk to the patients and relatives, time to teach the trainees, time to learn, and time to relax and freshen up. Consultants should not be over burdened by excessive NHS service work, nor by their private work, to the point where unacceptable compromises in the quality of service are inevitable.

In order to determine the most appropriate arrangements and programmes or duties, it is important for service planners to understand fully the comprehensive role of the consultant. Consultants are the leaders of the clinical team, undertake full and independent responsibility for the clinical care of their patients, and have extensive administrative, management, training and educational responsibilities locally, as well as a personal commitment to audit and continuing medical education. Some consultants also have additional external commitments to regional or national aspects of the NHS and its developments.[4]

The time commitment to each of these responsibilities will vary throughout a consultant's practising life, so contracts should either change to reflect these developments or be flexible enough to accommodate them. Post 'Calman', however, it should no longer be expected that the service workload will be routinely taken on by surgeons in training during the consultant's absence on other business.

When a consultant is appointed to be a clinical director or medical director, contracted clinical sessions will have to be dropped to accommodate the work involved. The number of dropped sessions will depend on the size of the hospital and the managerial support available. The larger the former and the less the latter, the more sessions will be required to do the work. The number of clinical sessions dropped will vary from two to ten. Acting as college tutor will also necessitate a reduction in the consultant's clinical sessions as the training and educational responsibilities for implementing structured training increase. The number of sessions required will depend on the number of specialty trainees.

The work programme of a consultant

For a consultant in any surgical specialty, the work programme will comprise a mixture of operating sessions, ward rounds, audit, postgraduate medical education, teaching, special interests/interdisciplinary clinical meetings, and flexible sessions to cover emergencies. The basic programme for a consultant general surgeon comprises three operating lists, two outpatient clinics, and a special interest session, which could be used as an extra operating or endoscopy session, or alternatively for research, teaching or management. Ward rounds are also an important component of a surgeon's work. They are used not only to assess and determine the clinical management of patients, but also to implement the doctrine of informed consent with regard to any intervention or operative treatment. They are an important component of surgical training.[5, 6] It can not be over-emphasised that emergencies are an essential and exacting component of all surgical specialties. In general surgery, emergencies comprise between 30% and 50% of admissions and constitute more than 50% of the 'occupied bed days' in a DGH[7]; they therefore create a very heavy workload. The same is true in trauma and orthopaedics, neurosurgery, and paediatric surgery. Two flexible sessions would be regarded as the 'norm' in general surgery and trauma and orthopaedics for consultants who share an emergency rota of 1-in-4 and 1-in-6.

Consultant emergency operating lists should be scheduled for a session during the day after a night on duty. This enables consultants to be involved in emergency surgery, whilst not expecting them to work for considerable periods at night. The Confidential

Enquiry into Peri-Operative Deaths (CEPOD)[8] has indicated that only a small minority of emergency general surgical admissions require immediate surgery during the night, and that most operations can be carried out more safely after a period of assessment and resuscitation during the following day. It might be sensible to organise the second session in the day after a duty night to be a flexible session in which the consultant could relax, sleep, or undertake private practice if so motivated.

In some larger centres, trauma and orthopaedic consultants are rostered to be free for a week from responsibility to elective orthopaedics and other commitments so as to be available for involvement in the care of all trauma cases.[9] Similar arrangements are currently being piloted in general surgery in Leicester.[10] This has significantly enhanced the quality of care to the traumatised patient and the teaching to trainees. The precise work programme and the elective workload for a consultant will therefore depend on the emergency work to which he is exposed and the frequency of his on-call commitments.[11]

Emergency operating lists scheduled for a daytime list will enable consultants to join trainees in operating on emergencies, without expecting them to work for considerable periods at night. For this to happen, staffed operating lists have to be available, and this commitment must be honoured by the consultant concerned. Table 12.1 shows a sample programme of duties.

'Calman' and training

'Calmanisation' provides impetus towards specialisation by encouraging the appointment of more consultants and creating the need for specialist training units. The Education Committees of the

Table 12.1   Sample programme of duties

	AM	PM
Monday	Ward round/X-ray/admin	Operating (elective)
Tuesday	Post-take/operating (emergency)	Flexible
Wednesday	Operating (elective)	OPD
Thursday	OPD	Flexible
Friday	Endoscopy	Ward round/teaching/audit/ post graduate education

Emergency duty = Monday, 1 weekend in 6

Specialist Associations and the Specialist Advisory Committees (SACs) are identifying such specialist units on the basis of the quantity and quality of experience that can be provided.[12] At the same time, patients are increasingly questioning the skills of the so-called 'generalist'. Is it fair for a patient to have his limb-threatening arterial occlusion dealt with by a general surgeon with an interest in coloproctology rather than by a vascular surgeon? The patient might well end up with an amputation rather than a potentially successful, albeit delicate and time-consuming, arterial reconstruction. This has obvious implications for quality of life.

The trend is therefore towards sub-specialists who practice their specialty by day but act as generalists at night. Provided that there is a policy for transfer to the appropriate specialist team as soon after admission as possible, this practice will probably remain as the cornerstone of emergency hospital practice in all but the largest hospitals. Training must reflect this. In general surgery, most consultant appointments will be of general surgeons with a major sub-specialty interest.

The Association of Surgeons recommended that the critical size for a hospital to provide comprehensive general surgical services is one serving a population of 300 000 or more.[6] Further sub-specialisation and the high cost of modern technological developments may lead to even larger units. Significant advantages accrue to larger units in the organisation of training. It becomes possible to organise prospective cover for 1:5 junior doctors' rotas — the maximum permissible to meet the hours of work requirement.[3] It also enables the training arrangements of the trainee to devolve to two sub-specialist consultants, which is regarded as ideal by the SACs.[12] This is regarded as optimal because it allows the trainee to gain wider experience and provides the opportunity for him or her to choose those elements of each of his/her chief's practices from which his/her training would gain, rather than being committed to what can sometimes be repetitive service work. The trainee's requirements, the patient's requirements, and indeed the consultant's requirements, all add up to the same need — an increase in the number of consultants.

Individual surgical workload

How can the workload of a consultant be calculated? In general surgery, agreement has been reached on the analysis and calculation of the components of workload.[4-6,11-16] Planned workload can be divided into that in the outpatient clinics and that in the operating theatres.

Outpatient clinics

It is accepted that for a satisfactory standard of consultation in a general surgical outpatient clinic, 20 minutes on average is required for each new surgical patient and 10 minutes for each follow-up.[4,5,11] This equates to seven new patients and about seven follow-ups per clinic. For planning purposes, in the post-Calman era, consultant outpatient clinics will have to be booked for a 44-week working year to allow for annual and study leave. This would ensure that all new patients were seen personally even if, on occasions, only briefly, to confirm the diagnosis and decisions made by trainee members of the surgical team.

With two clinics per week, one consultant working without support could see 600–650 'new' patients per year, and at least an equal number of old patients (7 × 2 per week per year = 616). Prior to the Calman era, it had been expected that a consultant team might see approximately 1000 new (referral) patients per year.[4] This was based on a major service contribution from the trainees. In 1991 it was agreed that higher surgical trainees were contributing service value equivalent to 0.75 of a consultant and that SHOs were equivalent to 0.5 of a consultant.[14] This value was known as the Service Equivalent Value (SEV), and enabled the calculation of appropriate workloads for surgical firms with different levels of trainee support.[11] Post Calman, these values are no longer appropriate. It is suggested that a specialist registrar might have an independent SEV of 0.4 of a consultant, and an SHO an SEV of 0.2 of a consultant.

Surgical training is, however, an apprenticeship. It involves gaining experience to act as an independent practitioner by seeing patients and making diagnoses and management decisions with a degree of independence commensurate with the level of training. Clearly, the more senior the trainee on a surgical firm, the more independent the outpatient and operating activity that would be appropriate.

For a general surgical firm with a higher surgical trainee offering assistance in one outpatient clinic and an SHO helping in a second, it would seem reasonable to expect the consultant firm to see 750–900 (new referral) patients per year. This figure would vary considerably with the sub-specialty, the complexity of the investigations carried out in the outpatient clinic, and the support available from the specialist nurses and others in the clinic. This figure is not significantly greater than that for a consultant working alone because of the time required for discussion between trainee and consultant.

Operative workload

All elective operating lists should be scheduled for consultants who can actively supervise and guide the developing operating skills of the trainees. This ensures the highest quality of technical expertise for the patient concerned, and also active teaching of technical skills to the trainee.

Assessment of surgical workload

Case load can be misleading as it does not take into account the complexity of the operative procedure.[15] Operative workloads are now compared using recommended values with a weighting index for each operative procedure based on the BUPA schedule of procedures, with each group given a relative value: minor = 0.5; intermediate (e.g. hernia repair) = 1.0; major = 1.75; major plus = 2.2; and complex major = 4.0. For planning purposes, 1 intermediate equivalent (IE) approximates to 1 hour's operating theatre time. This includes anaesthetic and turnover time in addition to surgical operating time. The average intermediate workload (IE) for one elective operating list is approximately 3.5.[5, 6, 14, 16]

A general surgeon carrying out three operating lists, including an emergency list, and one special interest list could thus undertake a weekly workload of 3.5 × 4 = 14 IE per week. The total operative workload for a 44-week year would then be 616 IE per year. A consultant-provided operating service would therefore enable 616 IE (weighted operations) to be performed by one consultant per year and 616 new (referral) patients to be seen in the outpatient clinic by one consultant per year.[11]

Analysis of a year's general surgical activity in a District General Hospital[7] showed that 643 new outpatients were seen per SEV, and 677 operations (IEs) were carried out per SEV. However, consultants only performed/supervised 48% of the operations and solo trainees performed the majority of the emergency operations (73.7%). This is what Calman seeks to remedy.

Training surgeons takes time, and operative procedures are likely to take longer when such training is taking place. Trainees, however, can undertake some independent surgery both as emergencies or on elective lists during consultant absences. It would therefore seem reasonable to calculate that a consultant-based surgical firm should undertake 15–20% more work than the consultant could provide alone, particularly if supported by a more experienced trainee. This equates to 700–850 IEs per year, as shown in Table 12.2.

It was found[17] that in Somerset for each 1000 population there was a requirement for at least 21 new patients per week to be seen in NHS outpatient clinics, with an operative service provision of at least 21 intermediate equivalent (IE) operative procedures (hernia equivalents). When private practice was taken into account, the total population requirements in Somerset for general surgery (1990/91) were found to be 25.1 new patient referrals per 1000 population and 28.1 intermediate equivalent (IE) operations per 1000 population.[17] The proportion of the total general surgical need that is satisfied by private practice varies widely throughout the country — in Somerset, 11% had private health insurance. These figures of surgical need broadly support the Association of Surgeons' Guidelines that one consultant-based surgical team could meet the needs of a 30 000 population.

Organisation of a post-Calman general surgical unit

A hospital serving a population of 300 000 or more would comprise 10 general surgeons, allowing:

- two specialists in upper gastro-intestinal disease
- two coloproctologists
- two breast/endocrine specialists
- four vascular surgeons.

Table 12.2 Workloads in the post-Calman era

	Consultant-led team[14] (pre-Calman)	Consultant-based team (post-Calman)
Service Equivalent Value	Consultant = 1 Reg/SR = 0.75 SHO = 0.5 1Con; ½ Reg; ½ SHO Team: SEV = 1.625	Consultant = 1 SpR = 0.4 SHO = 0.2 1 Con; ½ SpR; ½ SHO Team: SEV = 1.3
Outpatient activity of team (new patients)	616 × 1.625 = 1000/year	616 × 1.3 = 800/year
Operating activity	616 × 1.625 = 1000 1E/year	616 × 1.3 = 800 IE/year (range = 700–850)

In addition to this complement of general surgeons there would be 3–4 urologists. The services of other surgical specialties (i.e. plastic, cardio-thoracic, and neurosurgery) would be organised sub-regionally. Because vascular surgical emergencies in particular require special expertise, there should be both a general surgical and a vascular surgical rota for consultants. With ten or more general surgeons this is feasible, allowing a 1-in-6 general surgical rota and a 1-in-4 vascular rota. The trainees, one to each pair of consultants, would cover all the emergencies on a 1-in-5 with prospective cover rota.

To train or not to train?

The stipulation of the Calman Report and the *Guide to Specialist Registrar Training*[18] is that training requires time — consultant time. Not all Trusts nor all consultants may be prepared to devote time and resources for this purpose.[19] Trusts will increasingly be looking critically at whether it is in their overall interests to be a training hospital or not. Undoubtedly, more service work could be undertaken in a given time if the hospital were not a training hospital. The adverse effect of such a decision would be the likely erosion of standards in the absence of the stimulus to critical analysis which is engendered by enthusiastic trainees. The quality of specialist service in any hospital unit depends on the quality of the consultants appointed and their continued education, energy and initiative. Whilst continuing medical education and training in new operative techniques and methods of clinical management will help, the stimulus of teaching and the need to be one step ahead of the trainees gives constant encouragement to consultants to keep up-to-date and maintain standards. Without trainees, complacency might set in with existing working practices.

Conclusion

Many consultants have been appointed recently, both to meet increased workload demands and as a consequence of a reduction in junior doctors' hours. Further consultants will be required to meet the full impact of the Calman changes in higher specialist training. If the recommendations of the specialist associations are met and there is a doubling of the number of consultant trauma and orthopaedic surgeons[13] and an increase in the number of general surgeons to meet the recommended one per 30 000 target,[6] then it will be possible to implement the Calman proposals with every expectation that, whilst the training of specialists will be shorter because it is structured and concentrated, the standard of consultant produced will be higher, the working conditions of consultants in post will be enhanced, subspecialism will be enabled and the quality of patient care will be greatly improved. There appears to be a commitment from colleges, specialist associations, doctors in training and the Department of Health to achieve these goals over the next 3–5 years. The providers and purchasers have to recognise that the quality of patient care depends on the expertise and training of consultants. The NHS needs more consultants.

REFERENCES

Department of Health. Hospital doctor: training for the future. The report of the Working Group on Specialist Medical Training. London: HMSO, 1993.

Newton T, Grabham AH, Roberts G. Hospital medical staffing: achieving a balance: plan for action. London: DHSS, 1987.

Department of Health. NHSME. EL (91) 82. Hours of work of doctors in training, the new deal. London: NHS Management Executive, 1991.

The Senate of the Royal Colleges of Great Britain and Ireland. Consultant practice and surgical training in the United Kingdom. London: Royal College of Surgeons of England, 1994.

The Royal College of Surgeons of England. General surgical workloads and the provider/purchaser contract. Notes for guidance. London: Royal College of Surgeons of England, 1990.

Giddings AEB. Organisation of general surgical services in Britain: strategic planning of workload and manpower. British Journal of Surgery 1993; 80(11): 1377–1378.

O'Leary D, Collins CD. Analysis of a year's general surgical activity in a district general hospital. Annals of the Royal College of Surgeons of England 1994; (suppl): 176–181.

Buck N, Devlin HB, Lunn JN. The report of the confidential enquiry into perioperative deaths. London: Nuffield Provisional Hospital Trust and the King Edward's Hospital Fund for London, 1987.

Dawe V. Surgeons go on shift to aid A&E surgeons. Hospital Doctor 1994

Kelly MJ. Off duty for consultants in the week? It can be done. Annals of the Royal College of Surgeons of England 1995; 77 (suppl): 257–259.

Collins CD. Providing the ideal surgical service. Annals of the Royal College of Surgeons of England 1992; 74 (suppl): 126–129.

Joint Committee on Higher Surgical Training. Curriculum and organisation for higher surgical training in general surgery and its subspecialties. Specialist Advisory Committee (Gen Surg) at Royal College of Surgeons of England: 1996.

British Orthopaedic Association. Consultant staffing requirements for an orthopaedic service in the National Health Service. London: Royal Orthopaedic Association, 1995.

Collins CD. Recommended values for use in surgical audit and surgical workload analysis. Annals of the Royal College of Surgeons of England 1991; (suppl): 73–94.

Jones SM, Collins CD. Caseload or workload? Complexity scoring of operative procedures as a means of analysing workload. British Medical Journal 1990; 301: 324–325.

Pozo JL, Jones CB. What is a reasonable orthopaedic surgical workload? An analysis of elective and trauma workloads using two different complexity scoring systems. Annals of the Royal College of Surgeons of England 1993; 75 (suppl): 152–157.

Collins CD. How many doctors does Britain need? British Medical Journal 1993; 306: 647.

NHS Executive. A guide to specialist registrar training. London: Department of Health, 1995.

Collins CD. Government must meet the cost. British Medical Journal 1993; 306: 1756.

13. Involving doctors in contracting

Paul Smith

Introduction

The implementation of the reforms of the National Health Service in recent years has fallen into three distinct phases:

1. The separation of the purchasing and provider function by the creation of separate corporate bodies, i.e. health authorities (purchasers) and Trusts (providers).
2. The development of purchasing and contracting, including the establishment of GP fundholders.
3. Increasing the influence of GPs and their teams in purchasing and providing health care within agreed public health priorities. This is enshrined in the government's policy of 'a primary care-led NHS' in which decisions about purchasing and providing health care are taken as close to patients as possible.

Phase 1 is now complete. There has obviously been considerable interest on the part of doctors in the people appointed to sit on health authorities and Trust boards and whether such appointments have affected the overall management style of the organisation. However, this has probably had the least direct impact on doctors, other than the development of clinical directorates and medical directors.

Phase 2 — the development of purchasing and contracting — is, after a moderately quiet start, having a major impact on doctors in that it is affecting their work with patients and is also making considerable demands on their time. This involvement will be further increased as purchasing decisions are increasingly taken by local GPs as the NHS moves deeper into Phase 3.

The government has made perfectly clear how it wants these reforms implemented. In 1994 Dr Brian Mawhinney MP, who was the Minister of Health at the time, made a series of speeches under the heading of *Purchasing for Health: a framework for action*.[1] Key messages that were included in these speeches focused on the purpose of 'purchasing' following the NHS reforms.

Dr Mawhinney said that 'the development of purchasing is the next, and most crucial stage of the health reforms. Purchasing is now at the top of the Government's agenda for the Health Service'. He went on to say that 'Purchasing must reach out to the future, not simply replicate the past. Contracting between Purchasers and Providers is a powerful mechanism for change, but it needs development. Doctors and nurses must become closely involved in the contracting process'.

One of these keynote speeches was delivered to a conference at the Royal College of Physicians in which the Minister explained further what he meant by the involvement of doctors in the contracting process. He gave the following four important messages to the conference.

- Dialogue with doctors is essential in developing services and achieving health gain objectives because managers are simply not competent to make some of the judgements required.
- Realism in contracts can be achieved only if they take into account doctors' views on clinical need and practice, workload planning and medical developments.
- The commitment of doctors is required to develop the necessary guidelines for regulating activity if in-year pressures are faced.
- Access to the clinical audit process can inform both purchasers and providers on the effectiveness of interventions and the quality of the service.

These messages are now included in guidance and instruction by the Chief Executive of the NHS Executive. The expectation of the Executive is that doctors will be involved in:

- formulation of service strategies
- decisions on what services are to be purchased and the level of provision
- negotiation and agreement of contracts which will ensure the delivery of these services.

The recently published policy document by the Labour Party has indicated that although some of the present aspects of purchasing and contracting would not be acceptable to them were they to govern, the fundamental split of purchasing and providing would remain, with some modified type of 'service agreements' replacing existing contracts. It is reasonable to assume therefore that the purchasing and contracting framework will remain as the vehicle by which decisions regarding the provision of health care are taken for the foreseeable future.

Involving doctors

So how will doctors at a local level be involved in decisions about what services are to be purchased?

Firstly, doctors, whether they are working in hospitals or community services, general practice or public health, will increasingly be involved in dialogue concerning the formulation of strategies for health care. These strategies must be appropriate for their local populations as well as following national guidance and policies. The new health authorities established on 1 April 1996 have the statutory responsibility for developing and publicising local health strategies. They are reliant, however, upon considerable input from doctors from each of the branches of medicine described above and from other clinicians for expert advice. For example, the health authorities require advice on demography, need, effective treatments and evidence-based treatment, together with proposals on models and levels of service provision.

Secondly, decisions about what to purchase and, as importantly, what not to purchase will be in the hands of local primary care doctors in their capacity as GP fundholders. They will have ever-increasing budgets to purchase health care allocated to them by their local health authority and they will have the responsibility for purchasing services within an overall framework published by the health authority. They will have had considerable influence in the formulation of this framework.

The policy document, *Developing NHS Purchasing and GP Fundholding — Towards a Primary Care Led NHS*,[2] is quite explicit about how this will develop. It identifies how GP fundholding will expand with three levels of entry:

- *Community fundholding*, where GPs have budgets for practice staff, drugs, diagnostic tests and community health services but not the ability to buy hospital treatments.
- *Standard fundholding*, where GPs have budgets for the same components as the community scheme, but in addition have responsibility for purchasing virtually all elective surgery, outpatients services and specialist nursing services.

- *Total purchasing*, where GPs in a locality have budgets to purchase all hospital and community health services for their patients, including A&E services. In 1995/96 there were four national pilot schemes, with significant expansion during 1996/97. The pilot projects are being evaluated to identify the most appropriate model for the future. Under this scheme, fundholders in a locality normally form a purchasing consortium to spread financial risk, and develop a purchasing plan in collaboration with their health authority.

The vast majority of people in the country are now covered by one of these forms of fundholding. As fundholding expands, so will the responsibilities taken on by GPs. Fundholders will be required to remain properly accountable for the services they provide and their use of resources. This accountability framework is detailed in the NHS Executive publication *An Accountability Framework for GP Fundholding*.[3] Within this framework, GP fundholders are statutorily accountable to the NHS Executive, but will hold a day-to-day management contract with their local health authority. This contract details the objectives and services to be delivered by the fundholding practice. The GP fundholders will contract with NHS Trusts for the provision of health services for their patients. This will involve considerable dialogue and discussion with Trusts, and in particular with the clinicians who deliver services.

Available guidance for doctors involved in contracting

Guidance on how to undertake this process was given by the NHS Executive under cover of two Executive Letters entitled *1995/96 Contracting Review: Handbook*[4] and *Managing Activity and Change Through Contracting*.[5] The second of these — EL(95)10 — clearly spells out the respective responsibilities of Regions, purchasers, providers, and clinicians and other professionals. This important document has remained the bedrock of guidance on the contracting process from the NHS Executive. It focuses on:

- action to be taken prior to the signing of contracts
- action to be taken during the period of the contract
- managing change.

It contains several key messages for clinicians, shown in Box 13.1.

Box 13.1 Key guidance for clinicians on contracting

- Activity in contracts must reflect referral patterns and should be profiled throughout the contract period to account for seasonal variation.
- The level of activity must be clearly specified and 'trigger mechanisms' built into contracts to allow review. The respective actions of purchasers and providers once thresholds are reached must be clearly understood and agreed.
- The terms of contracts, purchasing specifications, schedules of service and activity levels must be understood and agreed with clinicians and other professional staff.
- Mechanisms for addressing issues of 'over-performance' and 'under-performance' against agreed activity must be identified in contracts.
- Arrangements must be in place for working with clinicians and other professionals to manage activity 'back into line' if over-performance occurs.
- Purchasers and providers have to be realistic about volumes of service to be purchased and the practicality and impact of changes in purchasing intentions. Doctors, nurses and other professionals need to be closely involved in drawing up purchasing intentions and plans, especially where there are proposals to change purchasing patterns.

The earlier guidance, EL(94)88,[4] included the specific requirement that 'Purchasers and providers must ensure that doctors, nurses and other professionals from provider units are actively involved in the contracting process'. It also stated that clinicians have a key role to play in the aspects shown in Box 13.2.

Box 13.2 Aspects where clinicians have a key role

- Determining capacity, throughput and case mix, and identifying new opportunities
- Clinical developments and change in volume
- Preparing service profiles and contract specifications
- Developing quality standards
- Agreeing referral and activity guidelines
- Addressing clinical concerns of GPs.

The involvement of clinicians is also crucial to the effective management and monitoring of contract performance.

The involvement of doctors in the contracting process

It must be remembered that the primary function and purpose of GPs and hospital doctors is to care for and treat patients. However, doctors have always had to manage how they provide services and have also been involved to some degree in the overall management of their own particular organisations. Purchasing and contracting is part of the management process which must have input from doctors. It is important to ensure that the best possible balance is achieved between direct patient care demands and management input to contracting without detriment to either.

A contract will include details of the items shown in Box 13.3.

Box 13.3   Items to be specified in a contract

- The type and profile of service
- The quality of the service
- The mode of treatment
- Referral and activity guidelines
- The volumes to be delivered, including type of cases
- Respective responsibilities for managing demand
- Cost of the contract and clear currencies to be used for payment
- Monitoring arrangements, including exchange of data.

The doctor will be part of a team of people within the particular organisation who will be involved in the agreement and monitoring of contracts. The team will also include or access the skills of financial, information management and technology (IM&T), quality and contracting, and marketing specialists. Input by doctors into this process requires the development of skills and commitment and, above all, time.

The expansion of fundholding and the movement towards specialty contracts will increase the amount of dialogue and discussion required. There is clear evidence from experience to date that effective relationships between GPs and hospital doctors result in the most effective contracts. A fundholding practice may have contracts with a number of Trusts with multiple specialties.

Conversely, Trusts will have contracts with a host of health authorities and GP fundholders, each for a range of specialties. The co-ordination of specialty contracts across a range of purchasers or the co-ordination of multiple specialty contracts for a particular purchaser will be a considerable management challenge.

The capacity to specify, negotiate and monitor such a multiplicity of contracts must be a key consideration in the process; if it cannot be properly measured, it cannot be properly managed. There is no point in agreeing contracts that are not deliverable. It is neither practicable nor necessary to undergo this process each year for each specialty. It will be appropriate to spread the annual task of contract negotiation by identifying those services that are suitable for a three- or even five-year contract, thus reducing the number of contracts that are reviewed and re-negotiated annually.

One of the key principles underpinning contracts between partners in the NHS is the sharing of risk. Contracts should not place all of the burden of risk on one party or the other. Clinicians are best placed to be able to identify the risk factors that exist for their own services. These could include shifts between emergency and elective admissions, shifts in case mix, increases or decreases in patient numbers, and pressures on community services. Parties to the contract must clearly understand both the impact on services and costs that may arise if shifts from the baseline contract occur and the responsibilities of each side to manage the situation.

The overall picture of how Trust contracts are performing across all purchasers, or how purchaser contracts are performing across all Trusts, will need to be closely monitored and a clear line of accountability for action to remedy any variances from contract will need to be identified. It is crucial that the clinicians involved in the delivery of the service are fully aware of the position with regard to all of the contracts for their particular service, and that they determine what action is necessary if any parts of the contract are not being met.

Skills and training required by doctors

This section identifies the skills and training that doctors need in order to contribute effectively to the contracting process. In 1996/97 current spending on the NHS is £31.5 billion. Of this, £23.2 billion is spent on Hospital and Community Health Services (HCHS). The vast majority of this HCHS expenditure will be the subject of contracts between purchasers and providers! There is very little formal training given to doctors in purchasing and contracting. In order to clarify training requirements, however, there must first be an understanding of the skill requirements. All doctors should have an understanding of the services they have contracted for, either as purchasers (e.g. GPs in a fundholding practice, public health doctors at health authorities) or as providers (e.g. hospital and community doctors working for Trusts or the independent sector). This should include understanding with whom they have contracted, the quality standards required, activity volumes, and price. They should be aware of the process of negotiation and know who is providing the medical input on their behalf. It is crucial that they should understand the importance to the contracting process of accurate clinical data regarding individual patients. This level of awareness should be attainable for each doctor without the need for any formal training or additional skills.

However, certain doctors within provider units will emerge as lead clinicians for their specialty; these people will have a clearly defined role in the management process of contracting. These clinicians may be complementary and supportive to clinical directors/medical directors, or they may fulfil the same role; individual organisations will determine how best to deliver this. This role requires special skills in the areas shown in Box 13.4.

Box 13.4   Special skills required by clinicians involved in contracting

---

- Liaison, discussion and negotiation with colleagues within their specialty as to the levels of service to be contracted
- Working as part of a contracting team with non-clinical colleagues from areas such as finance, information, marketing and contracting to agree the most appropriate type of contract for a particular service
- The ability to negotiate with purchasers regarding what is to be included in the contract
- The ability to monitor contract performance and discuss any required action with colleagues.

This does not mean that doctors will become accountants, but they will have to understand cost components of services and how these are reflected in the contract price. They will also have to understand how their budgets are affected by variations to contract.

Similarly, they will not need to be IM&T or marketing specialists, but they will need to understand the mechanics of data exchange and the importance of accurate and timely data in terms of contract income. The development of these skills will require a considerable time commitment and certain specialised training skills.

Conclusions

The purchaser/provider split within the NHS will remain for the foreseeable future. Some form of contracting will be the link between the branches of the service and the vehicle by which national and local priorities are delivered. This will include, in certain instances, the use of contracting to effect considerable changes to existing services.

The people involved in delivering care to patients — including GPs, hospital and community doctors — are best placed to determine priorities and models of care. They must have a major influence on the contracting process for it is they who ultimately have the responsibility for care and treatment of patients, and it is they who come face to face with local people who rely on the National Health Service. Health service managers therefore welcome their consultant colleagues joining them in contracting.

REFERENCES

NHS Executive. Purchasing for health. A framework for action. London: HMSO, 1994.
NHS Executive. EL(95)79. Developing NHS purchasing and fundholding — towards a primary care led NHS. London: HMSO, 1995.
NHS Executive. EL(95)54. An accountability framework for GP fundholding. London: HMSO, 1995.
NHS Executive. EL(94)88. 1995/96 Contracting review: handbook. London: HMSO, 1994.
NHS Executive. EL(95)10. Managing activity and change through contracting. London: HMSO, 1995.

Education, training and management development for clinicians

INTRODUCTION
Helen Jones   Mike Pedler

The changes in the NHS, especially since 1990, have brought into being new institutions, new structures and new roles which, to be successful, require the participation of clinicians in management. Self-governing Trusts, the purchaser/provider split, GP fundholding, and the relationship between primary and secondary care sectors arguably all need a creative partnership of managers and doctors to get the best performance in terms of improving health care with limited resources. The public/political requirement of 'more for less' or, at least, 'more for the same', is unlikely to go away in the near future, and can only be achieved by working in new ways, sometimes radically so.

It is still easy to find NHS Trusts where contracting for services is a wholly managerial preoccupation, not involving doctors in any meaningful way. Yet it is the doctors who must deliver the services being contracted. Why are doctors excluded from these and similar processes? Equally, despite the managerial involvement of many senior doctors, the Royal Colleges (with one or two exceptions) do not include management in their professional development curricula. Are doctors excluding themselves?

Whatever the conclusion, the personal, professional and managerial development of both doctors and managers appears ever more central to organisational and health care services development. Of particular importance is the quality of the relationships between all clinicians — not just doctors — and their managers. Doctors do, however, tend to set the tone for other professionals in health care organisations, and this is reflected in the chapters in this section of the book, which focuses on doctors, especially hospital doctors. Another crucial relationship which is underdeveloped in most parts of the country is that between doctors and doctors — between GPs and their secondary care colleagues. Some of the chapters included in this section show the links which are being made between hospital doctors and GPs, but this process is in its infancy and much more needs to be done.

Of the thirteen chapters in this part of the book, the first five address some of the *contextual factors* to our major concern — namely education, training and management development for clinicians. **Tony Winkless** discusses some interesting ideas about personality differences between doctors and managers; **Hugo Mascie-Taylor** considers the new roles, such as clinical and medical directors, which have developed recently; and **Bill Evers** looks at how consultants are appointed to their posts so as to recognise their managerial potential as well as their medical skills. In Chapter 17, **Mike Pedler**, **Hugo Mascie-Taylor** and **Tony Winkless** suggest that the underlying values of medicine and management may be difficult to reconcile, and offer a model of the positions which doctors may take in this dilemma. Finally, **Paul Watson**, **Graham Horne** and **Anna Firth** present an interesting experiment by Wakefield Health Authority to determine priority services.

The following two chapters (19 and 20) move on to consider the *management development needs of doctors*. **Tony White** and **John Gatrell** report on what is possibly the most comprehensive assessment of doctors' development needs ever carried out in the UK; whilst Chapter 20, by **Kath Aspinwall** and **Mike Pedler**, takes a wider view in considering the development needs of professionals in general, taking its examples from the world of the hospital doctor.

The next five chapters (21–25) deal with *specific approaches to doctor development*. **Julia Moore** is concerned about changes in the resourcing of management training and development, which may lead to the subject of 'management' being excluded from the curriculum for doctors. Chapters 22 and 23 both involve *action learning*: **Andrew Scott**, **Neal Jolly** and **Huw Griffiths** tell the story of a consultant and GP action learning set in Huddersfield; and a team from Law Hospital in Lanarkshire (**Liz Murphy**, **Liz Duncan**, **Jacqui Goldberg**, **Ian Gunn**, **Helen Jones**, **Jim McCallion**, **Donald MacLean** and **Grant Urquhart**) use an action learning approach to resolve a major difficulty facing the hospital. More broadly, Chapters 24 and 25 provide reports of practice in terms of doctors' management development in Northern Ireland (**Seamus Carey**) and Wales (**Stephen Prosser** and **Christopher Potter**).

Finally, in Chapter 26, **Margaret Attwood** takes an *organisational development perspective* in reflecting on her ten years of experience trying to create a learning organisation. She steps back to focus on the context of doctors' education, training and management development, trying to identify what sort of organisation is fit to house developing doctors.

14. Personality characteristics — medical consultants and NHS general managers

Tony Winkless

Introduction

A few years ago I was involved in running a development programme for consultants concerned with issues relating to their roles as clinical directors. The programme was run according to action learning principles, where the participants discussed issues of concern to themselves. One of the participants raised the issue: 'Are doctors normal people?' To my surprise, this was taken up by other members of the group with serious intent. The group looked at socialisation by doctor parents; the atypical nature of university life for medical students, which sets them apart from students of other disciplines; the strenuous hours of dedication to junior doctor training; and the professional 'islands' of later years.

As part of my work with doctors, I had also carried out many personality assessments to help in their self-development, particularly in relation to the growing demands of the post-Griffiths NHS management reforms. A favourite pastime of psychologists is to take psychological test data of an individual and manipulate, or normalise, the results in terms of comparisons with other groups of people. To shed some light on the question 'Are doctors normal people?', this chapter examines the issue in terms of the personality data I have generated in my work with doctors — in relation both to the general population and to NHS general managers with whom I have worked.

Describing and measuring personality

Before examining the data, we first need to consider some background information about how personality has been described and measured. Early attempts at describing personality differences can be traced back to medieval times, stimulated by the work of Greek medics, notably Hippocrates and Galen. Personality type was thought to be inherited by determining influences, termed 'humours'.

Humour	Type
Blood	Sanguine
Black bile	Melancholic
Bile	Choleric
Phlegm	Phlegmatic

Much later, Eysenck[1] proposed his type theory, which in some ways provides some similarity in its descriptions of personality types. This was also biologically-based, although in this case it was linked to the central and autonomic nervous systems. His dimensions are measured by the Eysenck Personality Inventory (EPI), shown in Figure 14.1.

INTROVERTED

moody sober	passive carefree
anxious pessimistic	thoughtful peaceful
MELANCHOLIC (sad)	PHLEGMATIC (cool + self-possessed)
rigid reserved	controlled reliable
unsociable quiet	even tempered calm
UNSTABLE	**STABLE**
touchy restless	outgoing talkative
aggressive excitable	responsive easy-going
CHOLERIC (angry)	SANGUINE (cheerful)
changeable impulsive	lively carefree
optimistic active	sociable leadership

EXTROVERTED

Fig. 14.1 The Eysenck Personality Inventory dimensions.

Although it is a reliable questionnaire, the EPI measures personality in just two, global, dimensions: introversion–extroversion and stable–unstable. Other workers have developed constructions and measurements of personality which provide a more differentiated approach. One such approach (and probably the most widely used in the western world over the past 40 years) is Cattell's 16PF[2] which, as its title suggests, provides scores on 16 personality factors. So, for example, rather than providing a single, global, score for introversion–extroversion, this dimension is differentiated in four ways: reserved–easy going; serious–enthusiastic; shy–venturesome; self-sufficient–group-oriented. The 16PF has been employed in this study.

The 16PF is based on clusters of related words for each pole of the 16 factors and aims to measure the underlying source traits of an individual. The practice in reporting is to present one- or two-word descriptions for each pole, but it is important to bear in mind that Cattell sought breadth in his factors. So, for example, the factor serious–enthusiastic embraces words such as sober, taciturn and cautious at one pole and happy-go-lucky, expressive and heedless at the other.

The sample

Doctors

My sample of doctors (164 NHS medical consultants) was obtained by testing delegates attending management courses sponsored by NHS Regions or business schools. The population is dominated by males (as is, of course, the consultant population at large) and includes a wide range of specialties, although it cannot be claimed to be statistically representative of all specialties. From this population the mean raw scores have been taken to establish 'Average Consultant' (AC). These raw scores have been compared or normalised with the two populations described below.

NHS Unit General Managers/Chief Executives

Data on NHS Unit General Managers/Chief Executives (n = 121) was obtained mainly from the managers' attendance on management courses and, to a lesser extent, through the selection process. It should be noted that applicants may have a tendency to produce socially desirable responses ('impression management'). The impact of such effects on the scores obtained from personality questionnaires is contentious. It is clear that people can 'fake' personality questionnaires under laboratory conditions; what is not clear is what they do under conditions where they may be subjected to cross-checks through the use of the other methods used in the selection process.[3] As with the population of medical consultants, the sample is dominated by males.

British general population

Data for the British general population (n=1104) is that for a total male population taken from *The British Standardisation of the 16PF*.[4] This population is accepted as a standard in terms of its being the largest and most representative study of British adult males between 16 and 70 years old. All subjects were tested at home by trained administrators. For the purposes of this study it is worth noting that social groups A and B accounted for 12.5% of the population.

Comparison

As noted above, the populations used are comprised mainly of men, probably reflecting accurately the sex distributions in these occupational groups in the years data was collected (1984–1992). In personality terms, there are differences between the sexes as measured by the 16PF (and comparable instruments) for the general population — for example, higher warmth and sensitivity and lower dominance for women compared to men. As more female doctors and managers occupy a higher proportion of the top NHS jobs, we may see different results and implications from those presented here.

Graphic representations of the comparisons are given in Figures 14.2–14.4. By definition, a profile of average Sten scores for a given population would be represented as a vertical line at 5.5.

Figure 14.2 shows AC compared with the NHS managers. Here AC differs in eight factors in comparison with these most senior managers. Thus, AC is likely to be more introspective and reserved, cautious and anticipating of difficulties, hesitant in taking risks and asserting himself, socially threat-sensitive, and self-sufficient in making decisions.

Additionally, AC differs in terms of the three factors which contribute most to anxiety. AC is thus likely to be rather more beset by apprehension and self-reproach, have a poorer tolerance of frustration, and carry a relatively higher degree of tension.

However, when compared with the general adult male population (Fig. 14.3), AC differs in just three factors. High differences can be

Low score Description	16PF profile	High score Description
	1 2 3 4 5 6 7 8 9 10	
Cool–reserved		Warm–easy-going
Concrete thinking		Abstract thinking
Easily upset		Calm–stable
Unassertive		Dominant
Sober–serious		Enthusiastic
Expedient		Conscientious
Shy–timid		Venturesome
Tough-minded		Sensitive
Trusting		Cynical
Practical		Imaginative
Forthright		Shrewd
Self-assured		Self-doubting
Conservative		Experimenting
Group-oriented		Self-sufficient
Undisciplined		Self-disciplined
Relaxed		Tense–driven

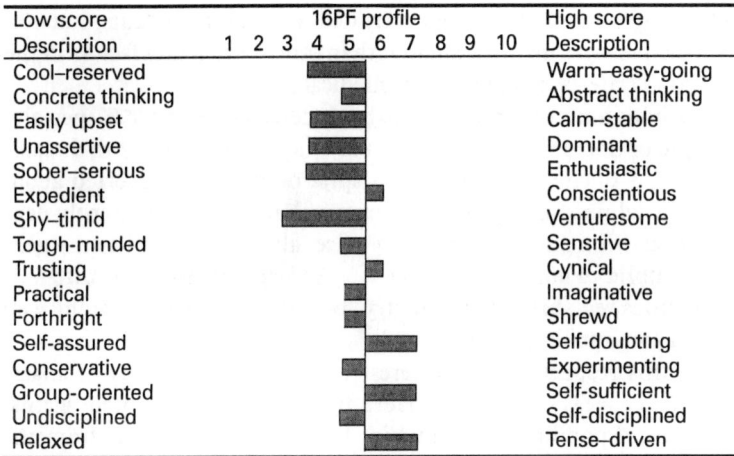

Fig. 14.2 Comparison of 'average consultant' and NHS managers

seen in abstract thinking and imagination, followed by a lesser difference in forthrightness. Perhaps not surprisingly, AC is more intelligent and conceptually-minded than most compared with this population, with a tendency to express views more directly. Thus it may be seen that AC differs less when compared with the general male population norms than when compared with senior NHS managers.

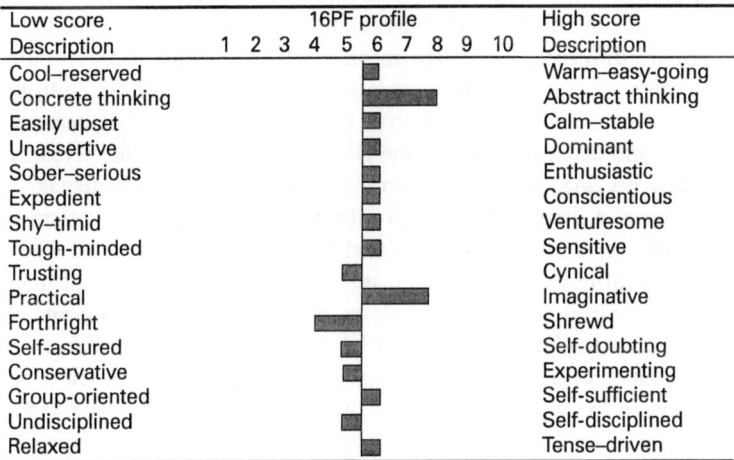

Low score Description	16PF profile	High score Description
	1 2 3 4 5 6 7 8 9 10	
Cool–reserved		Warm–easy-going
Concrete thinking		Abstract thinking
Easily upset		Calm–stable
Unassertive		Dominant
Sober–serious		Enthusiastic
Expedient		Conscientious
Shy–timid		Venturesome
Tough-minded		Sensitive
Trusting		Cynical
Practical		Imaginative
Forthright		Shrewd
Self-assured		Self-doubting
Conservative		Experimenting
Group-oriented		Self-sufficient
Undisciplined		Self-disciplined
Relaxed		Tense–driven

Fig. 14.3 Comparison of 'average consultant' and general adult male population

This may suggest that, when recruited as medical students, intellectual factors were more paramount than other personality factors in the selection criteria for entering the medical profession.

Although no other study has been detected for a cross-specialty sample of doctors in the UK, Cattell et al[2] report that for their sample of US doctors (n=170) '... in spite of all that is asserted about the special personality requirements in a doctor ... Apparently general practitioners are, personality-wise, almost as varied as the general public whom they serve ... An examination of different specialties, eg surgery, psychiatry, pediatrics, however, might well reveal some striking differences'.

In this respect, it is of interest to look at a UK study of anaesthetists (n=231) by Reeve.[5] Here findings were presented against the *general* population (as in Fig. 14.3). More deviations from the mean were found for this specialty compared to the wider group of specialties presented here in that the anaesthetists were found to be, for example, more socially withdrawn, cautious, self-sufficient, and anxious. This finding may suggest that there are indeed specialty differences in terms of personality. That is, just as the general population contains a wide range of occupational groups, perhaps this is true too of the medical profession when taken as a whole. It may well be that personality characteristics in doctors play a more significant part in their later determination of which specialty to pursue *following* initial medical training.

If, however, the mean raw scores from the general manager population are compared to the general adult male population (Fig. 14.4), there are differences from the mean in eleven factors. This strongly suggests that managers are not only selected on conceptual abilities, but on factors which contribute to a desire to be in control, relate to people, and take risks. Whilst the UK literature is sparse for personality data on doctors, there is more abundant material for managers, who have a longer history of personality testing. For example, Bartram,[3] in a study of short-listed UK managers, provides a very similar profile to that presented in Figure 14.4 in his study of managers (n=1796) of varying levels in the management hierarchy. In another study, McCredie[6] addressed the personality factors correlating with higher performance in *general* managers. His findings pointed to the personality factors of calm–stable, enthusiastic, trusting, and group-oriented as being supportive of the general manager's key role as a builder and sustainer of relationships. The evidence would therefore seem to suggest that managers are a much more homogeneous occupational group.

Low score	16PF profile	High score
Description	1 2 3 4 5 6 7 8 9 10	Description
Cool–reserved		Warm–easy-going
Concrete thinking		Abstract thinking
Easily upset		Calm–stable
Unassertive		Dominant
Sober–serious		Enthusiastic
Expedient		Conscientious
Shy–timid		Venturesome
Tough-minded		Sensitive
Trusting		Cynical
Practical		Imaginative
Forthright		Shrewd
Self-assured		Self-doubting
Conservative		Experimenting
Group-oriented		Self-sufficient
Undisciplined		Self-disciplined
Relaxed		Tense–driven

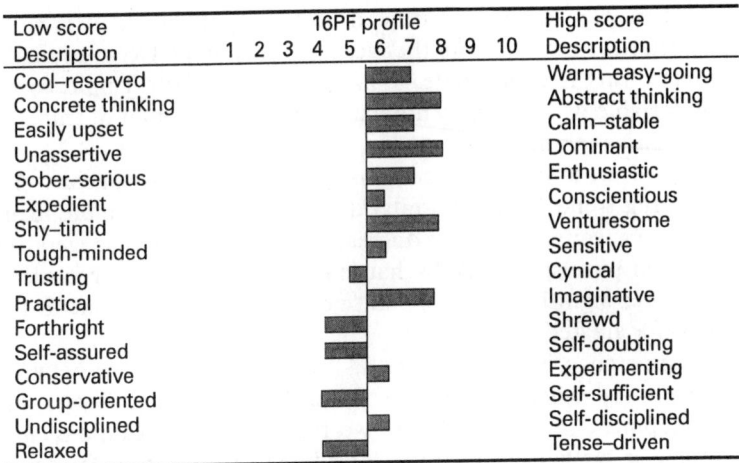

Fig. 14.4 Comparison of NHS managers and general adult male population

Personality factors may also be used to establish how an individual is likely to interact with his or her colleagues in a team setting.[7] In comparison with the managerial population, AC is highly elevated on both 'Monitor-Evaluator' (ME) and 'Completer Finisher' (CF). The ME role involves the monitoring of ideas and proposals in order to evaluate their feasibility and value. The CF role is concerned with practical translation and application of concepts and plans developed by the group. These roles are highly loaded by caution and anxiety, resulting in a drive to get things right. For comparison, the managers are prominent in 'Team Worker' and 'Resource Investigator' — both people-oriented roles.

Interpretation

Given all of this, what can we make of it?

In terms of the original question, 'Are doctors normal people?', with the exception of three factors there is a high correlation with the general population. This finding is of course based on the mean of the total population of doctors presented here. Just as, by definition, there will be people in the general population who are, statistically, strongly deviant from the mean, this will also apply to some doctors. Also, as Reeve's findings[5] suggest, there may well be personality factors associated with sub-groups of doctors (I hope to report later on psychiatrists and GPs).

When we examine the general manager population, it is clear that they are deviant from the mean in many ways. Occupationally applied, this is appropriate — managers need, for example, to be comfortable with a variety of relationships and tolerant of ambiguity and risk taking.

However, a sense of unease may arise when we consider the emerging trend for the hospital doctor to behave in a more managerial capacity. With the increasing influence of managers on selection panels, it is likely that managerial criteria are becoming of greater significance in appointment decisions; why not, in the quest for greater effectiveness?

A reference back to Figure 14.2 suggests differences between doctors and managers in some factors which may challenge this development. For example, do we really want less cautious doctors? Are we willing to trade considered introspection for social boldness and adventure? Would we not prefer our medics to be rather apprehensive about their decisions than be too self-assured?

There is, then, perhaps a need to think more in terms of celebrating the differences than attempting to reduce them — that is, to look at ways of working to complement each other, rather than conflict. For example, as suggested above, it is probably desirable for the doctor to be more cautious and the manager to be more able to make decisions in the face of ambiguity. These two personality characteristics do not sit easily together unless they are acknowledged for their respective usefulness. In the face of rising demands for consultants to act in a more corporate and client-centred manner (see, for example, Chs 15 and 17) these findings may provide additional perspectives and raise implications for the socialisation and development of both doctors and managers. Some potential areas for consideration are given below:

- orientations to decision making
- roles in team membership
- avoiding conflict
- specialty choice
- training of junior staff
- selection of medical students
- assessment of doctors for management positions (e.g. medical director, clinical director).

REFERENCES

Eysenck HJ. Fact and fiction in psychology. Harmondsworth: Pelican, 1965.

Cattell RB, Eber HW, Tatsuoka MM. Handbook for sixteen personality factor questionnaire. Champain, IL: IPAT, 1970.

Bartram D. The personality of UK managers: 16PF norms for short-listed applicants. Journal of Occupational Psychology 1992; 65 (2): 159–172.

Saville P. The British standardisation of the 16PF supplement of norms, forms A + B. London: NFER-NELSON, 1972.

Reeve DE. Personality characteristics of a sample of anaesthetists. Anaesthesia 1980; 35: 559–565.

McCredie H. The role and features of the general manager. Selection and Development Review 1992; 8 (4): 3–5.

Belbin RM. Management teams — why they succeed or fail. London: Heinemann, 1981.

15. Doctors and managers — roles and structures

Hugo Mascie-Taylor

Change and the NHS — prior to the NHS reforms

Prior to the NHS reforms, many would argue that the health service at hospital level was not managed in any coherent or proactive way. Few would dispute that doctors managed their patients, that administrators tried to help them to do so, and that no-one managed the doctors, except themselves.

With the exception of teaching hospitals, consultants were appointed by Regions and their contracts were held at regional level. Until 1990 the entire appointments committee was made up of other doctors fulfilling a variety of roles set out in the relevant statutes. It was possible that the majority of the interview committee might not have visited, or certainly might not be familiar with, the hospital to which the appointment was being made. This was not perceived as being a difficulty, because consultants were appointed on the basis of 'excellence' — that is to say academic excellence.

Following their appointment, consultants would join the staff of a particular hospital and set up a service which reflected their main interest, often their research interest. This was not necessarily inappropriate, but it was not planned in a market-driven sense. Some, however, would argue that it was this individualistic approach that was the strength of British medicine. The newly appointed consultant would set about building up a practice, feeling accountable, in an undefined but often real way, to his or her patients and, professionally, to the GMC.

Within this structure it was the role of the administrator to facilitate the development of consultant-led practices. Whilst to say that all administrators simply reacted to the wishes of the consultant body would be to overstate the case, the power of the consultants should not be under-estimated.

161

Within this structure there was no general management function and the doctors did not consider, probably could not consider, undertaking a general management role. The more ambitious and able developed a variety of representative roles. They sought on some occasions to represent their colleagues within the hospital and to chair doctors' representative committees, which were often powerful decision-making bodies. Outside their hospital they could develop a representative role within their College, the British Medical Association or a specialty Association. None of these roles involved accountability to a more senior colleague, managing other doctors, or indeed any line management other than within the medical team or 'firm'.

Change and the NHS — the NHS reforms

The NHS reforms of the 1980s were designed to produce a health service that was proactively managed. The rhetoric was that of internal markets. However, the most significant change was almost certainly the introduction of a contractual relationship between purchasers and providers. The purchasers were Health Authorities, later to become commissioners and to merge with the FHSAs, and GP fundholders, who were purchasers of secondary care as well as providers of primary care. In secondary and tertiary care all the providers became, over a number of years, NHS Trusts. These changes influenced the role of the consultants quite considerably, although perhaps not to the extent that might have been initially imagined.

The creation of purchasers and commissioners offered the opportunity to take into account 'the needs of the patient' or, put in another way, 'the needs of the market'. These needs were defined in part through the activities of a large variety of stakeholders, the most powerful being central government, and in part through such activities as health needs assessment. From the standpoint of the previously autonomous consultant, the important point was that, arguably for the first time, there was a voice outside the consultant body influencing his or her practice and coming largely from a managerial/political standpoint.

The purchasing organisations created a new set of managerial opportunities for consultants in public health medicine, who had the opportunity, indeed the responsibility, to become heavily involved in defining future health care strategy for their Districts. It is possible that some clinicians will also move into purchasing roles, again with a strong strategic rather than operational bias. As commissioning has developed, the need to take advice from clinicians has become clear and was ultimately made explicit (HSG(95)11).[1] Whilst offering advice to commissioners is not often seen by consultants as a managerial role, it is certainly a form of expert consultancy. Given that health authorities will, in the future, be able to take advice from consultants outside their own Districts, this type of consultancy may grow and may become a form of paid work for some consultants.

NHS Trusts

The creation of NHS Trusts was the key event for most consultants. Perhaps the most profound change was that in an explicit way consultants became employees of particular Trusts. This shift in their contracts from Region to their own hospital was resisted, presumably because it made the relationship clear in a way which had previously been confused. However, in spite of this clarity, behaviour has not necessarily changed dramatically, although an increasing number of consultant job descriptions talk about accountability. This accountability is often expressed in terms of 'managerially' or 'organisationally' to the Chief Executive, and 'professionally' to the Medical Director. The extent to which this really matters is very variable, and it is fair to say that consultants are not managed like other NHS employees. Indeed, some would say that in some ways the consultant body still stands at the edge of the NHS rather than at the centre of it. (It is interesting to observe the language that consultants use when describing where they work — they say they work 'at St. Xs', or in London they may say they are 'on at St. Ys', but they rarely, if ever, say 'I work for St. X or St. Y NHS Trust'.)

The creation of NHS Trusts was accompanied by the establishment of several specified senior management roles. One of these roles was that of Medical Director, and this role will be discussed next.

Role of the Medical Director

All NHS Trusts are obliged to have a Medical Director. To some extent the responsibilities of this role are unclear, but seem to be emerging in the following ways. The Medical Director has a corporate role and is accountable to the Chief Executive. The role is broadly to link the Board with the doctors and with some aspects of the external environment. There is also a professional activity which involves assisting with drawing up job descriptions, serving on appointment committees, being involved with disciplinary matters, and possibly being involved in merit award decisions. The Medical Director may well also have a lead or co-ordinating role in research and development and clinical audit.

In reality, the scope of the role is enormously varied, dictated by both the needs of the Trust and the competencies of the individual. The appointment should be made using a clear and open process and there should be an explicit contract. Some form of reward mechanism is appropriate. Performance review is very helpful and many medical directors need ongoing management development and training.

Medical directors have a strategic role in helping to determine the future direction of the services provided by the hospital. In this role they link with other doctors, and particularly, in many Trusts, with clinical directors. Rarely do Clinical Directors account to the Medical Director, and indeed this can only work well when the operational management issues are clearly resolved.

Medical directors are increasingly becoming involved with commissioners and purchasers, including GP fundholders. They may have links with their local university, with the regional office and with various colleges.

Role of the Clinical Director

Having attained Trust status, most chief executives rapidly recognised the need to 'get the consultants on board'. It became fashionable to establish Clinical Directorates or clinical groupings and to place a doctor in charge of these groupings. The extent, roles and size of these groupings vary considerably from Trust to Trust, as do the names given to them. However, the principle seemed to be that if doctors could be placed within the management structure then they would be 'brought on side' and behave like good corporate citizens. In some cases this worked, but unfortunately not in all. Some of the reasons for this failure will be explored further in this chapter, others have been described elsewhere (e.g. Ch. 17).

It is probably fair to say that in the initial rush to involve doctors in management many Trusts gave little thought to the way in which this might be done to best effect. Some of the problems which were, and still are, encountered are described below.

Lack of clarity about role

There sometimes is a lack of clarity about whether the Clinical Director or Clinical Co-ordinator role was a managerial role or a representative role. There had been a long history in the NHS of doctors electing their representatives within hospitals or Districts. One of the most recent examples, prior to the NHS reforms, would have been as Chairman of the Medical Executive Group (under the 'cogwheel' structure). The role of such elected representatives was variable, but frequently such figures were very powerful and had a major influence on the strategic direction of their hospital. Typically representatives were in post for three to five years and were elected by their colleagues, although the form of the election was not necessarily 'one man, one vote' in a secret ballot; sometimes a 'senior consultant' inherited the post. Nevertheless, the important point is that the consultant body felt that the elected representative was clearly charged with representing their views and therefore accounted to them.

In managed organisations, however flat their structure or complex their working relationships, managers are appointed by more senior managers. Negotiated power flows down the organisation and accountability up the organisation. Interestingly, doctors have no difficulty with this model within their own clinical firms, and the clear lines of accountability in these firms are probably of benefit to the patients.

However, there was no history of consultants accounting in meaningful ways to administrators, and when 'yesterday's administrators' became 'today's managers' they were often uncomfortable with the notion that consultants should account to them, even in a managerial sense. Equally, the consultants had never felt themselves to be accountable to administrators, many saw no need for it, and some actively fought against it.

In this context some chief executives choose to consult with the consultants about who should be their clinical director/clinical co-ordinator. There is of course some wisdom in this, in that it would be very difficult for any consultant to manage in the face of tough opposition from his or her colleagues. But the difficulty arises when there is a lack of clarity as to whom the consultant is managerially accountable. (In my experience of tutoring many management development courses for clinical directors, their most common dilemma was 'Do I account to my colleagues or do I account to the managers?'.)

Managing colleagues

In medicine there has always been a clear sense of hierarchy and an intuitive understanding that some consultants were more 'senior' than others. However, the formal position was that all consultants were equal, and no one consultant managed any other consultant. Indeed, to criticise or comment publicly on another's practice is regarded as professionally unacceptable. Therefore, when one consultant is made 'the manager', even if the appointment is made appropriately and not by election, great difficulties continue to surround the management of one consultant by another. This difficulty is often felt at least as much by the doctor-manager as by the other consultants. It may be that this is slowly changing.

Appointment of the 'Senior Consultant'

Like the doctors, the managers in the Trusts had a clear sense of the hierarchy amongst consultants. This was often based simply on the length of time in post, although sometimes it was influenced by other factors. In any event, the managers often felt that the most appropriate appointment as doctor-manager would be the 'Senior Consultant'. In fairness, this may have been the only option that had any chance of working, given that, had any other consultant been appointed, the most senior and influential consultant might have chosen to block any initiative made by his or her more 'junior' colleague. The difficulty was, and indeed often still is, that seniority does not necessarily guarantee managerial ability. In some cases the most senior consultants were actually those least likely to take a corporate view, and making them the manager simply allowed them to exercise their individualistic powers more easily.

Lack of clarity about accountability

Many doctor-managers are given the title of Clinical Director without any explicit statement as to who accounted to them and to whom they were accountable. Placing even an experienced manager in this situation would cause difficulties, and it often added considerably to the dilemmas of the doctor-manager.

Lack of development and support

Interestingly, many managers continue to make the assumption that because doctors can manage patients they can also manage organisations, or at least parts of organisations. Some doctors also make this assumption. Sadly it is not always true. If doctors are to be placed in managerial positions in organisations because they are doctors and not because they have a proven track record as managers, they require more development and support than other more experienced managers.

Appointment of clinical directors

Appointment as a clinical director should only be made if it is appropriate. If there is not an appropriate doctor to appoint as a clinical director, then it is unwise to make an appointment. The directorate should be managed in some other way, with the lead consultant having a representative or co-ordinating role. It is possible to have a mixed model in which some directorates are managed by doctors and others by non-doctors. Their hallmark should be competency.

Ideally, some reward, however small, should be made so that credence is given to the role. There should be a clear contract which states to whom the Clinical Director is accountable. This line of accountability should make organisational sense: in large Trusts clinical directors should probably account to the Director of Operations rather than to the Chief Executive (it is possible for clinical directors to have a strategic role outside their operational role — in fulfilling this they might meet with the Chief Executive or the Medical Director).

Clinical directors should have annual performance review and objective setting. Crucially, they need induction into their role and ongoing development. It is vital that they receive strong support, not only in the operational sense, but also in resolving the difficulties and dilemmas of their new roles.

Differing objectives of managers and doctors

Underlying many of the problems which have been described earlier in the chapter is the simple but crucial fact that doctors and managers often have differing objectives. In Deming's writings on quality the first point he makes is to stress the need 'to create constancy of purpose'.[2] That is to say, for an organisation to be successful the people within it must have agreed aims and objectives. Because of their previous experiences, consultants and senior managers do not necessarily share the same objectives. This is an area which is little explored; there is often an assumption that there is a shared set of objectives and that the only difficulties therefore are about process. However, doctors and managers do differ in significant ways. These will be discussed under the following headings:

● education
● preferred research methodologies
● socialisation
● views of the organisation.

Personality differences have been discussed in Chapter 14.

Education

Throughout a career in hospital medicine, academic attainment is perhaps the single most important factor leading to success. In order to obtain a place in medical school, an outstanding academic performance at school is required. Many medical schools do not interview at all; others only interview 'borderline' candidates. (In any event, one would have to doubt the value of an unstructured interview carried out by largely untrained assessors.) It is those students who are most successful academically at medical school who tend to obtain the best training posts. Career progression in hospital medicine remains very strongly linked to academic excellence — it is necessary to obtain further postgraduate qualifications, and, in many specialties, to publish in peer-reviewed journals and to speak at national and international meetings.

Academia remains very important to consultants. When doctors go to a medical meeting they usually expect to hear scientific papers presented rather than service delivery discussed. Although the merit award system is changing, a strong academic performance has been the most rapid way to a higher award. There is no convincing evidence that this has changed (even assuming that it should).

The education which doctors receive is very strongly science-based and it bears more of the hallmarks of an apprenticeship than of a broad-based liberal education. The academic background of managers is much more varied and unpredictable. In the past, many NHS managers were 'arts-based'. The managerial career is much more loosely structured and career progression is linked to output rather than to academic achievement. Performance-related pay, roughly the equivalent of the merit award, is also linked to the achievement of outcomes rather than to academic merit. If one compares the written curriculum vitae of a doctor and a manager the differences become very clear. In the medical CV the emphasis is on academic achievement, whilst in the managerial CV it is on achieving outcomes.

Preferred research methodologies

Medicine is strongly placed within the objectivist, positivist paradigm of research. In this paradigm, large groups are required in order to reveal 'facts'. It is the methodology which reveals the facts, and the paradigm is concerned with explanation and, crucially, prediction. Validity and reliability are statistically based. The methodology assesses the effect of one object on another (for example, drug on patient).

In teaching hospitals outpatient clinics are sometimes established in order to produce sufficient 'clinical material' on which to perform research. Whilst some may take the view that this does not fit easily with the service delivery ethos, it should be remembered that British academic medicine enjoys a very high international reputation.

Managerial science spans a broader range of the research paradigms. At one extreme, for example in some areas of psychology, the positivist paradigm is to the fore. However, some management research sits in a subjectivist phenomenologist paradigm. It is concerned with individuals and with meanings. The methodology reveals the meanings and the process is often descriptive or interpretative.

Whilst it might well be pointed out that the research methodologies used are appropriate to their subjects, and both can be useful, there is in practice often scant regard for one paradigm from the enthusiasts for the other. In practical terms the difficulty is that doctors sometimes say 'Well, prove it', when the subject under review is not amenable to a positivist form of research.

It is also interesting that the current demand for 'evidence-based medicine' from NHS managers has irritated some clinicians, who believe that their practice is strongly based on evidence. Such doctors not surprisingly respond 'What about evidence-based management?'.

Socialisation

This is a very powerful factor for doctors. Anyone who doubts this should witness the changes that occur from the age of 17 to about 27 years. A very bright and catholic collection of young people are heavily 'cloned' to become doctors. The most rapid change occurs when young doctors first emerge on to the wards and meet their role models. It is sometimes almost possible to predict which specialty the young student might enter — one can distinguish the budding psychiatrist from the budding surgeon!

Young doctors work for other doctors and not, in their perception, for the NHS. The service they deliver is in the name of consultants, not in the name of the NHS Trust. Their career advancement is in the hands of other doctors, not the NHS or NHS managers.

It was only in 1990 that a general manager was introduced to the Consultant Appointments Committee. Prior to that time, the entire consultant appointment procedure had been in the hands of other doctors. The great majority of interviewers continued to be doctors, although one could argue that they now tend to be more managerially oriented doctors (e.g. medical director, clinical directors).

For all these reasons, junior doctors feel that they work for consultants and not for the NHS, and some would say that the world of medicine is related to, but fundamentally different from, the world of the NHS (although they are probably becoming more congruent).

Until very recently, the distribution of merit awards has also been principally in the hands of the profession. The changes in the allocation of C awards may prove to be a significant change, although this has yet to be tested.

Socialisation of managers is, or at least appears to be, less strong and much more diverse. There were some changes following the NHS reforms. At that time one sometimes saw more aggressive behaviour from some of the managers. This was accompanied by sharper and more flamboyant dressing and a tendency to behave in ways which NHS managers perceived to be similar to those of managers in the private sector. This behaviour has to some extent abated and a more robust and satisfactory public sector management ethos seems to be emerging. NHS managers are very aware that they work for the NHS, and indeed see themselves as leading it.

Views of the organisation

In order to consider the views of the organisation of various employees, it makes sense to consider three types of organisation and to contrast them. Again, stereotyping is used in order to make the point. The three types of organisations considered are 'the university', 'the profession' and 'the service delivery organisation'.

The university. In the university, excellence is perceived in academic terms. It is the quality of research output which strongly influences the income of universities. Teaching may be less important. Within an academic discipline the true customer is the peer group, this being the only group with any real understanding of the quality of the research. The accountability is to academic standards; one should not falsify results or plagiarise.

In universities the power lies with the professors, although there may be a shift towards a new breed of entrepreneurial vice-chancellors. Professors like administrators who will to a large extent do their bidding and 'oil the wheels'. The service provided reflects the academic interest of the chair, and the service provided is therefore dictated by the provider.

Quality is formally assessed by research output.

The profession. In a profession, excellence is about judgement: in the medical profession it is clinical judgement which is valued by other members of the profession, and indeed, in as much as they can assess it, by the public. The customer is the individual and the professional is responsible to the individual, not to the collective. In the hospital-based medical profession, power lies with the consultants. Frequently in the past the service has reflected 'the interest of the consultant'. Consultants, following appointment, tended to establish services in those areas where they had a research interest. The service provided was therefore driven by their academic interest and not by a rational assessment of the health need of any population. There is some evidence that a more appropriate compromise is being reached. However, the service delivered still tends to be dictated by the person providing it rather than the person receiving it.

The professions appear to like administrators. They feel that administrators should react to their needs and should make sure that the organisation continues to function so that their practices can develop.

Quality within the profession is about the quality of 'an opinion'.

The service delivery organisation. In service delivery organisations there are large numbers of customers — excellence lies in 'delighting' these customers. Service delivery organisations have a corporate power structure and proactive management. They see themselves as responsible, in a utilitarian way, to a number of customers and the service they offer attempts to reflect the perceived needs of these customers. They are also of course accountable to their shareholders.

NHS managers see themselves as leaders of the service delivery organisation. Doctors see themselves as being within a profession although many doctors also see themselves as strongly university-based. This is particularly the case in teaching hospitals where all the consultants may well hold academic appointments. This professional/academic model has led to the high reputation of British medicine. However, many of the conflicts which occur in hospitals, particularly teaching hospitals, result from differing views of the organisation held by consultants and senior managers.

Summary

It is hoped that by comparing and contrasting the education, preferred research methodologies, socialisation and views of their organisation, it has been demonstrated that doctors and managers will often have different objectives. This does not mean the position is hopeless. It does, however, demand that the differences are acknowledged and made explicit so that the tension between the two can be constructive. Celebrate the differences!

REFERENCES

HSG(95)11
Deming

16. Consultant appointment — accessing the added value

Bill Evers

Background

The NHS Trust arrangements are providing an opportunity for Trusts to make major changes to the ways they have traditionally selected and appointed consultants. Under the traditional system, appointments were made by an Appointments Advisory Committee (AAC) which represented at least four interest groups: the Region; the District; the 'relevant' University; and the appropriate Royal College. Appointments were made with the expectation that they would be 'for life' — in practice for up to thirty years — and they were technically made to the Region, not to the hospital concerned. Furthermore, the AACs had, and still have, a legendary reputation for inefficiency, incompetence and political intrigue.

Under the Trust arrangements, appointments are made to the particular Trust, rather than to the Region, and may still be for life, even though Trusts may in theory offer different terms (e.g. a five-year rolling contract). Consultants have an increasing and major influence on the use of resources and the direction of development in the Trust, as well as having a position of leadership. There is thus a greater need for appointments to be successful, because the consequences of a poor appointment would be significant, with all the damage occurring within the confined space of the Trust concerned. Trust managements therefore wish to have more control over appointments, and to acquire the skills to minimise the risk of poor ones. They are increasingly aware of the development of more effective selection procedures in other occupational areas. In particular, Trusts may view the 'political' and somewhat subjective aspects of the AAC system as a major risk factor, and the consideration of factors beyond the medical credentials of candidates is now felt to be increasingly important.

The way forward was signalled by the Chief Medical Officer's agreement for Trusts to be 'more creative' about their appointment methods while retaining the statutory AAC, the constitution of the AAC having been modified to include Trust interests in the place of Region and District.

Huddersfield NHS Trust recognised these issues at an early stage. As a preliminary measure the Trust Board had decided to extend the statutory procedure by asking each candidate to give a short presentation on a topic relevant to the appointment before the formal AAC meeting. A candidate's performance in the presentation provided additional evidence for Committee members. This enhanced system was felt to be helpful but still not fully satisfactory. I was invited by Jim Feeney (the Medical Director) and David Walker (a Clinical Director) to make proposals for an improved selection process that would provide a more systematic and 'objective' process, and one that would further enhance the statutory AAC procedure, from which there is no escape.

First steps

Garrick Graham (the Chairman), Eva Lambert (Chief Executive), and Jim Feeney formed a Steering Group for the project. With them, I reviewed the typical components of processes used outside medicine for the selection of senior staff. We concentrated initially on the typical components of an assessment centre and how the evidence from these could be set against a set of criteria or attributes defining the requirements of the post to be filled. The first snag emerged: there was no clear and overt set of criteria against which a candidate could be assessed; each of the eight AAC members, representing very distinct interest groups, traditionally would follow his or her own private ideas and prejudices! By contrast, there were plenty of opinions of what constituted a bad appointment, and it was interesting to note that the vast majority were quite unconnected with medical skills.

The first step, then, was to develop a set of attributes, beyond medical qualification and competence, for selectors to use as a yardstick which would provide the context for making selection decisions for all consultant appointments. The next step would be to devise the means of obtaining relevant evidence from each candidate to enable judgements to be made.

Stage 1 — identifying the attributes

We needed to devise a set of attributes, or qualities, which all the parties in the selection process would recognise as relevant and appropriate to the appointment of a consultant. For this stage the Steering Group required a broad consensus between doctors and managers as an important element.

As a first step I conducted a series of in-depth interviews with a small sample of doctors, directors and managers. These followed a process of role-set analysis, examining the main points of contact a consultant has with others, and exploring the values and behaviour that would be accepted as appropriate in each case. The role-set included patients, patients' relatives, colleagues, junior doctors, nursing staff, support staff, the clinical directorate, hospital management, and a range of outside organisations including the purchasing authority and local voluntary bodies.

The critical questions in each case were: 'What role does the doctor play in this context?' and 'What would you regard a desirable/acceptable/unacceptable behaviour in relation to ... (e.g. patients)?'. A number of recurring themes emerged from the answers to these questions. These provided a specification for an 'ideal' consultant, who would almost certainly never exist, but against which individual candidates could be tested in a much more systematic way than before. The emerging themes represented a fairly typical list of professional and management qualities in any field outside medicine, but, in this case, qualities which needed the endorsement of a cross-section of medical and management opinion within the Trust. They are shown in Box 16.1.

Box 16.1 Professional and managerial qualities required by an 'ideal' consultant

---

- Communication ability
- Ability to work in a team setting
- Leadership qualities and ability to develop staff
- Willingness to support organisational processes
- Sensitivity to the general culture and needs of the Trust
- Sensitivity to patients' needs
- Potential to contribute to the development of the department/specialty/service.
- Self-management and self-development ability
- Potential to gain satisfaction from working in the (particular) Trust environment.

Each of these attributes was supported by some definitions of desirable behaviour. Whilst not exhaustive, these provide guidance to the selectors in interpreting and evaluating the evidence from interviews and other parts of the selection process. For example, in the case of the 'leadership and staff development' attribute, the important supporting behaviours include those shown in Box 16.2.

Box 16.2 Important supporting behaviours for the 'leadership and staff development' attribute

- Setting a good example, demonstrating the behaviour demanded of others
- Being aware of the impact one has on other people
- Clearly communicating goals, tasks, plans, etc. to those involved in achieving them
- Being prepared to develop team spirit and cooperation by involving team members in discussion and decision making
- Being prepared to take the clinical lead after listening to other professional views from colleagues and supporting staff
- When dealing with sensitive issues discouraging, and refraining from, personal attacks and keeping discussion focused on the matter at hand
- Accepting responsibility for those responsible to him or her: planning their development; supervising their work from an appropriate distance (or closeness); maintaining standards and discipline whilst recognising that those making mistakes and errors need support as well as guidance.

Stage 2 — consultations

A draft version of the attributes and the associated behaviours was discussed with a wider group of doctors and managers from the Trust who had not participated in Stage 1. This group was invited to discuss the attributes and comment on their appropriateness for the selection of consultants, and to add their own comments or reservations where they wished. This group had clearly recognised the problems surrounding consultant appointments and was very positive towards the need for change. Members gave a cautious approval of the attributes, with several suggestions for refinement, and of the proposed enhancement of the selection process.

We did not consider that more consultation at this stage would provide new information, so the Steering Group decided to implement the enhanced system on a trial basis without extending the consultation.

Stage 3 — obtaining the evidence

Initially, we considered a wide range of selection methods — group exercises, psychometric tests, in-tray exercises, behavioural interviews — in addition to the existing presentation and AAC interview. Most we ruled out at the outset. The major constraint was the time scale of the selection procedure which could not extend beyond one day for logistical reasons, and the afternoon would still be required for the (statutory) AAC interviews. Our strategy was therefore to use the morning session to collect as much relevant evidence as possible, which could then be summarised and reviewed before the main AAC interview.

Philosophically, our approach was based on the notion that the best predictor of future behaviour was past and present behaviour, rather than theoretical answers to hypothetical questions, so we were most interested in methods that would reveal and explore decisions and actions the candidates had taken in the past, and the reasons for them. We therefore narrowed our choice of method to two: a presentation on a specified topic, and a one-to-one behavioural interview focused on the particular attributes already identified. Between the two approaches all the necessary attributes would be covered.

Presentation topics may relate to the development of the specialty concerned within the Trust, to technological developments, or to any other relevant issue. The audience for the presentation would include the Chairman, Chief Executive, Medical Director, and the consultants from the Trust who would sit on the statutory AAC later in the day.

A behavioural interview asks questions about specific episodes the candidate has experienced, and explores why the candidate chose to behave in the way he or she did, and the eventual outcome. A typical example of such an approach might be 'Tell me about a situation where you had to deal with a junior colleague who was not performing up to standard. How did you tackle it? What was the result?'. The interviewer would probe the answers given to elicit what actions the candidate took and why, and whether the outcome of the episode was satisfactory (in the candidate's eyes). Answers are evaluated in the context of the relevant attribute, in this case 'leadership and staff development'. The interviewer would not necessarily look for a perfect outcome from the episode, but rather whether the candidate handled the situation in a way that was consistent with the attribute definition. If an outcome had been disappointing then what the candidate had learned from the experience is also relevant.

The interview questions were tested on a small group of senior registrars who volunteered for some interview experience. This pilot-tested several issues: whether the questions made sense to the candidate; whether the questions raised issues that were beyond the experience and scope of a typical senior registrar; whether the form in which each question was written was easily spoken by the interviewer; and the length of the interview. The outcome of the interview development process was initially two standard interview questionnaires, now reduced to one.

The choice of interviewers raised some questions. It was important that interviewers were of sufficient status within the Trust to have credibility with candidates, and that they were, or could become, sufficiently expert in the interviewing process. Initially two executive directors were trained — Yvonne Roberts (Finance Director) and Helen Thompson (Director of Operational Management). Neither was a doctor, but they had substantial experience of working alongside doctors and of staff selection and development.

Stage 4 — putting it together

When a vacancy for a consultant occurs, a view needs to be taken of how the attributes might relate to the vacancy — for example, are there any special features in the job which would require a greater than normal response to a particular attribute? It may be that a stronger than normal ability to deal with conflict is needed, or the need to train juniors may be emphasised. This 'profiling' of the attributes is applied to all the elements of the selection process.

Within the wider selection process the purpose of shortlisting is to eliminate all (medically) unappointable candidates and to select the four most promising of the appointable ones. This is still largely done in the traditional way from the evidence of the CV, from impressions gained from any visit to the Trust by the candidate, and from any personal knowledge of a candidate.

On selection day itself, during the morning session each candidate gives a short (20-minute) presentation, with some questions from the audience, on a topic relating to the vacancy and undergoes a 30-minute behavioural interview. At lunchtime, interviewers and AAC members meet to review their impressions of each candidate in relation to the attributes.

From this provisional review AAC members are able to plan and co-ordinate their questioning strategy for the AAC held in the afternoon. Questions are devised for the follow-up of any area where a candidate is felt to be weak or borderline, or to supplement areas where more information would be helpful. The members of the AAC who have not been involved in the morning's proceedings, usually the University and Royal College representatives and a non-executive director of the Trust, are welcome to attend this lunchtime meeting.

When the full AAC assembles, the Chairman reminds the members of the job and of any special qualities sought in relation to the attributes. The College Adviser and the University representative, who have probably not been involved in the morning's proceedings, are usually invited to concentrate on the qualifications, training and medical appointability of each candidate. The AAC proceeds as it always has done, with each member being given an opportunity to ask questions. The important differences are that questions are now co-ordinated between members, and that each question will have a specific purpose in relation to the particular evidence sought about particular attributes. Many questions will still be asked of all the candidates, but some will be 'personalised' as indicated by the lunchtime review.

After the interviews decision making is assisted by the ability to refer the evidence on each candidate to the original attributes. Comparison of candidates is thus more systematic and more objective, and there is less opportunity for one member of the AAC to try to dominate the others. Decision making is more transparent and a full consensus is usually forthcoming. The Medical Director reports that decisions appear to be made for the right reasons, and that it is also much more clear when it is right not to make an appointment, as has happened in a number of cases. Under the original system, it would have been much less clear if a potential appointment was risky.

Organisational learning

Clearly the main learning outcome has been how to apply a more systematic selection process to the appointment of consultants. However, there has also been some important learning for the directors involved, both individually and collectively.

From the start, the directors recognised their learning need and, fortunately, held an extremely positive attitude towards it. The greatest single need was to help doctors with a high level of skill in the interviewing of patients to transfer and adapt that skill to the interviewing of job applicants, something that was not happening of its own accord. The AAC members invited me to sit in on the meetings and to listen and give feedback afterwards.

The main problem to overcome was the perceived need to ask impressive questions, usually in the form of long, complex questions, and sometimes in the form of a statement rather than a question. The difficulty here is that the candidate may have a problem in identifying the real question being asked, or may even answer the wrong question, and be marked down for it! We concentrated on the straightforward use of open questions — 'what, how, and why?' — and emphasised the importance of one question at a time. In addition, the AAC members from the Trust jointly plan the questions they will individually ask in response to the feedback from the lunchtime meeting, learning from each other.

Most of those from a management background had previous experience of management selection. The challenge for them was to unlearn old skills and to be willing to learn new skills, in particular to move away from a less structured approach and to submit to the discipline of asking standard questions of a behavioural kind, within a strict framework and time scale. They also had to learn how to present their assessments clearly and concisely to the lunchtime meeting. Again, there has been a high degree of willingness to be supervised, coached and to listen to feedback.

Achievements of the project

The project is still continuing and the Chairman and directors of the Huddersfield Trust are pleased with the outcomes so far. They have developed an ability for the managers and doctors in the Trust to work coherently as a team in the selection of new consultants, individually and collectively developing interviewing and selection skills. They are more confident that the decisions they make will be good ones. More importantly, they have the confidence to recognise when a particular appointment may be risky, and to decide not to appoint. Most important of all, they feel that they are in control of the process.

In the course of the project we have successfully obtained the cooperation of the various consultants from the Trust who have participated in AACs since the new system started, though some openly claim to be suspending judgement, for a while at least. We have successfully obtained the cooperation of the various college advisers and university representatives, who seem happy to fit into their modified role and do not regard the change as an attempt to channel or limit their contributions unduly.

Conclusions

Huddersfield Trust are pleased with the appointment system we have jointly developed. They are confident that they have made good appointments when using it, and they are continuing to improve and refine the system. We have twice reviewed and refined the behavioural interview questions in the light of feedback from the interviewers and from candidates.

We still need to improve the production of a personnel specification and the tailoring of the attributes to meet more precisely the needs of individual vacancies, i.e. deciding which of the attributes are going to be more critical and which less. This work is now under way.

Any NHS Trust could adopt similar enhancements to the selection process, but to do so would require much more than the 'bolting on' of an interview and a presentation to the AAC procedure. Each element in the procedure should relate carefully to a coherent context, which itself needs to be sensitively developed in a way which gains the commitment of all parties to the process.

Looking back over the exercise, much more seems to have been achieved than improvement of the selection system:

- Doctors and managers have collaborated to introduce this significant cultural change, breaking down barriers and building trust in the process.
- The attributes developed for consultant appointments are now used for senior management appointments, representing the building of a significant bridge between doctors and managers.
- The attributes can be adapted for the purposes of doctors' appraisals.

ACKNOWLEDGMENTS

A number of factors have clearly contributed to the success of the exercise, for which I am eternally thankful:

- the commitment of the Chairman, Chief Executive and Medical Director to the development of the process, and their ability to take advice and guidance

- the sensitive interviewing skills and enthusiasm of the other directors involved — Yvonne Roberts, Helen Thompson, and Jan Freer
- the practical help and enthusiasm of Linda Dunne (Personnel Manager) and of her director, Ruth Hodgkinson.

17. Doctors and dilemmas

Tony Winkless   Mike Pedler   Hugo Mascie-Taylor

Introduction

Recent policy in the NHS has been concerned with strengthening the managerial function to achieve efficiency and effectiveness gains. These changes involve doctors in more managing: their personal practices; their work teams and colleague groups; their departments and organisations. However, the greater use of 'rational' management methods, together with many private sector assumptions and values based on the market metaphor, creates profound difficulties for many doctors. For such doctors, managing the 'new health service' is not just a matter of acquiring new knowledge or skills — it calls into question central medical values and beliefs.

The authors conducted research funded by the NHS Training Division (NHSTD) on the alternative positions which doctors may take with regard to the resolution of the common dilemmas which arise in fulfilling the role of today's hospital consultant.[1] The underlying source of these dilemmas can be summed up in the question 'How can the values of medicine and management be reconciled?'.

This paper summarises the main findings of the research, including the model of 'ideal types' which represent alternative resolutions of the dilemmas facing hospital consultants. It also contains brief details of the *Doctors and Dilemmas Workbook*[2] which has been developed from the research as a self-development guide. Before discussing the research and its findings, there are brief notes on the importance of values, beliefs and attitudes and of two alternative sets of values — 'managerialism' and 'medicalism' — which are particularly relevant to this discussion.

The importance of values, beliefs and attitudes

The performance and commitment of people is crucial to organisational effectiveness. Nowhere is this more true than in the NHS.

Central to people's ability and willingness to commit themselves is the question of how any given task squares with their values, beliefs and attitudes.

Stevens[3] defines 'value' as 'an individual's criteria for judging the worth of things' and 'beliefs' as 'assumptions about the possibility that an object exists, that it possess certain characteristics or that it is related in certain ways to other objects'. Here values are, in a sense, 'inner'; beliefs are more 'outer' — in the world. 'Attitudes' are consequences of a valuing process and are defined as 'positive and negative feelings about the objects in (his/her) psychological world'. In this chapter we use 'values' to refer to these three taken together.

Value systems are deeply rooted structures, built up throughout life, and are enduring and slow to change. Though unique to each of us, they reflect the collective culture in which we have been brought up and educated. Their significance lies in their potential to influence actions. If our actions and behaviour are a function of our knowledge, skills and *values*, it is usually easier to recognise the limits of our skills than it is to judge the impact of our values.

The first step is for a person to understand his or her own values and how these influence what he or she does. A further step is to be aware that there are other, alternative sets of values which can apply to any given situation. Awareness of alternative value sets can give more choice and freedom of action.

'Managerialism' and 'medicalism'

Alternative sets of values associated with doctoring and managing in the NHS can be perceived. Piper and Aitkenhead[4] suggest that 'managerialist' beliefs, held by most (but not all) managers, include the primacy of securing and controlling resources, which are limited, competed for, and secured through the delivery of agreed outcomes. This requires organisational control through a hierarchy. By contrast, 'medicalist' beliefs are based on those of the 'personal doctor' responsible for providing the best possible care to each individual patient and accountable to peers and professional bodies.

Both of these beliefs may be held in 'strong' or 'weak' forms along a continuum. A strong form of 'managerialist' beliefs would verge at the extreme on 'macho management', using the power to hire and fire to enforce performance management and control. For strong 'medicalists', doctors are not accountable to managers, who are there to administer and resource clinical decisions. At the weaker end of both sets of beliefs there is more of a belief in consensus, with managers, doctors and other groups needing to work together to agree and produce desired outcomes.

In daily experience we can see how these values operate to influence people's actions beyond the particular skills and knowledge which a person may have. If a person is not clear about his or her values, and is not aware of alternatives, then it is likely that he or she will act according to those values, irrespective of how appropriate they are to the specific situation.

The Doctors and Dilemmas Model

The model presented here is based on the research study[1] mentioned above and suggests four possible alternative positions which doctors may take with regard to the resolution of the common dilemmas which arise in fulfilling their role.

The purpose of the study was to explore and test a model of 'ideal types', representing alternative resolutions of these dilemmas, and to evaluate critically ways of employing the results of the research in the development of doctors.

A panel of judges — senior doctors and managers — was presented with the matrix shown in Figure 17.1 and asked to identify representatives of each 'ideal type' — A, B, C and D. Panel members were then interviewed using a repertory grid approach to elicit their personal constructs about the differences between the representatives they had chosen. Full details of the sample, the method

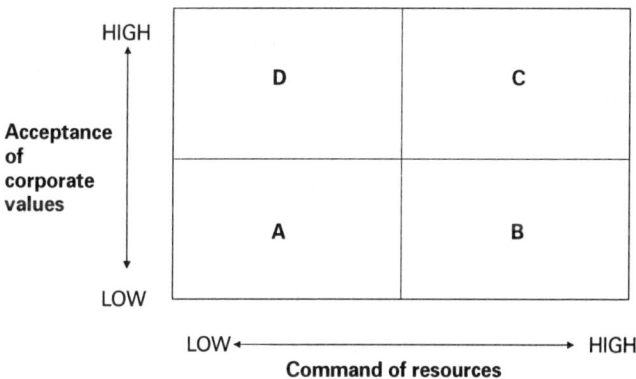

Fig. 17.1   The matrix

for eliciting constructs, the interview protocols, and examples of interview data can be found in Mascie-Taylor et al.[1]

Findings

The sample liked the model and thought that it worked well, although the A type was difficult: 'I understand the model very well ... it works except for A ... that is more difficult ... you need to define it more'. Respondents commented on the model as if it were a map or plot in which people might move around, occasionally in short-term tactical terms, but usually in longer-term career terms:

Perhaps everyone starts at A. People soon move through except for very low achievers. Some people go to B and stay there ... they could become a C perhaps ... no, I don't think they could ... they might try if it suited them. It takes time to become a C, although some people do it very quickly. I think Ds would often like to be Cs, but something stops them. Either they lack the skill or vision, or they just want an easy life. I'd like to be a C.

Another said: 'A can go to D or B ... B is usually an end point, but D can go back to A or on to C. C is a transitory position ... it is such hard work ... they go to D or A'.

These quotes illustrate the use of the model as a heuristic device, both in terms of illustrating the various possible alternative positions and as an aid to career planning. In addition to their constructs, respondents made many comments about the different types, and these have been incorporated into the 'identikits' below.

One respondent thought that the model was an over-simplification, and suggested having more boxes:

The model is a very limited choice — only four styles ... I'd like to see eight — this reduces people ... it was difficult to think of people who fit into boxes ... people are all shades ... I tried to make a caricature of these people to fit them ... that is why I included myself, because I felt better for putting myself in when talking about others. Another way would be to have different levels of value system, and let people choose their position on a line ... It would be fairer.

The same person nevertheless was able to talk about her own situation with considerable insight using the model:

In my team I would be a C ... especially at a time of change, but for the whole unit I'm often a D, doing labouring, less skilled management work. The struggle is I want to move from D to C, but I've never been able to make that move with regard to the whole unit. Much of this is to do with personal psychology — 'you can't do this big job; you must delegate too much of your work with patients ... patients are also my friends; my sub-specialty will go to pot, and so on' ... a struggle ... fears of having to confront unpleasant people and even use devious tactics — that would be difficult. I do use them, but I have to be well-prepared because I'm not skilled ...

Four identikits

We reduced the mass of data to four 'ideal type' descriptions — pen pictures, caricatures or *identikits*. In doing this we tried to make all four boxes 'habitable', despite the managerialist bias of our sample. Three identikits emerged with clarity, but Type A turned out to be a catch-all of sub-types.

The identikits are presented in a clockwise order, starting with Type D. Each is described in terms of 'focus', 'abilities and skills', and 'beliefs and values'. Each also has a 'below the line' description, which can be interpreted better as a 'shadow side' to the type rather than as a 'downside'.

Box 17.1   Ideal Type D

Ideal Type **D**	TEAM PLAYER 'Good corporate citizen'
Focus	* Primarily to the team, but with awareness and interest in the whole organisation * Team leader advising rather than leading organisation.
Abilities and skills	* Takes leadership at team level and is prepared to accept it at corporate level * Plays by the rules within corporate goals of the organisation, node/building block of the organisation * Participative, cooperative, loyal, supportive, shares responsibility, team worker * Good interpersonal skills, good communicator * Economical with resources * Personable, well-respected.
Beliefs and values	* Service orientation * Recognises 'added value' and complementary skills of management * Democratic process, participation, consultation * Loyalty to medicine and medical values together with valuing the whole organisation.

Below the line

Type Ds form the backbone of the organisation, often being dedicated clinicians, 'the sort you'd like to take your mum to', but are also interested in playing their part in the whole.

Ds can be 'big fish in small ponds' who might be Cs, but lack the confidence or have fewer skills. In some ways they resemble Cs but are less inclined to take risks and may prefer to avoid tough decisions. Some may have been Cs but have chosen a quieter life to pursue other interests or to focus on their medical role.

They are less likely to have or take on a formal management role than Cs, but as they are parsimonious with resources they may take too much upon themselves and be somewhat self-sacrificing in meeting the demands of others.

Box 17.2   Ideal Type C

Ideal Type **C**	LEADER 'Strives on behalf of the whole'
Focus	* Commitment to the organisation as a whole * Wide view, broad vision, strategic thinking.
Abilities and skills	* Change agent, politically astute * High interpersonal skills, influential, good communicator, good listener, assertive, can be tough * Manages resources on behalf of the whole * Develops people and teams * Manages conflict — constructive and supportive, tolerant of ambiguity and dilemmas.
Beliefs and values	* Quality service and value for money requires doctors and managers to work together * Capability in the whole system is what counts * Pluralistic — different sources of loyalty are legitimate; conflict is inevitable, endemic and needs to be managed * People (including self) can learn and are developing beings.

Below the line
From a managerial perspective Type C is perhaps in danger of being too good to be true and lacking a 'shadow side'.

Though Cs are often highly committed and very able leaders, Bs and perhaps As may see them as having 'gone over to the other side' or as having failed to make it in medicine and now seeking an alternative career. Some Cs may be Bs in temporary disguise, playing the corporate game in order to secure advantage. Others may indeed be more interested in personal career advancement than with the rather altruistic 'good of the whole'. A strong motivation may be the desire to learn and to explore new possibilities, not just for career but for personal development.

Cs are widely liked and respected for their leadership qualities, especially by Ds.

Box 17.3   Ideal Type B

Ideal Type **B**	INDEPENDENT 'Fights for own patch'
Focus	* Me and my specialty * Me and my profession.
Abilities and skills	* Confidence, dominance, determined, may be aggressive * Political skills, well connected, knows 'right people' * Entrepreneurial, energetic and hard working * Uses conflict * Good ideas — sometimes functional, sometimes dysfunctional for the organisation.
Beliefs and values	* Self belief, self-worth * Individuality, individual excellence is what counts * Specialty is all-important * Doctors don't need managing, but need administration * Rules are to be broken or 'my rules'.

Below the line
The shadow side of Type Bs is that they have little in the way of corporate loyalty or values. Uninterested in corporate management, they see managers (at best) as means of acquiring resources for their patch.

They often lack sensitivity to others, and may appear aloof, overbearing or arrogant. They arouse strong feelings and may be admired, feared or disliked. They express themselves well in advancing their own work or specialty, but are poor at team-work, chairing meetings or achieving agreement. They can be extrovert, convivial and amusing.

Their ability to command resources, in the hospital or via external funding (e.g. University, BMA, Royal College), whilst lacking an awareness and concern for the whole, makes them often the most difficult people to manage — 'you can't herd cats'.

Box 17.4   Ideal Type A

Ideal Type **A**   'CONTRACT CLINICIAN'   'Uninvolved'

Focus   * One-to-one patient care and clinical management, with no interest, awareness or involvement beyond this level.

This 'ideal type' is a 'catch-all' of several sub-types. Classified as low on both corporate values and command of resources, this type has few abilities, skills, beliefs or values which are relevant from a managerialist perspective. For this reason the format for Type **A** is different, and consists of a brief description of four possible sub-types:

1. The new starter. The learner doctor, on the way to **B**, **C** or **D**. May be naive, idealistic and dedicated, with little awareness of how the hospital or Health Service works, and with little energy or attention to spare for learning the role.

2. The dis-engager. Winding down and preparing to separate from the organisation through retirement, tiredness, ill health, etc.

3. The contract worker. Personal doctor working '9 to 5' who does-n't want to get involved in anything outside one-to-one patient care. May have domestic responsibilities or consuming interests outside work. Does a good job for the hospital within the strict limits of the contract.

4. The isolate. The loner who may be good, bad or indifferent, but is essentially unrecognised in terms of contribution. May work in a remote location or specialty, or be isolated for some other reason.

Below the line

Type **A**s have least impact from a managerial point of view because they contribute little to the organisation as a whole beyond their immediate task. This is not a commentary on them as people or as doctors — they may be effective or ineffective at that task. They may be learners or about to retire; they may have a limited contractual relationship with the organisation or have a deep moral involvement in patient care. They may be 'tongue-tied clinicians' (in the words of one respondent).

They share a certain isolation from the run of events and may be candidates for further personal and professional development.

The Doctors and Dilemmas Workbook

As a result of this research and a series of seminars based on the findings, a *Doctors and Dilemmas Workbook*[3] has been devised to help doctors who are involved in managing in the Health Service to:

- assess their own values and understand how these affect their actions
- understand the alternative sets of values associated with managing the NHS, especially how managerial and organisational values differ from medical ones
- choose more appropriately between medical and managerial values in given decision situations
- persist, where values conflict and dilemmas are met, in continuing to struggle to reconcile differences in values in particular decisions.

The *Doctors and Dilemmas Workbook* adopts a self-development approach and contains a self-diagnostic questionnaire together with structured activities built around the Doctors and Dilemmas Model. These activities are accompanied by chapters on Life and Career Options for doctors (often a question of great interest to those who, in pursuing their careers to date, have often not given much thought to what future options may be open to them) and various resources to help with further development.

Whilst the *Workbook* is designed for individuals to work through on their own, great value may be obtained in involving other people in the process of personal and professional development. For this reason, advice is given on how to engage other people in the process:

through forming small development groups, through mentors, or through using the *Workbook* as part of a management or professional development programme.

Conclusions

The research study[1] had various limitations, mainly the smallness of the sample size and its managerial bias — four of the judges were managers (all being Chief Executives), whilst the other four doctors classified themselves as either Ideal Type C or D. Unsurprisingly, the construct descriptions display this bias; for example, Cs and Ds tend to be described in favourable terms, whilst As and Bs are described in markedly more negative terms. For the purposes of the study the 'managerialist' view of doctors in hospitals was central, but clearly very different results might be obtained with a more representative sample of doctors. In the study it was stressed that we were talking about doctors as *managers* or in terms of their values and attitudes regarding management, and were not commenting on a doctor's clinical ability, which lies outside the scope of the model.

There are other limitations. We have assumed that, in referring to the 'managerial' role of the doctor, we can lump together all those activities which contribute to the effective running of the complex collective which is the hospital. Thus 'managerial' includes resource allocation, ward closures and clinical developments, which are the stuff of medical director or clinical director roles, and also the help and counselling of colleagues, the teaming and ladling of everyday duties and responsibilities, and the micro-organisational side of patient management, without which the 'negotiated order' of the hospital could not happen.

Allowing for these limitations, the research suggests that the model provides a useful and thought-provoking way of thinking about the alternatives in resolving the dilemmas of working with both medical and managerial values. The main value of the research may lie in its applications to personal, professional and organisational development work with doctors and other health professionals who may find themselves in analogous positions.

REFERENCES

Mascie-Taylor H, Pedler MJ, Winkless AJ. Doctors and dilemmas: a study of 'ideal types' of doctors/managers and an evaluation of how these could support values clarification for doctors in the Health Service. Bristol: NHSTD, 1993.

Mascie-Taylor H, Pedler MJ, Winkless AJ. Doctors and dilemmas workbook. Bristol: NHSTD, 1996.

Stevens P. Attitudes. Open University Press, 1976.

Piper J, Aitkenhead M. The relationship between doctors and managers. Internal consultants' report to members of Leicestershire Health's Mental Health Services Unit Management Board. 1992.

18. Prioritising new services — the Wakefield experience[*]

Paul Watson   Graham Horne   Anna Firth

Introduction

Since 1991, District Health Authorities have been charged with the assessment of the health needs of their local population. However, they have to meet these needs within the limitations imposed by overall spending limits. The implicit philosophy behind needs assessment is a zero-based approach, that is, a complete and thorough-going review where all current investment needs to be justified. Some commentators have instead advocated an approach based on marginal analysis. This approach accepts the bulk of current activity as a given, and attempts to ensure that decisions concerning marginal changes around this baseline are informed by evidence of cost-effectiveness.

Marginal analysis can, in principle, be applied to decisions concerning proposals to increase or decrease funding in any particular area. In reality, there are enormous problems for a health authority embarking on a course of disinvestment in any particular health care activity, and examples of successful disinvestment are rare.

There is, however, one area where health authorities can make an informed decision on the allocation of health care resources — when deciding whether or not to invest in new developments such as the introduction of a new drug or a new clinic. Once a new service is introduced, expectations of continued public funding in that service quickly become established, and so the decision to introduce a new service can be seen as the cutting edge of NHS purchasing.

This chapter describes a process developed by Wakefield Health Authority to manage the introduction of service developments around a set of values and principles developed to guide the strategic thinking of the Authority.

---

[*] This article first appeared in the *Health Services Journal*, March 14th 1996.

The prioritisation process

The first stage in making decisions on new service developments is to ensure that deliberations on individual proposals are made in parallel. An individual proposal assessed simply on its own merits is an inadequate guide to decision making. Most proposed developments can be seen as a 'good thing' in themselves, but what is required is a consideration of the 'opportunity cost' — i.e. a consideration of what other developments are being sacrificed in order to support the service under consideration. This kind of discussion can only take place if all the potential developments are considered simultaneously so that the trade-off between developments can be made explicit.

Local providers were thus invited to submit proposals in October 1994 for funding during the 1995/96 financial year. General practitioners were included in this process if a Health Authority contract for a service was being sought. Health Authority officers were also invited to submit bids, either in partnership with the potential provider or simply as ideas for new services. Thirty-nine bids were received, of which 4 were later withdrawn by the provider, leaving 35 to undergo formal prioritisation, as shown in Table 18.1 (see p. 199).

Once the bids had been received, a mechanism was required to allocate a score to each bid. This scoring system was adapted from the Authority's statement on values and principles which is intended to give a guide to the issues that should be considered in making purchasing decisions in Wakefield.

The task of converting these criteria into a usable scoring system was formidable. The method adopted was to allocate each development a number of points up to a maximum of 50. Individual criteria were scored as described below.

Potential health gain

This is derived from the degree of benefit expected and the number of people likely to benefit:

Degree of benefit	
Life saving with full recovery	6
Life saving with residual problems	5
Produces full and sustained relief of disability or pain	4
Produces partial sustained relief of disability or pain	3
Produces temporary relief of disability or pain	2
Improvement in service quality with no direct effect on fatality, disability or pain	1

Number of people	
Up to 10	1
Up to 100	2
Up to 500	3
Up to 1000	4
Up to 10 000	5
Over 10 000	6

The total score would be derived from summing the individual scores — for example, a life-saving service which leaves residual problems and affects 40 people would score 5 + 2 = 7. The maximum score would be 12 (i.e. 24% of total score).

Strength of evidence of clinical effectiveness

This is an assessment of the strength of the research evidence, not a measure of the effectiveness itself (which is covered by the previous section). The following allocation is proposed:

Several randomised controlled trials (RCTs) or of unchallengeable benefit (an example of this would be penicillin)	9
Single RCT plus several unrandomised controlled studies	7
Single RCT or several unrandomised controlled studies	5
Single unrandomised controlled study	3
No controlled studies	0

The maximum score is 9 (i.e. 18% of total score).

Prevention over treatment

If two alternative interventions produced the same benefit then an intervention that prevented disease would be favoured over one that cured it:

Intervention prevents a problem for which there is no specific treatment	9
Intervention prevents a problem where treatment short of total relief exists	6
Intervention prevents a problem where total relief is possible	3

The maximum score is 9 (i.e. 18% of total score).

Appropriate setting

This means a setting which improves patient access whilst maintaining clinical quality. The following scores would be allocated only if the improvement in access did not undermine clinical effectiveness:

More appropriate	6
No change	4
Less appropriate	2

Promotion of equity

Equity has a number of elements: a service development could bring Wakefield into line with other health Districts; a development could address geographical inequity within the District or a development could be targeted at people with particular problems (e.g. thalassaemia screening for ethnic minorities). Alternatively, a development could promote equity by making an existing service more acceptable or accessible to certain people (e.g. provision of transport child care to enable women to attend screening):

Development addresses intra-District inequity	6
Development brings Wakefield into line with other health Districts	4
Development promotes access to an existing service	2

The maximum score is 6 (i.e. 12% of total score).

Public preference

This was obtained by using the Authority's Local Voices panel. The panel consisted of members of the public who had previously agreed to act as a 'sounding board' for the Authority's strategic thinking. In order to simplify the process, the 35 bids were grouped into 14 broad service areas — for example, the hospice bids were grouped together, as were all the proposed counselling services. Respondents were then asked to list their top five services in order of preference. These 'votes' were then used to allocate a score of 0–4 points to each development (i.e. 8% of total score). The response rate was 50%.

General Practitioner preference

This was obtained by writing to each practice in the District and

Table 18.1   Summary of bids received

Bids received	£
Development of the paediatric occupational therapy service	63 275
Development of speech therapy for adults with learning disability	55 721
Speech and language therapy for children	32 936
Development of speech therapy for dysfluent clients	24 250
Development of multi-disciplinary team to support child and adolescent mental health services	166 784
Assessment and respite care for children with learning disabilities	426 100
Increased occupational therapy services	85 200
Additional support for the Youth Advisory Service	12 177
Specialist school nurse for asthma	22 000
Community-based menopausal clinics	40 000
Increased psycho-sexual counselling services	25 000
Triage system for accident and emergency	80 313
Improvement to outpatient pharmacy waiting area	14 309
Upgrading of hospital pathology equipment	15 048
Upgrading of hospital X-ray storage facilities	11 200
Additional consultant radiologist (part-time)	31 360
Improved hospital specimen transport service	62 530
Additional consultant chemical pathologist (part-time)	24 106
Pain clinic based in a GP practice	25 000
Hysteroscopy/endometrial biopsy in a GP practice	20 000
Medical termination service based in a GP practice	20 000
Psychology support for palliative care services	25 000
Chiropody service based in a GP practice	107 200
Consultant medical support for palliative care services	27 600
Cervical cytology recall equalised across the District to every three years	62 000
Increase in NHS funding for terminations	23 560
Community-based infection control nurse	22 000
Additional counselling for people with HIV	16 745
Counselling services for victims of sexual/physical abuse	43 570
Young people's worker for alcohol services	33 547
Extension of breast screening to 65–69s	80 000
GP-based counselling services for mental health problems	100 000
Dedicated health visitor sessions for mother and baby unit of local prison	1 500
Homestart — a self-help scheme for families with young children:	
• continuation of existing pilot	60 000
• roll-out to entire District	530 000

Note. Not all developments were formally costed by providers, and some costs are thus estimates.

asking the practice to list their top five preferences as for the public score. Practices were sent details of all 35 bids to assess separately. The practice 'votes' were then used to allocate a score of 0–4 points to each development (i.e. 8% of total score). The response rate was 33%.

Scoring was carried out by a panel involving managers and public health physicians drawn from across the organisation. Each development was scored independently by two members of the panel using the information submitted by the applicant. The final score was allocated by taking an average of the two independent ratings. Where there was a substantial discrepancy between scorers, the bid was discussed by the panel as a whole and a score agreed by majority opinion. The General Practitioner score and public preference score were then added to the panel rating to give a total score. The bids were then placed in rank order, as shown in Table 18.2.

The next step was to decide how many developments could be funded. It was at this stage that the Authority received notification of its funding allocation for 1995/96. This was to involve a loss of £2.1 million non-recurrent funding from the District. At the same time, the effects of the new capitation funding formula on individual Districts were announced. The new formula meant that Wakefield was 4.5% above its capitation funding target (i.e. £7 million). The result of these two financial changes was that development funds were to be in short supply both for 1995/96 and for the foreseeable future.

Despite the scarcity of development funds, it was felt important that some of the proposals should be adopted as strategic priorities for 1995/96. After some debate three of the top four bids were adopted: counselling services in primary care; improvements in palliative care services; and improved access to termination services. The bid to reduce the recall interval for cervical screening from five years to three years was not adopted since there was considerable disagreement within the panel as to how this development should be scored.

The funding of the three prioritised developments is now under consideration; the bid for termination services has been taken forward by the negotiation of a contract with the independent sector. The use of mental health reprovision funds is being explored for primary care counselling services. However, the source of funding for palliative care service development has yet to be identified.

Discussion

The process described is an attempt to bring clarity and transparency to the difficult area of priority setting — an activity that has traditionally been carried out away from the public arena. There are a number of observations that can be made about our experience in Wakefield.

Table 18.2   Prioritisation of service development proposals: ranked list of combined scores

Position	Proposal	Scores			Total
		Panel	GP	Public	
1	GP-based counselling service	29	4	1	34
2	Cervical cytology	28	2	0	30
2	Palliative Care Medical Support	27	2	1	30
4	Terminations – increased funding	25	3	1	29
5	GP Chiropody service	28	0	0	28
6	GP Medical terminations	26	0	1	27
7	Menopausal clinics	24	0	2	26
8	Triage system	20	1	4	25
9	Breast screening	23	1	0	24
9	Youth Advisory Service	23	0	1	24
9	Infection Control Nurse	22	0	2	24
12	Psycho-sexual counselling	18	3	2	23
13	Sexual/physical abuse counselling	20	1	1	22
14	Chemical Pathologist	17	2	2	21
15	Alcohol Services	19	0	1	20
15	Pharmacy waiting area	19	0	1	20
15	Speech therapy for learning disability	19	0	1	20
15	Asthma School Nurse	17	2	1	20
19	Palliative Care Psychological support	18	0	1	19
19	Paediatric occupational therapy	18	0	1	19
19	Occupational therapy	17	1	1	19
19	Home Start (pilot scheme)	17	0	2	19
19	Child & Adolescent Mental Health	16	1	2	19
24	Home Start (district roll-out)	16	0	2	18
24	Consultant Radiologist	16	0	2	18
26	Respite care for children with learning disabilities	16	1	0	17
26	Speech and Language therapy for children	16	0	1	17
26	Hospital pathology equipment	16	0	1	17
26	Speech therapy for dysfluent clients	16	0	1	17
30	Prison Health Visitor	16	0	0	16
30	HIV counselling	15	0	1	16
30	GP Pain Clinic	14	1	1	16
33	GP Hysteroscopy/endometrial biopsy	11	0	1	12
34	X-ray storage facilities	9	0	1	10
35	Specimen transport	8	0	1	9

The first observation concerns the unscientific nature of the process described; there are a number of criticisms that can be made about the process, for example: the attribution of health gain according to the number of people affected is non-linear; the apportioning of appropriateness is highly subjective; there is no consideration of cost in the process. However, focusing on these technical aspects would be to miss the point; the purpose of the exercise was to introduce clarity into the process of priority setting. The driving force behind this was an intention to move away from making decisions behind closed doors using implicit values to a process carried out in public using an explicit statement of underlying principles.

We would contend that we have moved some way to achieving this in Wakefield. Each purchaser, however, must develop its own way of reaching decisions — values are not necessarily shared — and ultimately there is no simple technical fix to what is essentially a process of making value judgements. Critics might, however, point out that there is a technical fix available, i.e. economic appraisal. When the process was being designed the possibility of basing the process on economic appraisal was considered. However, it quickly became apparent that the health economics literature was generally not applicable to the developments the providers were likely to submit. The majority of the literature focuses on assessing discrete interventions such as hip replacements or cholesterol screening. However, the debates that Health Authority purchasers have with providers tend to be about the development of service infrastructure rather than about levels of discrete treatments (other than a few high-cost treatments such as renal failure); this makes it difficult to apply health economics thinking directly to Health Authority purchasing. One solution would be to commission specific evaluations of the bids that were submitted; however, the volume of bids and the short time available to make decisions preclude this as a viable option. The real value of existing economic appraisal will probably lie in GP fundholding, where contracting is more concerned with the volumes of discrete treatments rather than the discussions on service infrastructure which underlie Health Authority purchasing.

The third issue is the dependence on growth in funding that this model assumes; the lack of specific development funds in the District has proved an obstacle to implementing the scheme. This is an issue for many purchasers and there is a need to look at reducing funding which is relatively ineffective or in low priority areas in order to release funding for high priority new developments. There is no reason why the process described above could not be used to guide decision making on disinvestment, but what is really required is for purchasers to have the determination to weather the political storm such moves would cause.

19. Management development for doctors: research in South and West Region

Tony White   John Gatrell

Introduction

In 1894 John Shaw Billings wrote: 'The education of the doctor which goes on after he has his degree is, after all, the most important part of his education'.[1] In considering that education, we must include management education and management for doctors. This involves three closely inter-related topics: decentralisation, clinical freedom and the cultures of managers and professionals.[2]

The historical perspective

Historically, hospitals were cottage industries. The craftsmen were doctors with complete authority over their own beds. With specialisation, new departments were created. They provided a service to patients, but little thought was given to their function in a unit. The idea of a health care team is still beyond the comprehension of many people in hospitals. Doctors have moved from professional independence to interdependence, although some fail to recognise this, resulting in stresses within the system.

According to Klein: 'Implicit in the structure of the NHS was a bargain between the State and the medical profession. While central government controlled the budget, doctors controlled what happened within that budget. Financial power was concentrated at the centre; clinical power was concentrated at the periphery'.[3] The bargain was frustrating for the doctors as the price of preserving clinical freedom was accepting the constraints of working within fixed budgetary limits. Individually, doctors often could or would not do this; tribalism and rivalry between specialties and departments prevented them from doing so. Equally, doctors fear that government and managers threaten their professional independence and seek more accountability. The phenomenon of managerial control is developing in every western country.[4]

The bargain was equally frustrating for managers. Enthoven[5] states: 'The consultants have accepted long term contracts with the NHS and limits on total expenditure in exchange for job security and "clinical freedom". Thus NHS management has very little leverage to make their services responsive to patient needs'. Managers felt that clinicians constrained managerial choices: firstly, by extending the range and cost of their activities without taking account of the resource implications; and secondly, by shifting clinical direction to personal interest rather than the needs of the hospital. Managers thus experienced frustration that actions by clinicians could unbalance programmes designed for a hospital, and therefore faced the difficult task of persuading doctors to accept that their clinical freedom must be counterbalanced by an awareness of, and responsibility for, the effective management of resources. For example, decisions by consultants to keep patients in hospital longer than necessary have implications for the NHS as a whole.[6] However, real power has moved from individual consultants and shifted to the purchasers, particularly GP fundholders, challenging the idea that clinical freedom bestows an automatic right to use public resources without scrutiny or limits.

Doctors' managerial roles

Research has increasingly focused on observing what managers do rather than on what they should do. Boyatzis tried to identify the characteristics of excellent performance.[7] He concluded that a job is performed most effectively when three elements are congruent: the job demands; the organisational environment; and the competence of the job holder. There are certain characteristics which seem to distinguish successful doctors in management. Turrill et al,[8] in a study of excellent doctors in management, referred to these types of characteristics as competencies and found that: 'These occur with sufficient frequency to suggest that they are too important to the role to be ignored. They may be termed the threshold variables in that they suggest the minimum conditions for fully acceptable performance'.

In Wessex, a project to explore clinicians' needs and their understanding of management in its broadest sense and how those needs and values could be incorporated into their professional development has been under way since 1992. The key objectives were to identify managerial knowledge and skills from undergraduate to medical director, with the aim of developing a core management training strategy for medical staff in the region, and thus define a long-term management training and development programme for doctors, which should be transferable on a national basis.

The study explored managerial activities of all grades in a wide range of specialties and organisational settings, including hospital medicine, general practice and public health. It was not undertaken as an isolated project on possible involvement of doctors in managerial issues, but rather as a recognition that all professionals, including doctors, perform a range of tasks in common with managers.

A national survey of management development activity was undertaken, followed by a questionnaire study of doctors and senior managers and an in-depth interview programme. The decision to use a questionnaire developed with a series of pilots, and compared raw data from one previously published nationally, based on the need to obtain information about the 'management techniques' used by doctors during their work. The assumption was made that if the outcome was to be important to doctors they had to be the first reference point. The wording of the questionnaire was critical as previous experience suggested that the use of the word 'management' alienated some potential respondents. Loosely based on the published structure of competence outlined by the Management Charter Initiative, it was eventually refined after four iterations into a 59 task characteristics version applicable to most doctors.

The interview programme had five aims:

- to validate the information from the questionnaires
- to identify what could have been taught earlier that might have been helpful
- to identify the skills where interviewees felt they needed most help
- to identify those methods which would receive a favourable acceptance by the profession
- to identify at what stage this would occur.

230 interviews were divided between grades of doctors and sites, covering hospital and general practice, public health doctors and some senior managers and targeted doctors (both receptive and non-receptive to management).

The interviewer was an active clinician. A short pilot programme was conducted to verify the process and develop a consistent pattern. The participants were not self-selecting. Interviews were carried out with representatives from all groups shown in Box 19.1.

Box 19.1 Groups interviewed

Medical students

Hospital
- Pre-registration house officers
- Senior house officers
- Registrars
- Senior registrars
- Consultants
- Clinical directors
- Medical directors
- Medically qualified chief executives

General practice
- Trainees
- Partners in general practice
  — Fundholders
  — Non-fundholders
  — Members of consortia

Community and public health doctors
- Purchasers
- Providers

Others
- Part-time women doctors
  — General practice
  — Hospital specialties
- Combined clinical assistants/general practitioners
- Staff grade hospital doctors

Managers
- Senior managers
  — Personnel directors
  — Finance directors
- Chief executives
  — Purchasers
  — Providers

Also interviewed were a number of established academics and management trainers throughout the country. Participants were selected by a variety of methods. Three hospitals provided one- or two-day programmes of interviews, otherwise doctors were

contacted at random by telephone and interviewed at their conve-
nience. A division of location was necessary to differentiate the
nature of work (see Box 19.2). Some interviewees were also
selected on the basis of their declared antipathy to management.

Box 19.2   Sites of interviews

Teaching hospitals	Small DGH
Large DGH	Trusts
Directly managed units	GP practice more than 5
Community hospitals	doctors
GP practice 2–4 doctors	Single-handed practices
Purchasing authorities	Health commissions
FHSAs	Regional Health Authority
Postgraduate hospital	

From the information gathered it was possible to synthesise a
model from a range of existing models set in the context of doctors
working in the health service. The model was developed through
iterations of the questionnaire during its pilot stages and in discussion with doctors and managers throughout the service. Task characteristics were derived which divided into five broad clusters of
capability, as shown in Box 19.3.

Box 19.3   The management model for doctors

- Contextual awareness
- Strategic thinking
- Functional and operational skills and knowledge
- Interpersonal and team skills
- Self-management skills.

Contextual awareness is the understanding and ability to operate
effectively at all levels within the NHS organisational structure,
including knowledge of central government health strategies, NHS
funding, roles of major constituents, the purchaser-provider concept,
senior organisational roles and the structure and process of local units.
Strategic thinking is based on an understanding of essential
processes and the ability to apply them.
Functional and operational skills and knowledge apply to a
range of activities and processes associated with the daily operation

of units in health care organisations. These include the recruitment and selection of non-medical staff, pursuing equal opportunities policies, non-clinical staff training, staff appraisal and implementing disciplinary procedures, negotiating contracts, monitoring business planning and performance, managing a budget and generating income, managing organisational crises, handling official complaints, using information systems, problem solving and decision making. Quality issues include managing quality, implementing patient satisfaction indicators and clinical audit.

Interpersonal and team skills include communicating sensitive information, counselling colleagues and subordinates, chairing and contributing to meetings, making presentations, dealing with the media, negotiating, conducting interviews for appraisal, selection, grievance and discipline, delegating work, resolving conflict, and goal setting for others.

Self-management skills used in the management of career and personal effectiveness at work include learning from experience, implementing difficult non-clinical decisions, acting independently and using initiative, time management, handling uncertainty, self-awareness and effective self-presentation.

Further evidence to support compatibility with other models was drawn from recent research.[9] In addition, a very high Cronbach's alpha reliability coefficient enabled the use of a relatively simple method to analyse the data, the aim being to identify the key managerial elements of doctors' work which they determined were significant. For each of the 59 items, respondents were asked to signify on a scale from 1 (low) to 4 (high) the importance they attached to each in the performance of their work; a zero (0) option indicated no involvement. The outcomes were later cross-referenced to the data collected from the interview programme. The value of the information derived was to enable the strategic use of resources to develop doctors in management. The means used to determine those task characteristics which were regarded by doctors as significant was to select those items which had been identified by more than 50% of respondents as important (either 3 or 4). This resulted in some important general conclusions:

- It is possible to separate management learning needs of doctors according to grade.
- The management development needs of doctors are progressive, and are dependent on grade of appointment.

- A number of key skills relating to management pervade all levels of appointment. These include team working, self-presentation, assertiveness, self-development, time management, and communicating sensitive information.
- Another set of skills and knowledge can be classified according to doctors' direct involvement in management. These include contextual awareness, strategic thinking and an array of functional capabilities.
- Learning needs are progressive and there is a high level of consistency in the clusters of need expressed at different levels.

It is impossible to report on the whole range of findings here; those who are interested should refer to the full report.[10] The generic nature of the managerial skills identified is believed to be useful in determining realistic training and development activities in the context of the opportunities and constraints facing the NHS. Management development for doctors is provided unevenly around the country. Regions which have been most successful in initiating and sustaining this development have been those with specialist support functions, staffed with professionals who have had appropriate management training. This has been most effective where specialists with sound knowledge and experience of the issues are employed.

Just as there is clear evidence for an overlap in professional and managerial characteristics, so there appears to be a broad 30:70 split between those doctors who are receptive to the concept of management as part of their role and those antagonistic to it. Sabin,[11] writing about his experiences of research in medical and managerial views, quotes highly committed doctors as describing management as 'the syphilis of the NHS'. Our own research attracted questionnaire responses which attacked the researchers: 'You're a traitor, call yourself a doctor?' and 'I have influence and will not forget your name'. An equally enthusiastic manager said that 'before the reforms the NHS was run by consultants who in the past would have been buccaneers on the high seas'.

Despite initiatives to enhance the position of 'softer' skill development in the undergraduate curriculum, many believe there has been little real change. Doctors at and above senior registrar level often found management training to be of interest, but only committed themselves to learning if there was a perception of its relevance to their clinical work.

Parker[12] says: 'Although doctors have many of the necessary skills — such as communication and problem-solving skills — there are other skills most do not have — such as financial and planning skills and knowledge of organisation dynamics and leadership styles. A great deal of training is needed to make doctors into effective managers and they have to learn the management trade as rigorously as they learned their medical trade'.

It is more accurate to say that doctors *should* have these skills. Unfortunately many do not have good communication and interpersonal skills.[10] Doctors and consultants in particular have a very high assessment of their own interpersonal skills, but there is a significant gap between senior doctors' self-assessment and the perception of those with whom they work. A matching study for general practitioners gave similar results. This correlates with the Audit Commission Report[13] which drew attention to the need for better communication between doctor and patient.

Clinical freedom

Despite the American Medical Association's rejection of socialised medicine, because of its supposed threat to clinical freedom, the British doctor by and large maintains more freedom of action than his American counterpart. Hoffenberg[14] speculated that British doctors possessed far greater clinical freedom than their counterparts in America, where three main forces had combined to curtail their clinical freedom. Advances in medical technology have resulted in patients resenting the authority of doctors, demanding a greater say for themselves: patient power. Pellegrino[15] describes the 'irreversible shift in the locus of decision-making from physician to patient'. Eddy[16] adds that 'physicians are slowly being stripped of their decision-making power'. The dominance of litigation also forces doctors to surrender much of their freedom of action and to adopt defensive medicine. Lastly, the costs of health care are encouraging payers — whether government, insurers, industry or individuals determined to regulate costs — to implement controls on the doctors who initiate the expense.

The same process now threatens the profession in Britain. Such practice and demands suggest there might no longer be grounds for justifying unmanaged status, other than in the provision of personal clinical services; perhaps a move towards agency medicine makes doctors easier to manage. There are consultants who are amenable to practising where no clinical priority can be established, and who accept that the hospital has to earn its money from somewhere. Patients are described as consumers, customers or clients. Relman[17] wrote: 'The present trend towards market competition is clearly weakening the traditional values of our profession'.

Clinical freedom concerns the relationship between a doctor and the patient being treated[18] and does not directly affect managers. Clinical freedom is not about decisions regarding future patients. One of the issues that surfaced in a number of interviews[2] was the question of the effect that limited resources would have on clinical freedom. The consultant has the discretion to make decisions about patients under treatment without those decisions being reviewed or overturned by anyone else, even someone from the same discipline. These decisions may be shared in peer review by discussion, but it is voluntary; no-one can overturn or alter treatment.

It is the issue of resources through contracts that seems to be the major threat to clinical freedom, although some doctors believe this is not a bad thing. A more popular view amongst those consultant clinical directors most convinced about the need for change[2] can be summarised as: 'What a clinician wanted was clinical freedom and that required resources because if you didn't have the resources, you didn't have the clinical freedom. The question was, would we be able to direct more resource into clinical work as doctors than if we weren't involved? If we could increase the efficiency of our work we would maximise our clinical freedom.... By being involved, you can make sure that the money available is used in ways which make the most medical sense to improve clinical freedom'.

Doctors are now becoming aware of the finiteness of resources; some of them are prepared to make changes and no longer regard this as an infringement of clinical freedom. To make doctors cost-conscious, budgets should be devolved as low as possible, even to individuals if necessary.

Decentralisation

The essence of decentralisation is to increase the involvement of all staff in the operational management of the service. It is important that responsibility and authority should be equally devolved and commensurate with the task; there is a tendency for management to decentralise responsibility, but not to decentralise financial or operational authority. Equally, clinicians in decentralised management structures may wish to acquire authority but not the responsibility and accountability. These issues must be openly discussed and resolved for a decentralised system of clinical management to be effective and, according to Musch,[19] decentralised units are always smarter than 'top-down' management.

The four requirements for successfully involving doctors in management are, therefore:

- agreement
- responsibility
- accountability
- authority.

All need clear understanding, particularly authority, which is an area some managers and consultants find difficult. Clinical directors should be part of the major decision-making machinery, with real responsibility and authority (including financial). There needs to be a single management body with the clinical directors and executive directors.

It is important when setting up a new organisational structure to consider its remit. Frequently too much attention is given to structures and very little, or none at all, to the rules by which it will work. The means of approaching problems should be clear even if the solution is not.[20] It is also important to define the roles, responsibilities and relationships of medical directors and clinical directors. Doctors are highly motivated but frequently have their own objectives which may be different to those of the organisation. Mechanisms for maintaining relationships between directorates and the consultant body within the hospital need to be supported by such bodies as a Medical Staff Committee separately from the management structure.

Professional/manager relationship

Few developments take place in the delivery of health care which do not involve the relationship between clinicians and managers, and progress must depend on the two cultures having a mutual understanding and recognition of their respective skills and knowledge. The IHSM *'Medicine for Managers'* philosophy[21] states that it is also important that each is prepared to empower the other to apply that understanding in day-to-day management and professional practice.

Managers have divided opinions about doctors and divided views about the need to involve them in management. Although a majority felt that partnership was needed, there were fears surrounding this concept. Some managers are envious of doctors' apparent freedom, jealous of their education, dismissive of their values, angry at their arrogance; and frightened of their own position if the doctors' role in management turns out to be a 'sleeping tiger'. Equally, many managers have genuine feelings of admiration, and a willingness to support and help doctors in their work.

Actions of some managers can result in the clinician's rejection of management, such as breaking promises and showing naivety rather than seeking advice. Lack of clarity over financial limits devalues the idea of sticking to a budget. Money will always be found if it is politically unacceptable for a hospital to become bankrupt, resulting in a large barrier to cooperation.

Discussion

Many doctors admitted that the profession had neglected to become involved in management because of lack of interest and time, and the poor image associated with such involvement.[2] The way doctors choose to react to changes in the fields of clinical and resource management will substantially influence the type of career available to consultants in the 1990s. Perhaps at no time since the beginning of the National Health Service have the choices and decisions been so important. If consultants become involved, their clinical leadership can be enhanced. Doctors did not at first grasp the opportunity created by the reforms, nor the idea that their involvement in management would strengthen rather than weaken their position.

Management in hospitals is broadly divided into two parts: guidance or strategy management, and delivery or operational management. The task of a clinical director is *mainly* concerned with operational management. Although not a representative of a specialty, a clinical director reflects the views of clinicians as a group and should have a voice in hospital strategy and policy formulation, and contribute to effective decision making, for which he or she should recognise corporate responsibility. In successfully decentralised hospitals, the Management Board is chaired by the Medical Director and attended by all clinical and executive directors.

Much has been said and written about managerial power in the NHS and how it has changed over the last few years; there are many accounts of the various aspects of this.[2-4, 22-29] In the view of one senior executive: 'Whatever we say about managerial power in the Health Service, and there is no question, managerial power has increased greatly since I was a lad, doctors are still the single most powerful group in the service'. Nearly all those managers inter-viewed recognised that doctors should be involved in managing the organisation and that this involvement would be beneficial to the success of the establishment. Those who did not were in a minority.

Conclusions

Consultants are divided between those who are now active in sup-porting the new management initiatives and keen to play a full par-ticipative role in management, and those who are not. There are several indications which suggest that about 30% are favourably inclined with 70% against.[10]

Fitzgerald and Sturt [30] highlight evidence suggesting that clini-cians need incentives and support to perform management roles. There is evidence from other professions which underlines the problems facing professionals moving into a second career or adding an additional set of knowledge to their specialty.[31-33] The old attitude to doctors' involvement in management was summed up by Musch:[19] 'Doctors in hospital management are like eunuchs in a harem. They know how it is done. They have seen it done. But they cannot do it'. This attitude is changing.

There is a need for trainers to take account of the preferred learning styles of doctors. Recommendations by Gatrell and White[10] are based on the assumption that those with power and responsibil-ity exert considerable influence on organisational culture. They propose a model for the management development of doctors which sets up a process for the development of a national approach to training and development. There is also a need for managers to improve their image within the medical profession and for organi-sations to integrate learning into the fabric of the operational lives of their members to become 'learning organisations'.

Senior doctors agreed that more support and training from their organisations would have been useful, if only to identify areas of weakness requiring development. Clinical directors frequently commented on the lack of training opportunities provided by their organisations. Managers are generally supportive of the concept of doctors becoming involved in management, although some har-bour doubts about doctors' willingness to make the move success-fully. Others are concerned about the effects such moves will have on established management career structures. There is evidence of reluctance by managers to 'let go' of responsibility and authority.

Jones[34] stresses a partnership approach to engaging doctors, together with managers, in management development.

There remains the unresolved conflict between the clinical role as advocate of the individual patient and the managerial role of providing the maximum possible benefit for the greatest number of patients. Problems also arise for the doctor who leaves a managerial role and expects, or is expected, to re-enter clinical work, but who may have lost clinical expertise and acceptance by colleagues, to say nothing of the loss of expert management resource to the organisation.

There is an important role for a 'regional head', perhaps under the authority of the Postgraduate Dean, in encouraging and facilitating the design and implementation of relevant training and development activities. Doctors assuming management responsibilities must be fully supported by training and development in their new roles; real change can occur only when a new generation of doctors is in place. As William H. Welch[35] said: 'Medical education is not completed at the medical school: it is only begun'.

REFERENCES

Billings JS. Boston Medical and Surgical Journal 1894; 131: 140.

White A. The role of hospital consultants in management decision making and change. PhD thesis. Bath University, 1993.

Klein R. The politics of the NHS. 2nd ed. Harlow: Longman, 1989.

Loveridge R, Starkey K, eds. Continuity and crisis in the NHS: the politics of design and innovation in health care. Buckingham: Open University Press, 1992.

Enthoven AC. Reflections on the management of the National Health Service. London: Nuffield Provincial Hospitals Trust, 1985.

Higgins J. The business of medicine. Basingstoke: Macmillan, 1988.

Boyatzis RE. The competent manager. A model for effective performance. New York: Wiley, 1982.

Turrill T, Wilson D, Young K. The characteristics of excellent doctors in management. NHS Management Executive, Resource Management Unit. Thirsk: Turrill, 1991.

Simpson J. British Association of Medical Managers. Clinical Directorates Survey, 1992.

Gatrell J, White T. Medical student to medical director, a development strategy for doctors. Bristol: NHS Training Division, 1995.

Sabin JE. Mind the gap: reflections of an American health maintenance organisation doctor on the new NHS. British Medical Journal 1992; 305: 514–516.

Parker R. Healthcare Management. January 1993; 56–7.

HMSO. What seems to be the matter? Communication between hospitals and patients. London: HMSO, 1994.

Hoffenberg R. Clinical freedom. Rock Carling Lecture. London: Nuffield Provincial Hospitals Trust, 1987.

Pellegrino ED. The relationship of autonomy and integrity in medical ethics. In: Allebeck P, Jansson B, eds. Ethics in medicine. New York: Raven Press, 1990.

Eddy DM. Clinical decision making: from theory to practice. The challenge. Journal of the American Medical Association 1990; 263: 287–290.

Relman, 1987.

White T. Clinical and professional freedom. In: White T, ed. Textbook of management for doctors. London: Churchill Livingstone, 1995.

Musch K. Managing clinical services — decentralisation in action. Conference organised by BMA/IHSM/RCN/BAMM 24–25th September. New Connaught Rooms. London, 1992.

Chantler C. Interviewed for research into 'Role of hospital consultants in management, decision making and change in acute hospitals'. PhD thesis by A White. Bath University, 1991.

IHSM. Medicine for Managers. Annual series of programmes for managers in the health service run in collaboration with the Royal College of Surgeons of England. 1994.

West PA. Understanding the NHS: a question of incentives. London: King Edwards Hospital Fund, 1988: p 99.

Riseborough PA, Walter M. Management in Health Care. Bath: John Wright/Butterworth, 1988.

Nelson MJ. Managing Health Professionals. London: Chapman and Hall, 1989.

Stewart R. Leading in the NHS: a practical guide. Basingstoke: Macmillan, 1989.

Harrison S, Hunter DJ, Pollitt C. The Dynamics of British Health Policy. London: Unwin Hyman, 1990.

Strong P, Robinson J. The NHS – under new management. Buckingham: Open University Press, 1990.

Spurgeon P, Barwell F. Implementing Change in the NHS: a practical guide for managers. London: Chapman and Hall, 1991.

Pettigrew A, Ferlie E, McKee L. Shaping Strategic Change. Broughton Gifford: The Cromwell Press, 1992.

Fitzgerald L, Sturt J. Clinicians into management. On the change agenda or not? Health Services Management Research 1992; 5 (2): 137–146.

Perucci R. Engineering: professional servant of power. In: Friedson E, ed. Professions and their prospects. London: Sage, 1973.

Schneller ES, Weiner TS. The MD — JD revised. A sociological analysis of the cross-educated professionals in the decade of the 1980s. The Journal of Legal Medicine 1985; 6 (3): 337–372.

Earl MJ, Skyrme DJ. Hybrid managers. What do we know about them? Research paper. Oxford: Oxford Institute of Information Management, undated.

Jones H. Engaging doctors in management. In: White T, ed. Textbook of management for doctors. London: Churchill Livingstone, 1995.

Welch WH. Bulletin of the Harvard Medical School Association 1892; 3: 55.

Gale R, Grant J. Managing change in a medical context. Guidelines for action. London: The Joint Centre for Educational Research and Development in Medicine, 1990.

HMSO. Government White Paper. Working for patients. London: HMSO, 1989.

Hoffenberg R. (1991). The Harveian Oration, 17th October 1991. London: Royal College of Physicians, transcript p 1.

Kaluzny AD, Hernandez SR. Organizational change and innovation. In: Shortell SM, Kaluzney AD, eds. Health care management: a text in organization theory and behaviour. 2nd ed. New York: Wiley, 1988: pp 380–381.

Lincoln YS, Guba EG. Naturalistic inquiry. California: Sage, 1985.
Pope C, Mays N. Opening the black box: an encounter in the corridors of
    health research. British Medical Journal 1994; 306: 315–1.
Templeton Series on DGM's Issue Study 5. Managing with doctors. Working
    together? NHS Training Authority. Aldershot: The Academic Publishing
    Group, 1986.
Winkenwerder W, Ball JR. Transformation of American health care. The role
    of the medical profession. New England Journal of Medicine 1988; 318:
    317–319.

20. Management development for professionals: the case of hospital doctors

Kath Aspinwall   Mike Pedler

Introduction

In many organisations the aim is to create partnership between managers and *professionals* rather than managers and *employees*. Yet, too often, the two groups are found to be in conflict, with managers trying to exert control over professionals who resist. Managers who work from a developmental perspective will seek a more productive relationship, aiming to create mutual respect and trust between managers and professionals and working 'with the grain of professional interest in quality'.[1] This approach will require specific skills, for example in the area of values clarification and reconciliation. Work will be needed at two levels; within the individual, especially when a professional becomes a manager and, most crucially, between individuals in developing the manager/professional partnership.

Where there is little or no commitment to development and partnership there can be negativity and conflict. Managers may perceive the professionals in their organisations as self-willed and intractable, hiding behind professional smoke screens; the latter may see the former as obsessed with control and budgetary constraints regardless of the effect on standards. For some, the difference is irreconcilable: 'There was also spirited debate about how closely doctors could work with managers ... some thought the value systems of doctors and managers were in fundamental conflict'.[2]

Professionals have been more widely accused of abusing their power, of having 'captured' the services they provide, and of having become answerable only to themselves and their professional bodies.[3] Sometimes they accuse themselves: 'I hate the idea of professionalism because it is a class system within the working environment, a way of being superior and at the same time submissive to exploitation'[4]; whereas some professionals see themselves as the last supporters of the old values, standing against a simplistic focus on financial efficiency.

However, neither the picture of self-indulgent recalcitrants who need to be brought into line, nor that of heroic resistance fighters for the old values, fits the situation where many managers and professionals work together in partnerships, or where professionals increasingly take on managerial roles in their organisations.

If professionals and professionalism are a growing force in organisations and society, what kind of management development can help professionals make their best contribution? First, we consider the notion of professionalism itself, and of the requirements for managing professionals in organisations. In this context, what are the most appropriate kinds of management development for professionals?

We take our main examples and cases from the world of hospital doctors — a group who meet the strict criteria of what it means to be 'professional'. Their case is particularly relevant at the moment as they grapple with the new managerialism of the UK National Health Service.

What is a professional?

The term 'professional' can be used in a variety of ways. Three common definitions of professional are as:

- distinct from amateur — being paid for it
- working to high standards — doing a good job
- having particular knowledge, skill and training — belonging to a professional group.

The last of these, and the one used in this chapter, is elaborated in Flexner's seven criteria for the designation 'professional', which are shown in Box 20.1.

Box 20.1 Flexner's seven criteria for the designation 'professional'[5]

1. Possess and draw upon a store of knowledge that is more than ordinarily complex.
2. Secure a theoretical grasp of the phenomenon with which it deals.
3. Apply its theoretical and complex knowledge to the practical solution of human and social problems.
4. Strive to add to and improve its stock of knowledge.

> 5. Pass on what it knows to novice generations not in a
>   haphazard fashion but deliberately and formally.
> 6. Establish criteria of admission, legitimate practice and proper
>   conduct.
> 7. Be imbued with an altruistic spirit.

A group of NHS hospital doctors were asked to complete the sentence: 'I am a professional because ...'. Their responses reflected Flexner's criteria and included:

- of the long training period which I served
- the training is an apprenticeship — there is a 'right way'
- I have a licence to practice (which can be taken away)
- of the need for professional 'refresher' training throughout my career
- of my membership of professional bodies — the British Medical Association, the Royal College of Psychiatrists, etc.
- access to the profession is controlled and restricted by the professional bodies
- only my peers can judge my competence — through medical audit, etc.
- I conform to a clear ethical code
- my commitment is to medicine, not to the particular hospital I work in
- I am responsible for my own work and for no-one else's
- medicine has a long history — it has become a profession over time
- my first responsibility is to the patient — I am judged on how well I do for that person.

An accompanying group of hospital managers showed more mixed responses as to whether or not they saw themselves as professionals. It was obvious when they looked at the doctors' list that they did not meet the strictest criteria of 'professional' (e.g. restricted access to the profession, formal apprenticeship, licence to practice); however, the term was entirely relevant on the basis of:

- possessing specialist knowledge and skills
- a constant need to update their knowledge and skills
- being competent and effective
- having ethical standards
- doing their work in a serious and 'professional' manner.[6]

At first sight the characteristics of the professional — self-motivation, adherence to ethical standards, possessing specialist knowledge and skills, being self-regulated, and taking responsibility for one's further training, together with a general lack of dependence on the organisation — are both attractive and useful. Yet this autonomy creates a potential problem for management.

Managing professionals

The autonomy and self-judgement of professionals makes their managing a demanding task. Scholes[7] suggests that these independently minded, self-motivated, self-regulating individuals may respect leadership, but they are very often resistant to being 'managed'. Added to this is their tendency to be loyal first to the profession and not to the employing organisation. Handy[8] explores the implications for organisations that employ professionals:

1. Professionals demand a lot of independence and autonomy, the right to do their own task in their own way.
2. Professional organisations are flat structures, with perhaps three steps in the formal hierarchy.
3. A professional career means advancement in one's profession not necessarily in the same organisation — professionals are mobile.
4. On the other hand, professionals have effective tenure and it is hard to get rid of them except on the grounds of unprofessional conduct.
5. Professionals prefer networks rather than formal bureaucracy.
6. Professionals prefer to be managed by fellow professionals but regard management and administration as a chore.
7. Professionals train the next generation themselves, professional organisations have therefore to be schools as well as work organisations.

The use of the words *demands* and *rights* as well as the softer *prefer* indicates why professionals can conflict with their managers. Since Handy's words were written, many professionals have found these demands and rights challenged by the changes that have swept through some of their organisations. It is in the public sector that professional autonomy, rights and demands have received the greatest battering.

Whilst by no means all professionals work in public services, the changing relationship between managers and professionals here throws the potential for struggle into particularly sharp relief. What has been happening can be most clearly illuminated in the context of accountability. The notion of professionals being self-accountable remains, but new accountabilities have been added. Simkins[9] draws these together, as shown in Table 20.1.

The new emphasis on consumers or users is often welcomed. Most professionals (at their best, at least) would wish to put their patients, pupils or clients at the centre of the work they do. The political dimension is very familiar to those in the public sector. National and local government have long set budgets and other requirements for these services. However, the particular dimensions of devolution on the one hand and of centralisation on the other are new; these constitute a factor that has profoundly changed the relationship between managers and professionals. The growth of managerial power has threatened professional autonomy, and it is not surprising that: 'The prospect of "outsiders" refining *their* goals, streamlining *their* professional decision procedures and inspecting *their* feedback was not an overwhelmingly attractive one'.[10]

However, this is not the only reason for professional reservations. There has also been considerable concern that matters such as 'social needs, professional standards, deprivation, community or equity' play little or no part in traditional managerialist ideology.[10] It is not just awkwardness that leads hospital doctors to question the fact that they may not treat patients because of end-year financial constraints.

Professionals and managers as partners

How can managers best help professionals deal with these expanding accountabilities in order to serve the organisation's users and customers?

Table 20.1

	Professional	Managerial	Political	Market
Key actors	Professionals	Managers	Representatives	Consumers
Influences factors	Peer review	Hierarchy	Governance	Choice
Success criteria	Good practice	Effectiveness and efficiency	Policy conformance	Competitive success

Barrett and McMahon[11] note how the search for efficiency, the shift of power from doctors to managers, and the change towards market values has changed traditional 'welfare' assumptions and increased the sense of chaos and uncertainty for managers, professionals and politicians. Observations of a learning set of senior managers over a five-year period produced certain conclusions about the nature of managerial work in the health service and, perhaps, in other sectors employing large numbers of professionals. An emphasis on trying to 'increase top-down managerial control through techniques that involve tighter accountability for achieving ever more narrowly defined goals and objectives ... ways of thinking that draw heavily on management practice in the private sector ... *actually hinders rather than helps managers' ability to cope with change*' (our emphasis).[11]

They found that managers did not act on these prescriptions at all. Rather, they appeared

to spend much of their time negotiating with individuals and groups which, although part of the organisation, seem to have scant regard for its goals, but seem instead to be following their own sectional interests ... They spend a great deal of time using their 'networks' to establish who is making what deals with whom. They also seem to work hard to keep their team of senior managers loyal to their cause. They do not appear to be in control, but are able to exert influence, and their ability to do this depends on a much more subtle melange of factors than the simple exercise of managerial authority.

This is akin to what Strauss[12] describes as the 'negotiated order' of the hospital, which is reached via negotiated processes between groups with different values, interests, stakes, power bases and relative autonomies — where conflict is normal, indeed, endemic. Commenting that uncertainty comes as much from inside the health service as from without, Barrett and McMahon suggest that managers can add value to their professional organisations in the three ways discussed below.

a. By providing a 'sense of direction' — not a detailed plan, but a broad vision based on core values to provide a template against which operational decisions can be made. As part of this, a steering system is needed to co-ordinate disparate incremental changes to allow for longer-term purposeful shifts.

b. By helping people and groups come to agreements about directions rather than relying on coercion — as well as obtaining a clear strategic direction, it is important, particularly in times of uncertainty, to have a good process for arriving at this direction.

This is primarily a negotiating process: '(managers) ... are actually holding the ring; managing the network of negotiation and bargaining. In other words, we see managers using their *formal* position of authority to facilitate and steer the *informal* process of negotiation, rather than ignoring it or attempting to control it away. So we can see formal authority as a bargaining counter which legitimises managers' central role in the negotiating process'. Barrett and McMahon note that negotiating tempo actually increases in times of uncertainty, and that managers are always negotiating on many issues at once, so that they are able to generate power through getting consensus on one issue whilst making concessions on another.

c. By working with endemic conflict — as conflict cannot be avoided, managers need to find ways of dealing with it as positively as possible. 'Political mapping' is the process by which managers determine the key 'players' on a particular issue and assess their interests and bargaining power before deciding how to act.

The conflicts and dilemmas involved in managing with professionals appear strongly in the inner tensions felt by those increasing numbers of professionals who are also managers. For example, in the NHS, Piper and Aitkenhead[13] posit alternative sets of 'managerialist' and 'medicalist' beliefs which are incompatible in their strong forms. There is clearly great potential for conflict and ineffectiveness wherever these interface.

Mascie-Taylor et al[14] studied the positions which doctors may take with regard to the resolution of dilemmas which arise in confronting the day-to-day reconciliation of medical and managerial roles. This necessitates both *inner* reconciliation and position-taking by the individual and *outer* negotiation with, and between, often complex webs of interest groups.

These observations provide some useful insights as to how managers might best manage and 'add value' to their professional colleagues rather than trying to control them. Many difficulties remain, however, with regard to the management/professional divide and the dilemmas to which this gives rise. Whilst there is a basis for bringing doctors and managers together for joint working where a 'weak' or moderate form of each set of beliefs is held, if 'strong' versions are held on either side this may not be advisable or possible. Initially, doctors can sometimes be more open to reflection on the nature of management if managers are not present.

What sort of training and development?

What, then, are the implications for management development for professionals? In the NHS, accompanying the continuing managerial reforms, there has been more provision of training for doctors. However, much of this seems to be designed on the assumption that if the appropriate managerial knowledge and skills are provided, doctors will then be enabled to fulfil their new roles. This ignores the conflicts and dilemmas rooted in sometimes incompatible value positions. Professionals' management development is not just a question of acquiring new knowledge or learning new skills, but of dealing with and, indeed, learning from the inevitable value clashes which they will experience.

For example, doctors who become involved in managing need to think through and clarify their values in relation to their medical and managerial roles. Increased investment in the knowledge and skills of managing may actually add to the problem if doctors take on managerial tasks and roles with these dilemmas unresolved.

From a management perspective, people's ability and willingness to commit themselves to a particular task depends upon how that task squares with their values. Commitment to anything requires first that we value that thing. From a management development perspective, people tend to find it easier to recognise the limits of their skills and knowledge, and therefore to make appropriate decisions about their actions, than to judge the impact of their values. In clarifying values, the first step is for a person to understand his or her own values and how these influence what he or she does. Another step is to be aware that there are other, alternative, sets of values which can apply to any given situation. Awareness of alternative value sets can give more choice and freedom of action.

In addition, for doctors whose main experience of education has consisted of medical training followed by conferences tightly packed with formal presentations on the latest clinical developments, their first contact with management development can be surprising. The questioning and reflective processes of management development are quite different from the traditional and didactic methods they are used to, and can seem difficult and threatening.

Self-development and action learning

Action learning[15] can play a useful role here, providing a confidential setting to work with peers on issues of concern; it is not uncommon for people to say that this is the only setting in which they have discussions of this kind. Winkless[16] describes a series of management development programmes for doctors using this approach. He noted the issues with which they were concerned, on which they sought advice, and in which they looked to develop themselves. These were classified into four categories:

1. Self-management/development:

- coping with feelings of being threatened/isolated
- developing and practising assertiveness
- building self-confidence in dealing with management and colleagues
- reducing 'Type A' (stress) pressures from the environment

2. Colleague relationships:

- introducing change in the face of opposition
- separating friendships from professional relationships
- negotiating in and between committees
- negotiating teaching sessions
- negotiating workload commitment
- managing approaches to research

3. Managing relationships:

- managing the political and economic environment
- clarifying the roles of doctors vis-a-vis managers
- challenging a perceived undemocratic management decision
- negotiating the content of a job description
- role clarification in hospital reorganisation

4. 'Small m' management (as distinct from 'Big M' management involving hospital managers; those aspects of the job which, although managerial in nature, were not normally described as such by those practising them):

- 'time and motion' study in the clinic
- dealing with low staff morale
- balancing work priorities
- developing a working strategy
- managing the clinical and support team
- bed utilisation and numbers
- apportionment of study leave
- design of wards.

Conclusion

The emphasis on partnership between managers and professionals raises the question of the role of the manager as developer in this particular context. Where there is conflict or a clash of values there will need to be both inner reconciliation and outer negotiation. Managers will need to be in a position to work constructively and creatively on their own needs in this area, as well as those of their professional colleagues. Managers working as developers have the opportunity to create a new climate of mutual trust and respect in which a true partnership can be grounded.

For any organisation working in a knowledge-based field, its professionals are amongst its most prized assets. Their recruitment, further professional development and retention become critical strategic issues. Professionals, operating within an extra-organisational 'community of practice', produce new knowledge as part of their work. The professionals' ability to research and develop new ideas into practice, which then generate public demand, is the source of 'new business' and yet may in turn create funding and other difficulties with which other managers and politicians have to deal.

Not all hospital doctors (or any other group of professionals) are great researchers or pioneering developers, yet all value the autonomy, self-regulation and peer review which they inherit on membership. Seeking to manage them in a controlling way can only have value as a temporary measure to achieve some short-term order; in the long term it is likely to result in a sterility of ideas and an inability to deliver a speedy and flexible response to the user or customer.

If this line of argument is accepted, two approaches to the management of organisations employing key numbers of professionals suggest themselves. One possibility is to recruit and train more professionals for managerial roles, in order that professionals might be managed by professionals and that there might be a critical mass of responsible managers who are more likely to be able to see both sides and therefore collectively be more able to grapple with the dilemmas. A second route is the creation of partnership relationships between professionals and managers at all levels with dual accountability and responsibility.

In the first of these cases, knowledge and skills-based management appropriate to the role to be performed may be useful. However, both the nature of managerial work in such organisations and the inevitability of value conflicts and value-based dilemmas presenting themselves, mean that this is not sufficient. Action learning can provide a forum in which managing professionals or managers of professionals can voice their concerns and queries and receive the assistance of their peers in seeking to negotiate their way through.

We have argued that the values of professionals and managers inevitably conflict at some point, and that the dilemmas caused by these conflicts may cause intrapersonal and interpersonal difficulties with resultant stress and disorder. Becoming aware of one's values, of how they affect one's actions, and of how they might differ from the values of others, and having the means for dealing with such differences, will not remove the conflicts or the dilemmas but may help to resolve them.

The Practice Development Unit[17] at Seacroft Hospital in Leeds (which is part of St James's and Seacroft University Hospital NHS Trust) is clear about the management style that brings out the best in their professionals: '... a clinical climate which encourages and empowers nurses and therapists to be knowledgeable, reflective and autonomous practitioners who work in harmony together ... (through) ... facilitating, coordinating, enabling, resourcing and providing a global view and vision'.

REFERENCES

Wrigley L, McKevitt D. Professional ethics, government agenda and differential information. In: McKevitt D, Lawton A, eds. Public sector management: theory, critique and practice. London: Sage in association with The Open University, 1994.
Smith R. Medicine's core values. British Medical Journal 1994; 309: 1247–1248.
Wilkinson D, Pedler MJ. Strategic thinking in public service. In: Garrett B, ed. Developing strategic thought. Maidenhead: McGraw-Hill, 1995.
Windsor, 1991.
Solomon, 1992.
Pedler MJ, Aspinwall KA. Perfect plc? The purpose and practice of organisational learning. Maidenhead: McGraw-Hill, 1995.
Scholes K. Strategic management in professional service organisations (PSOs) — the finders, minders and grinders. Sheffield: Sheffield Business School, 1994.
Handy C. The future of work. Oxford: Blackwell, 1984.
Simkins T. Policy, accountability and management: perspectives on the implementation of reform. In: Simkins T et al, eds. Implementing educational reform: the early lessons. Harlow: Longman, 1992.
Pollitt C. Managerialism and the public services. 2nd ed. Oxford: Blackwell, 1993.

Barrett S, McMahon L. Public management in uncertainty ... a micro-political perspective of the Health Service in the United Kingdom. Policy and Politics 1990; 18(4): 257–268.

Strauss, 1979.

Piper J, Aitkenhead M. *The relationship between doctors and managers.* Internal Consultants' Report to Members of Leicestershire Mental Health Service Unit Management Board, 1992.

Mascie-Taylor H, Pedler MJ, Winkless AJ. *Doctors and dilemmas: a study of ideal types of doctors/managers and an evaluation of how these could support values clarification for doctors in the Health Service.* Final report. Bristol: NHS Training Division, 1993.

Pedler MJ, ed. *Action learning in practice.* 2nd ed. Aldershot: Gower, 1991.

Winkless AJ. Doctors as managers. In: Pedler MJ, ed. *Action learning in practice.* 2nd ed. Aldershot: Gower, 1991.

Practice Development Unit. *The team approach to better health: Practice Development Unit Profile.* Department of Medicine, Seacroft Hospital, Leeds, 1994/95.

21. Doctors as change agents — developing a corporate perspective

Julia K. Moore

Introduction

The NHS is going through a period of rapid change, which poses both threats and opportunities for the organisations and individuals involved. If the threats are to be managed and the opportunities harnessed we need a flexible, forward-looking workforce and management. This has been recognised by the Management Executive and Regional General Managers who have given management development 'the highest priority' and have emphasised the need for 'managers at all levels to have management development as a particular and personal responsibility which sits at the heart of the management function'.[1]

Our perception of a *manager* may well be that of a career manager, perhaps rising through the NHS management training scheme, collecting competencies and a portfolio of skills and ending up at the top of an organisation dealing strategically with culture, change and organisational development. However, most NHS managers no longer fit this mould: a significant proportion of managers are 'clinical' managers. Their training is unco-ordinated and separated from the mainstream of management development. These issues must be addressed if health service organisations are to grow and develop.

Doctors determine the health spend

Although relatively small in numbers, doctors initiate 70–80% of health care spending. They determine the use of resources, deployment of staff, organisation and delivery of services and the development, or otherwise, of new modes of care. They are respected and act as opinion formers and leaders, both at work and in the community. Wielding such power, doctors need to accept that they also

233

have major responsibilities, not only to individual patients but also to their organisation and the wider health service. This requires training and development.

Management skills complement clinical skills

The NHS exists to serve the needs of patients, who expect the very best treatment to be available when they need it. To deliver this within a cash-limited budget requires a close working relationship between doctors and managers.

Investment in management development should be targeted particularly at consultants. In this respect, the terms 'manager' and 'management development' may be a disadvantage, as they carry strong connotations of 'us and them' and implications of a command and control hierarchy. To engage doctors' interest and commitment, it may be valuable to emphasise opportunities for personal and organisational development as well as management development.

A rose by any other name ...

Tietjen[2] comments that she is unable to differentiate between management development and organisational development, but 'that we must focus on ensuring the organisation's objectives are delivered, and in doing so one is usually developing managers'. In the health service our key objective is to deliver a more responsive and effective service. Development and training should be explicitly geared to this objective, and this link must be explained to the recipients of training. For doctors, training should include personal, management and organisational development to identify and enhance the individual's skills, encourage the wider investigation and evaluation of options, promote teamwork, accept complexity and diversity and find 'new ways of doing things'.

Who pays?

Currently, 80–85% of NHS education and training expenditure is on statutory professional education and training, the remainder being devoted to continuing education and training, and management education and development.

The prime responsibility for management development rests with the individual and line manager. Management development is considered an integral part of an organisation's investment programme, being expected to maximise effectiveness and produce added value and a return on the investment.[1] With education and training being funded by providers, the advent of the purchaser-provider split led to a potential squeeze on investment, as providers pared costs down to the minimum. Recent changes are designed to address this by setting up three separate funding streams:

- patient care
- research and development (Culyer proposals)
- education and training.

Research and development and education and training will be funded by a levy on purchasers (detailed below), encouraging explicit recognition and protection for the wider costs of the health service.

The national picture, pre April 1995

The NHS view of the importance and direction of management development began to change with the NHS Training Authority publication *Better Management Better Health* in 1986.[3] This superseded the previous 'scientific management' view of the 1970s which concentrated on sending different 'levels' of clinical manager away on courses.

The NHSTA paper reflected the philosophy espoused by the Griffiths report — the transition from hospital 'administration' to 'general management'. It recognised the need for managers to be involved in service direction, clinical practice and quality issues, and set up several initiatives to speed management development. These included Individual Performance Review (IPR), new General Management Training Schemes and the Management Education Scheme by Open Learning (MESOL). Management development moved away from attending courses towards career development and the acquisition of a portfolio of skills.

The publication of Working Paper 10 in 1989[4] required Regional Health Authorities to assess workforce requirements and then to contract for, and oversee the quality of, non-medical education and training (NMET) to produce this predicted workforce. In contrast, professional education is regulated by the statutory professional bodies, who are not required to take account of health care employers' views. The NHS reforms of 1991 ensured the devolution of staff, and the associated human resources function, to providers, giving them a greater incentive to introduce educational activities and approaches which would address the needs of the organisation as well as those of the individual.

New arrangements, post April 1995

The new arrangements expect employers to assume responsibility for workforce planning. Together with health care purchasers, they also become responsible for purchasing the education and training required to generate this workforce. Various safeguards have been built in to ensure that regional and national perspectives are also considered. The main features are shown in Box 21.1.

Box 21.1   Main features of the new arrangements

- Assessment of future workforce requirements becomes the employer's responsibility. This information is forwarded to the ETC (see below).
- Purchasers and providers come together in *Education and Training Consortia* (ETC) to prepare proposals for commissioning education and training, including management development. Consortia cover a defined area (usually geographical) and include GPs, local authority, private and independent sector representatives.
- The *Regional Education Development Group* (REDG) takes a strategic view of education, training and management development and validates the ETC's investment proposals.
- The Regional Office sets up the consortia and the REDG, devolving all functions associated with the commissioning of education and training once the consortium is ready.
- From April 1996 the education and training so commissioned has been funded by a national levy on purchasing authorities, to which consortia may choose to add an additional local element. A separate levy is raised to fund Postgraduate Medical and Dental Education (PGMDE), which remains within the remit of the Postgraduate Dean.

How to cut the cake?

The levy will be determined nationally, although the quantum is still under discussion. In addition it is still not clear how the funds will be devolved to consortia. In Northern and Yorkshire it has been suggested that funding should initially reflect the level of student training commissions currently in place. In the medium term, devolution might be on the basis of numbers of staff in post, with the final aim being to devolve funds on a population basis.

The minimum level of funding will be set by the national levy. An individual consortium then has the option to top up the levy locally. This additional charge must be met by the consortia's purchasers, providing an incentive to keep training costs down and ensure value for money.

Once devolved to consortia, the cake will need to be split between professional education, training and management development. Individual consortia, or even individual members of a consortium, may have very different views about the value of management development. With the drive to reduce the cost of education, funding for management development may be squeezed out by the need to continue professional statutory education. Proponents of management education will need to be well represented on both consortia and Regional Education and Development Groups.

Can we deliver?

For the last ten years, the NHS has taken management development seriously and there has been no shortage of activity, provision and exhortation, with some notable local or individual achievements. However, there are still many people who need management development but are slipping through the net. The recent changes introduce a market philosophy to education and training, with the intention of improving quality and driving down costs. Will this new scheme lead to real improvements?

Potential problems and opportunities

Time scale

The time scale for implementation is tight, with devolution of budgets and contracting to ready consortia from April 1996. Most, but not all, regions have defined and appointed consortia and lead organisations, but there is still a huge amount of work to be done defining workforce requirements and training needs.

Squeeze on management development

Evaluation. Consortia may fund statutory courses at the expense of management development. To make a strong case for management development, training programmes must be subject to a more critical economics-based evaluation of outcomes, to demonstrate added value. Key steps would include:

- objective setting at the strategic planning stage
- prioritisation of investment in training
- provision of training and development
- validation and feedback on training activities
- measurement of success against the objectives set.

Publication of evaluations should also be encouraged, to disseminate knowledge and experience of valuable tools for change[5] and provide pragmatic evidence to assist investment decision making.

Complementary roles. Consortia and individual organisations should revisit ways of delivering management development training, develop complementary roles and move the emphasis away from short-term, quick-fix, initiatives. The roles of the organisation and the consortium are shown in Box 21.2.

Box 21.2 The roles of the organisation and the consortium

The role of the organisation:
- Local opportunities:
  — mentoring
  — extended roles
  — project management
- Human resources function:
  — workforce planning
  — identifying individuals 'ready' for management development

The role of the consortium:
- Selection of external development programmes provided by:
  — in-house group training association
  — links with higher and further education
  — partnerships with external consultancies.

The opportunity should also be taken to learn from other public and private sector industries, who have expertise in change management.

Special groups

The Regional Office will retain responsibility for non-medical education and training (NMET) where staff numbers are too small to devolve training to consortia. It may also be appropriate for some top manager programmes to be held at regional or national level, to allow participants to be selected from a wider area. A mechanism would need to be found to fund these programmes, such as that in Northern and Yorkshire, where purchaser chief executives have agreed a joint funding initiative.

Medical staff

Clearly, much thought has gone into the proposals for non-medical education and training (NMET). The situation regarding clinicians is much less clear, however, even though management development for clinicians will be critical to the success of organisations. More pragmatically, if change is about teamwork, committed doctors are also needed to facilitate successful management development for many other staff groups.

There are two main issues surrounding management development for medical staff:

Who pays? The budget available to the consortium is for non-medical education and training, with no direct remit to fund training opportunities for doctors. Medical education continues to be purchased by the Postgraduate Dean, and will be funded by a separate levy. The Dean will be a member of the REDG, but, as with manpower predictions, the consortium and REDG can only advise the Dean in this area.

Continuing medical education (CME) for doctors. The Medical Royal Colleges requirements for CME have recently been published, and have been described as 'regimented and restrictive'.[6] CME points are collected for attendance at internal and external educational events, but points are only generated by 'accredited' professional educational meetings. Management education is not recognised and does not generate credits. The impact of fulfilling CME requirements will make it more difficult to increase clinicians' uptake of management development opportunities for three reasons:

- There will be increasing pressures on clinicians' time. For most colleges, achieving the necessary points will require attendance at external educational events for 10 days a year — as consultants receive an allocation of 10 days a year study leave, CME will absorb all study leave.

- The increased uptake of study leave will be extremely costly, both in financing attendance at meetings and also in covering the clinical work that would otherwise be lost. The financial burden will fall on Postgraduate Deans, who may have no resources left to support management development; on providers, who will not be able to spare their reduced medical workforce for additional in-house development; and ultimately on purchasers, whose contract may not be delivered.
- The final, and most important, barrier CME creates is a psychological one. The colleges' exclusion of management training and development from professional recognition sends strong signals to the medical workforce that professional excellence can stand in isolation from the rest of the service, militating against all moves to improve understanding and collaboration between all those who have to deliver patient care.

Unless these issues are resolved, management development for clinicians will be the exception rather than the rule. Widespread investment in management development for clinicians requires support from Postgraduate Deans to finance programmes and to lobby for recognition, and, if necessary, accreditation by the Council of Colleges. The professional colleges must widen their view from a requirement for continuing medical education (CME) to one of continuing professional development (CPD). CPD begins with the identification of learning needs and includes aspects of management and personal development. This shift was emphasised in the recent SCOPME report,[7] but appears not to have taken root.

Whom to target?

Management development opportunities are currently targeted at consultants and, increasingly, at senior registrars, who are beginning to recognise the need to broaden their skills as they face complex managerial problems. This opportunistic approach must gradually be superseded by teaching undergraduates about management and its relevance to health care delivery. Medical student training is currently under scrutiny, and medical schools and Undergraduate Deans must be encouraged to include the basics of management training in the new curriculum. Continued emphasis throughout professional training would then ensure that doctors practised management as part of practising medicine.

Local commitment to implementation

Impact on the organisation. Despite the rhetoric, there is still ambivalence about the potential impact of management development for non-managers. Offering development opportunities to non-managerial staff may provoke anxiety in the organisation's management. The NHS has functioned for many years along strong hierarchical lines and this is threatened by staff empowerment. This may be particularly true where doctors are involved, as they are already perceived to be a powerful and articulate body.

A serious commitment to management development includes the recognition that the organisation must be prepared to support 'developed' staff, who are more likely to challenge the organisation's culture and style, and may become frustrated if they are unable to effect change. This may be a problem both at local level and nationally, where the 'light touch' is sometimes more theoretical than real.

Impact on the professional manager. There may also be a more personal threat to the 'professional' manager, in career structure and advancement. Since the Griffiths report, jobs in NHS management have become more influential and rewarding. As more non-managerial staff receive training it becomes clear that many are very talented and that some aspire to move into full-time managerial roles with the support of organisations such as BAMM (British Association of Medical Managers). Increasing competition between clinicians and managers for senior management posts may lead to resentment from the professional manager.

Impact on doctors. Resistance to management development may come from the clinicians themselves, who may passively or actively oppose change. Management encompasses the concept of responsibility as well as power. Using 'the manager' as scapegoat is a useful means of abrogating responsibility for difficult decisions. As Erica Jong put it, 'take your life in your own hands, and what happens? A terrible thing: no one to blame'.

The future

Management development has the explicit support of the Executive in its quest to stimulate dynamic change in the NHS. To achieve all that is claimed for it, professional managers and educationalists must address the above constraints. In particular, managers and doctors will need to accept the consequences of staff empowerment. The changes to commissioning and delivery of training and development could then give organisations access to structured management development opportunities for many more of their staff. The role of doctors will be critical in moving the service forward; if they, their managers and their professional bodies do not pursue the benefits of management development they will be left behind in 'splendid isolation', to the detriment of the NHS and the patients we serve.

ACKNOWLEDGEMENT

I would like to thank Mr B Scott, Wirral Hospital NHS Trust, for his helpful comments.

REFERENCES

Department of Health NHSME. A management development strategy for the NHS. Bristol: NHS Training Directorate, 1991.

Tietjen C. Management development in the NHS. Personnel Management 1991; May: 52–55.

Donne J. Better management, better health. Bristol: NHS Training Authority, 1986.

HMSO. Education and training. Working for patients: Working Paper 10. London: HMSO, 1989.

Moore JK, Neithercut WD, Mellors AS, Manning CA, Jones H, Alman RJ, Al-Bachari M. Making the new deal for junior doctors happen. British Medical Journal 1994; 308: 1553–1555.

Hayes TM. Continuing medical education: a personal view. British Medical Journal 1995; 310: 994–996.

SCOPME. Continuing professional development for doctors and dentists. SCOPME Working Paper, London: Standing Committee on Postgraduate Medical and Dental Education, 1994.

22. Clinical and management development through action learning

Andrew Short   Neal Jolly   Huw Griffiths

Introduction

With recent changes in the NHS establishing clinical directorates and fundholding general practitioners, it is no longer sufficient for doctors to rely upon their clinical skills alone. An understanding of management is essential in order to implement change.

Whilst many clinicians can now avail themselves of management development programmes, these may often appear distinct from the real issue of patient care. Action learning provides an exciting opportunity to develop personal management skills whilst working as part of a team towards solving problems which influence clinical practice.

What is action learning?

Action learning is an approach to management whereby participants learn through the exploration of a practical problem. A successful action learning group must not only address a problem and make recommendations, they must also implement the necessary changes, as there cannot be 'learning' without 'action'. According to Revans,[1] who developed the 'action learning' approach, learning must continue at a greater rate than changes occurring in an organisation in order for that organisation to survive. This approach has not been widely used in the National Health Service, although a recent success story in the Wirral achieved through action learning has been described in the *British Medical Journal*.[2]

Action learning requires a small group of committed individuals who wish to address problems which directly influence them. Each individual must be willing to work as part of a team to explore possible solutions to the problem. Whilst tackling the problems, team members will also focus on what they learn about themselves, ensuring this knowledge remains with them to be utilised in other situations in the future. Whilst the solution to the problem is important, the process by which that solution is reached is equally relevant in action learning. It is hoped that, in the process of action learning, individuals will also attain greater understanding of organisations and how they work.

Getting started

The project originated thanks to the enthusiasm and vision of a local consultant with extensive experience of medical management. Discussions with various directors on the local NHS Trust Board had established a need for management development for hospital medical staff. The local FHSA were also approached and showed a similar commitment to developing management skills for local GPs. Funding was agreed by both the Trust and FHSA for a pilot project, including the provision of locum cover for GPs to allow them to attend without fear of financial disadvantage.

Information was sent out to local GPs and hospital consultants explaining the nature of this innovative project and inviting applications for further information. Eight hospital consultants and eight GPs were selected, with a bias towards younger clinicians or those already in management roles.

Participants included clinical directors, members of the local commissioning group, and members of the local audit advisory group. Three clinicians dropped out at an early stage because of constraints of work, but this did not adversely affect the structure or function of the group.

At the introductory meeting, senior representatives from the sponsors attended to outline their hopes and aspirations for the project. The Trust Chief Executive identified six key areas causing concern:

- activity
- clinical effectiveness
- understanding the purchaser's agenda
- public expectations
- medical staffing
- finance and efficiency.

The senior officer from the FHSA identified similar areas of concern:

- reorganisation in primary care
- GP fundholding

- joint protocols of care
- clinical effectiveness
- 'locality' projects.

Having listened to the concerns of both primary and secondary health care providers, the participants split into small groups to identify possible projects. The main areas that were felt to be relevant and manageable included:

- clinical effectiveness
- prescribing
- communication between GP and hospital
- explaining increase in activity
- junior doctors' training
- access to hospital service.

Once the areas for further consideration had been identified, subsequent discussions established that some subjects might be too sensitive or threatening, particularly in areas of clinical effectiveness and increased activity. These areas having been excluded, two subjects remained which were to form the basis of subsequent work for the two action learning sets: communication and prescribing. At this point, therefore, the group was divided into two sub-groups to work on these projects, with regular updating sessions to keep each group informed of the other's progress, and to allow mutual support and criticism.

Team selection

The initial action learning group consisted of 13 doctors and two facilitators. This size of group was felt to be too large to work at one unified project, and was therefore divided into two sub-groups. The process of team selection was democratic and allowed for personal preferences, whilst aiming to provide a good mix of hospital and community doctors. To maximise the chances of successful team working, we made use of the Belbin team characteristics which had been established at an earlier session. The success of a team has been shown by Belbin[3] to be dependent upon the combination of qualities brought by individual members. Diametrically opposed traits, such as innovative free-thinking and meticulous attention to detail, will not be shown by the same individual, and therefore the right balance is required regardless of the brilliance of any one team member. Belbin was able to identify eight separate team roles, each with separate but overlapping skills.

Armed with the knowledge of our own Belbin roles, we were able to ensure that our team of six doctors had an admirable mix of roles, and included a 'chairman', a 'resource investigator', an 'implementor', a 'shaper', a 'team worker', and a 'monitor evaluator'. The role of 'plant', suggest new ideas and strategies and assess the approach of the team to potential problems, was filled by the group facilitator. The lack of a completer-finisher was of some concern, although this trait had been demonstrated by at least one of the group scoring highly in initial assessment. It was a source of great comfort for the group to know that they represented a balanced team with commitment to succeed in all aspects of the proposed project.

Project planning

The initial aim of the action learning group was to establish what project would be addressed over the ensuing meetings. Project criteria had already been established after discussion with the sponsors, who hoped for some tangible benefit from their support. It was thought to be essential that the project decided upon should:

- help improve services
- allow participants to develop their management skills and knowledge
- address a real problem
- be interesting and worthwhile
- have measurable outcomes
- be feasible
- implement rather than simply recommend change
- improve relationships between general practice and hospital services.

Guided by the facilitator, the group systematically addressed the project through 'the seven Ps' of project planning.

The *purpose* of the project was to improve communication between general practitioners and junior hospital doctors in order to develop a partnership approach, leading to improvements in the quality of patient care. This purpose was chosen because of a number of concerns about the current *position*, which included ineffective discharge procedures, delayed notification of deaths, delayed responses to requests for admission by GPs, and variable standards of both admission and discharge letters. Many of these concerns involved tasks mainly undertaken by junior hospital doctors, and it was therefore essential to involve them at all relevant stages of the project. The *power* to ensure that the project succeeded was provided by the make-up of the group with backing from both the Chief Executive and the FHSA.

The *people* in the group had, by volunteering for the project in the first place, demonstrated their desire to implement change. A large number of other interested groups were also identified (e.g. audit committees, quality managers) and were to be involved in the initial stages of the project. The *process* was in some ways decided by the limited time available — six half-day sessions over a six-month period. There was an initial commitment to attend all these sessions, work as a team, take individual responsibility where appropriate, review the work of the group and learn together. *Plans* were drawn up taking into consideration the tight time scale, with specific tasks assigned to individual team members. Ultimately the *product* would be a project report with specific recommendations to be presented to the sponsors and all interested groups at the final meeting.

Process evaluation

Continuous evaluation of the content and process of each meeting was an integral part of the programme. Participants were asked to assess both the content and style of the programme, and the benefit they had derived from it.

People attending the introductory half-day were asked why they had joined the programme. A list of rather vague reasons was compiled, including:

- concern over morbidity in the community
- curiosity
- to find out about action learning
- 'space'
- self-preservation.

A more focused response was obtained later when participants wrote their expectations on flip charts. A wide variety of topics, ranging from specific requests for factual information ('outer world tasks'), to desires to improve personal skills ('inner world tasks'), was produced and displayed. Most topics were related to personal and interpersonal skills; only a minority of requests were for factual information (e.g. 'how the Trust works'). Common themes were:

- time management
- assertiveness
- delegation
- understanding and influencing each other and our organisations
- balance between work and leisure.

These 'expectations of outcome' were collected and discussed again on the final day, but in addition the groups reviewed their activities at the end of each meeting. The review took a variety of forms, including discussion by participants of what they had achieved, or failed to achieve, during the day; how the members of the group had interacted; and observations by an external facilitator on the group's dynamics.

Several devices were employed to improve self-awareness and to enhance the functioning of the group. Belbin scores have already been described as an aid to forming balanced teams. The Myers–Briggs Type Indicator (MBTI) was used in a session called 'Understanding Yourself and Others' to determine personality types. It consists of four scales, each measuring a pair of behavioural preferences (extrovert/introvert, sensor/intuitor, thinker/feeler, judger/perceiver). A subject is scored by means of a detailed questionnaire concerning preferences when dealing with people and problems. Knowledge of one's MBTI type provided an insight into how people interact with each other and why certain environments are stressful for some people, but not others. It was possible to recognise leadership styles from the classifications given to members of the group.

Several other important subjects were covered in depth, including assertiveness, time management, and coping with change. Formal presentations on NHS structure and management were provided by guest speakers. The practical work required for the projects also provided valuable insights into the managerial structures of the Trust and FHSA.

On the final day, after presentation of projects, participants assessed whether their learning objectives had been met, and evaluated the content and process of the programme, using flip charts for presentation. The opinions expressed were generally favourable, examples of personal benefits cited being:

- knowledge of NHS
- awareness of power play of purchaser, FHSA and Trust
- understanding of structure and access to key members

- knowledge of how to use MAAG and hospital audit
- understanding and managing oneself
  — knowing when to say 'yes' or 'no' and sticking to it
  — not taking conflict personally
  — realising I am a 'monitor evaluator' and expressing rather than concealing my feelings
- technical skills
  — better at prioritising and time management
  — I sound out stakeholders before 'jumping in'
  — at meetings I observe and spot key players
  — practice meetings better organised.

In addition to meeting specific learning objectives, participants were complimentary about the nature and process of the programme. Many mentioned the camaraderie of the group and the high level of commitment of all concerned. Some stated that the projects had worked better than expected.

Some reservations were also expressed. The programme was felt to be less successful when dealing with pure management; sometimes the projects were given too much priority, so that there was insufficient time for review and evaluation. Greater feedback from the facilitators was also desired.

Positive comments greatly outweighed the negative, however, and the general feeling was that the programme had been a great success, with many surprises and a feeling that collaborating on project work had provided an opportunity for personal growth and understanding.

Project evaluation

All participants feel that the project has been a success; this is supported by the positive feedback received by the programme's sponsors. Having identified areas of concern relating to communication between doctors in primary and secondary care, the project set out to address these concerns with a view to improving patient care.

The first step was to devise a questionnaire which was to be sent to all local GPs and junior hospital doctors. This questionnaire specifically addressed five areas involving direct communication between GPs and hospital doctors:

1. telephone communications for advice or acute admissions
2. written communications for referral to hospital
3. written communications on discharge from hospital

4. notification of deaths
5. future proposals to improve communication.

The questionnaire response rate was 41.3% for junior doctors and 53.0% for general practitioners. Responses to the questionnaire confirmed that problems existed in all the above areas.

1. Telephone communication. The majority of GPs and junior doctors were happy with the information exchanged during phone calls for advice or admission. There were occasional problems for GPs being unable to speak to the appropriate junior doctor, and occasional delay in establishing a destination for patients. Some GPs were also concerned about the time taken to get through to the hospital switchboard. The project recommended that a telephone line specifically for GPs should be established, and that no pre-registration house officer or senior house officer should refuse hospital admission if this was requested by the GP — this has now been established as Trust policy.

2. Written referral letters. The questionnaire established that GPs were including less information than they had thought in referral letters, which often lacked essential medical information. The standard of referral letters, as judged by junior hospital doctors, was considerably lower than when judged by those writing the letters. The group recommended that a minimum data set for referral letters be established; this work is proceeding through the Clinical Audit Department.

3. Discharge letters. The questionnaire confirmed previous concerns about the quality and speed of written discharge letters. A separate Trust initiative had been established to address this problem and information from our results was forwarded to this group. As a result we are currently piloting written discharge letters completed by nursing staff to establish whether the service will be improved.

4. Deaths. Two thirds of junior doctors were unaware of any existing guidelines regarding who should be notified in the event of a patient death. Only 15% regularly informed the GP. When questioned, junior doctors felt that it was reasonable to inform GPs within two working days. GPs, on the other hand, felt that this should be done within one working day, although there was wide variation in who was felt to be the most appropriate person to perform the task. As a result, the group recommended that the notification officer should be empowered to phone the GP for all patients dying in hospital. This proposal has also been accepted and acted upon.

5. Future proposals. All doctors were in agreement regarding the need for greater understanding of each other's roles. Suggested means of achieving this included a greater input from general practitioners for junior doctors' induction courses, and the possibility of workshadowing. This might include pre-registration and post-registration doctors spending a day with a nominated GP, and GPs having the opportunity of spending days with junior or senior hospital staff. The Trust has agreed to build in one day of study leave for each pre-registration house officer every six months to allow attendance at a local practice to workshadow a GP. In addition, there is an open invitation for all hospital doctors to avail themselves of the same service. Enquiries are continuing to establish whether GPs workshadowing a hospital consultant might qualify for post-graduate medical education accreditation, in which case this offer is also likely to be well subscribed.

As a result of the action learning project, which was conceived, conducted and published in six half-day sessions, nine separate recommendations were made and presented to the interested parties in the Trust and FHSA. An indication of the success of the work is that four of these have already been implemented, and work continues on the remaining five, with both Trust Managers and group members showing an active interest in completing the first phase of this action learning project.

Summary

This chapter described the successful establishment of an action learning group consisting of enthusiastic local clinicians committed to improving patient care. Both the local NHS Trust and FHSA were willing to support the project and identified mutual areas of concern. By employing management tools that may be alien to some clinicians, effective team building led to successful project planning. Provision of an external site and financial support for locum cover ensured that all participants were able to give the necessary commitment to the project.

While the successful completion of the project has been an important step towards improving patient care, of equal importance are the personal development and management skills acquired by each individual member of the team. An external facilitator is invaluable to ensure that the participants spend some time focusing on the process of their project work, not just the content. The management skills acquired in the process of action learning will lead to improved understanding of the roles of management within the NHS. As we have demonstrated, this can lead directly to improvement in patient care as well as in working relationships for all clinicians within the NHS.

Conclusions

Action learning is a management tool that is ideally suited to use in the NHS to promote individual development. We learn how to influence colleagues and bring about change. We learn how to approach a problem systematically. Most importantly, we learn how to listen to others' views and work effectively in a team. With current changes in medical manpower within the NHS, this is a vital skill to ensure its continued success.

ACKNOWLEDGEMENTS

This project would not have been possible without the vision and commitment of David Walker (a clinical director at Huddersfield NHS), and the enthusiasm and support of both Eva Lambert (Chief Executive, Huddersfield NHS Trust) and West Yorkshire FHSA.

We would also like to acknowledge the contribution of the other members of the Action Learning Group:

> Felicity Matthews – Facilitator
> Julie Manning – General Practitioner
> David Seeley – General Practitioner
> Rabi Paes – Consultant Radiologist

REFERENCES

Revans R. ABC of action learning. Chartwell-Bratt, 1983.
Moore JK, Neithercut WD, Mellors AS, Manning CA, Jones H, Alman RJ, Al-Bachari M. Making the new deal for junior doctors happen. British Medical Journal 1994; 308: 1553–1555.
Belbin RM. Management teams — why they succeed or fail. London: Heinemann, 1981.

23. Changing the Law through action learning

E. A. Murphy   E. Duncan   J. A. Goldberg
I. R. Gunn   H. Jones   J. McCallion
D. MacLean   G. Urquhart

Introduction

In this paper we describe an alternative approach to management within the NHS which successfully bridged the management–clinician divide. The paper outlines the development of an action learning set based in a District General Hospital. The problem tackled was that of junior doctor recruitment, which is one faced by many hospitals.

Law Hospital is a 700-bedded District General Hospital situated in South Lanarkshire about 20 miles from Glasgow and 40 miles from Edinburgh. Recruitment of pre-registration house officers (PRHOs) previously relied heavily on graduates from the University of Glasgow. In recent years, recruitment has become increasingly difficult, largely as a result of an increasing shortfall of local graduates (there are now about 200 graduates each year for 350 posts in the West of Scotland). Law Hospital has eight surgical and eight medical PRHO posts every six months and increasing use was being made of overseas graduates, some provided by agencies. Whilst some of these doctors were of a high standard, the quality was unpredictable, and posts were often not filled until the last moment. This chapter describes the way in which a group of consultants tackled this problem.

Getting started

Tackling the problem of junior doctor recruitment was the subject of an article by Moore et al in the *British Medical Journal*.[1] This paper from the Wirral addressed many of the problems we were encountering and one of our group approached several consultants within the hospital to sound out the possibility of adopting a similar approach at Law. From an initial group of about a dozen interested individuals, a core of six enthusiasts met informally at one of our homes in July 1994 and decided that there would be benefits in setting up an action learning set to look at the problems of PRHO recruitment at Law. It was decided that it would be advantageous to include a general practitioner in the group, and that we would seek an external facilitator. The idea was put to the Trust management and this in turn led to a preliminary meeting on the 6th December 1994, when Helen Jones and Julia Moore from the Wirral project came to Law and spoke about their experiences. Approval was given for the project to proceed and a first meeting was arranged for January 1995. The composition of the group was as follows: Helen Jones as facilitator; 1 general practitioner (ED); and 6 consultants. The consultants were 1 biochemist (IRG), 1 radiologist (GU), 1 surgeon (JAG), 2 physicians — a rheumatologist (EAM) and a geriatrician (JMcC), and 1 anaesthetist (DMcL). All were under 40 years of age and had been consultants for less than 10 years.

Action learning

Action learning sets bring together small groups of people to tackle workplace problems using a technique developed by Revans.[2] The philosophy of this approach is that, for effective problem solving, present (inherited) knowledge is not enough and new knowledge needs to be sought, that the best way to find new knowledge is to work with others, and that people learn most effectively by experience (doing). The aim of action learning is to find a solution to a real-life problem and to use critical reflection to enhance the learning value of the exercise. The group analyses the problem and examines possible solutions. Actions are then agreed and tried in the real-life setting, and at subsequent meetings the situation is reviewed and further strategies agreed if necessary. By discussing problems, sharing experiences and reflecting on successful and unsuccessful actions, the group learns new knowledge and skills which are applicable to a variety of situations. Each action learning set establishes ground rules which set the boundaries within which the team must work and which facilitate good team work. The principal characteristics of an action learning set are listed in Box 23.1.

Box 23.1 Characteristics of action learning sets

- Each individual makes a voluntary commitment.
- The problems are real.

- The group works together to explore alternative actions which solve the problem or make it more manageable.
- Following each action, there is reflection on its consequences by the group.
- There is an emphasis on learning not just about the problem being tackled but also about oneself, so that the learning is transferable to other situations.
- Each group has a facilitator whose role is to help the group identify and develop the necessary skills.
- The group should provide a balance of support and challenge for each individual.
- The members of the group should have a broad base of experience.

Identifying the problems

It was clear from the outset that the major aim of the project was to improve junior staff recruitment. We felt that an important first step was to gather information from the current PRHOs to ascertain what they perceived as the good and bad aspects of the posts. A survey was therefore commissioned and was carried out by Gaynor Bennett-Emslie, a health and social services researcher, using the nominal group interview technique. She interviewed four medical and four surgical PRHOs in January 1995; her survey highlighted several areas which the PRHOs felt required improvement, as well as several good points. All of the doctors indicated that they found Law to be a friendly and relaxed environment in which to work. They felt that the hospital was a good size, not too busy but providing a wide variety of patients and good experience. Negative features included inappropriate working practices, insufficient teaching and supervision, poor communication, a low standard of accommodation, insufficient on-site facilities, and the lack of a hospital social committee. This report was available at the first meeting of the action learning set and, together with an early brainstorming session, established the agenda for actions required.

Actions

The group met on 12 occasions between January 1995 and November 1995, with eight whole-day scheduled meetings and

four extra evening meetings. The actions taken over that period
can best be summarised under a series of headings:

Working conditions

A summary of appropriate duties for junior house officers (JHOs)
was drawn up and measures taken to remove inappropriate
duties. A statement of the philosophy of the PRHO posts was formulated (see Box 23.2). The surgical posts have been reorganised
so that each PRHO works as part of a team attached to a specific
consultant. Several steps have been taken in both medicine and
surgery to remove routine tasks which could be done by other
members of staff. A nurse practitioner post is being piloted
within the medical directorate, and so far seems to be very successful. All medical and surgical wards are now staffed with ward
clerks and there is a seven-days-a-week phlebotomy service for
routine samples. The handbook issued to junior doctors in the
hospital has been revised and the procedures for employing
locums to cover sick leave have been improved. The personnel
department has been enthusiastic in cooperating with these
changes, and regular meetings now take place which we hope will
improve communication and facilitate prompt resolution of any
problems which do arise.

Box 23.2   Law Hospital's PRHO philosophy

The Trust aims to provide the best possible pre-registration
house officer posts in order to attract high quality candidates
who will actively contribute to the medical care provided for the
people of South Lanarkshire.

Purpose
The purpose of the pre-registration year is to consolidate undergraduate education with supervised clinical experience. The
year should be enjoyable and stimulating, with opportunity for
continuing education and personal development.

Environment
The pre-registration house officer is respected as an important
member of the health care team. We strive for a friendly, supportive working environment. High quality accommodation and
living conditions are provided. Holiday, leisure and study time
are protected.

> *Education*
> The posts provide a broad range of general clinical training. Everyone is expected to participate in the formal education programme. Emphasis is placed on personal development through the acquisition of appropriate responsibility and skills. Career guidance and regular feedback are integral components of the programme.

Education

Weekly tutorials are now organised in both medicine and surgery. These run throughout the six months and cover a variety of topics of relevance to PRHOs. Finding a time which is convenient for both tutors and juniors, and ensuring that the time is adequately protected, are problems which have not yet been completely resolved.

Mentoring

A mentoring system has been established. There was a good response from consultants volunteering to be mentors. The mentors have come from a variety of specialties and include some senior consultants. Each mentor is allocated no more than two JHOs, and no mentor is allocated a junior from his or her own specialty. Meetings are generally informal and the initial feedback from the PRHOs is that they find this a useful development. A study day in mentoring skills was arranged for January 1996, and attended by 12 consultants.

Accommodation

The Bennett-Emslie report detailed the problems with accommodation. Meetings were held with the estates manager and the hotel services manager and plans were drawn up for a series of refurbishments to upgrade the accommodation. These were approved by the Trust Board and an initial sum of £10 000 allocated. This was sufficient to start work on one corridor of rooms providing accommodation for nine doctors. A further £40 000 was subsequently released, allowing completion of a further nine rooms and upgrading of the public areas. The accommodation is now furnished to a high standard with no more than two doctors sharing a bathroom.

There are four well-equipped kitchen areas, two laundry areas and a comfortable sitting room. Free newspapers are provided and there is cable TV.

Mess steward

Two mess stewards have been employed. These individuals prepare and serve a complimentary breakfast to the resident staff each morning and take care of general housekeeping in the mess. They deal with day-to-day problems which arise with the accommodation and ensure that the bedrooms and public areas are well maintained.

Social

A social committee has been established with representatives from a variety of departments within the hospital. Several events have been organised in recent months including a ceilidh and a sports day. A hillwalking club and weekly keep-fit session have flourished and a hospital soccer league has been established. Funding for a gymnasium and shower area within the hospital has been approved.

Marketing

A brochure was produced for potential PRHOs. This included information about the hospital and the posts. It has been distributed to students from Glasgow, Edinburgh and Dundee Universities and was followed by a series of open evenings when interested students could come to see the hospital and meet consultants. There was an encouraging amount of interest in posts following these initiatives, which made us hopeful that most of the posts for the coming year would be filled in the near future.

Techniques

Throughout the period of the action learning project, we were exposed to a variety of techniques which helped the group to work more effectively both as individuals and as part of a team. These included:

- time management
- problem-solving strategies

- project leadership
- stakeholder analysis
- problem-based learning
- models of assertiveness and influencing skills
- negotiation skills and management of conflict
- communication and listening skills.

Exploration of learning styles and team roles, career anchors, the Egan model of change, and personal construct psychology were used to encourage the development of insight with regard to the best methods of dealing with problems. Personal and group success criteria were established at the beginning and were reviewed regularly. Reflection on progress and difficulties was a regular feature of the meetings.

Presentations

Midway through the project, a half day was devoted to presenting progress to date to a group of invited stakeholders (the postgraduate tutor, some other consultants, and members of the Trust management team and Trust Board). The meeting was chaired by one of the group. This was an important meeting since it demonstrated what progress had been made, and also generated a good deal of support for future developments from colleagues and management. This support has been crucial to the success of the project. An informal open meeting was held at the end of the project with posters summarising the various aspects.

Outcomes

These can be considered in terms of:

- the aim of the project
- the wider impact in the Trust
- individual success criteria
- the success of the group.

At the time of writing it is too soon for us to know if the main aim of the project — successful recruitment of PRHOs — has been achieved. This will require to be evaluated over the next year or two. Regardless of this, several important outcomes have been achieved. The refurbishment of the mess, the development of a mentoring scheme, the establishment of a social committee, and improvements in the working and educational arrangements for PRHOs are already improving the JHO posts at Law. To ensure that progress continues, a steering group is now being established to co-ordinate and monitor various issues of relevance to junior doctors.

The visible success of the project has demonstrated to many within the Trust that change can occur when appropriate energy and resources are directed at a problem. The format of the group has also been useful in demonstrating that the directorate structure is not always the most useful model for achieving change and that there are other ways for doctors (none of whom were clinical directors) to work successfully with management. There have been potential drawbacks in that there has been a tendency for management to expand the original remit of the project by delegating additional associated problems (and thus increasing workload for the group members), some of which involved areas of conflict between management and others within the hospital. It has therefore been important for the group to decline to deal with issues which it did not feel were appropriate and for the group to maintain control of the agenda for the project.

The individual members of the group have perceived several advantages, most notably the achievement of the specific outcomes listed above. The personal development aspect has varied for each individual, but the group has been unanimous in finding the project a useful experience. The personal success criteria defined at the outset varied enormously and it is difficult to generalise in this regard. All members of the group found the project hard work, but were encouraged by the amount that was achieved when protected time and adequate resources were allocated to a task. The value of the group as a support structure in a professional and personal sense was important, although again this varied for individual members of the group.

Our group worked well as a team; this was an important aspect of its success. Some of the factors which helped the team to develop are shown in Box 23.3.

Box 23.3   Some factors helping team development

- There was a clear objective to which each member of the team was committed.
- Motivation and commitment were high.
- Cooperative working was achieved.

- Good communication was established as a priority at the outset.
- Individuals volunteered for tasks.
- Tasks were evaluated at each meeting.
- Team members were supportive of innovation.
- The climate was one of support.
- Information sharing was excellent.
- Humour and fun were integral to the working of the group.
- Each individual had influence over decision making.
- Regard was given to other groups within the organisation.

Conclusions

Recent changes in hospital management have developed the clinical directorate structure as a way of involving doctors in management. We have described an alternative model where doctors who were not clinical directors worked with management to tackle a staff recruitment problem. This approach has the advantage of allowing those who do not wish to take on the responsibilities of a clinical director to contribute to management by becoming involved in projects in which they have a particular interest. We feel that project management of this type is important and that the technique of action learning has several particular advantages, as shown in Box 23.4.

Box 23.4   Some advantages of action learning

- It provides the opportunity to focus on particular areas of professional life and to discuss these at a level that is not usually possible at work.
- It provides the opportunity to gain a new perspective on a problem based on the experience of others.
- It provides the opportunity to develop and practise new skills in a relatively safe environment while at the same time focusing on a real problem.
- It provides personal and professional support, and friendship.

ACKNOWLEDGEMENTS

We wish to acknowledge the support and cooperation of the Trust Board at Law, Susan Johnstone for organisational and administrative support, and our consultant colleagues who helped to make things happen.

REFERENCES

Moore JK, Neithercut WD, Mellors AS, Manning CA, Jones H, Alman RJ, Al-Bachari M. Making the new deal for junior doctors happen. British Medical Journal 1994; 308: 1553–1555.

Revans R. Action learning projects. In: Taylor B, Lippet G, eds. Management development and training handbook. London: McGraw Hill, 1993: pp 266–279.

24. Clinicians in management in Northern Ireland: a personal perspective

Seamus Carey

Background

Since the 1970s there have been successive attempts to involve doctors more closely in management through a variety of reforms and policy initiatives. In addition, there have been a number of internal and external environmental factors relating to the provision of health care within the UK and outside which have influenced the development of a 'clinicians in management' agenda.

This chapter reviews the range of management and organisation development initiatives concerning clinicians in management being undertaken by my organisation on behalf of our core clients.

In reviewing the context in which clinical management has developed, research published by the BMA, BAMM, IHSM and RCN[1] arrived at three broad conclusions:

a. Decentralisation of clinical management, moving the responsibility and authority for decision making on the use of clinical resources as close to the patient care setting as possible, is developing as the preferred model in the UK.
b. There is a move away from the notion of 'one right structure' for decentralised clinical management, to the use of more flexible solutions to meet the needs of the individual provider organisation and its patients.
c. A multi-disciplinary team approach to decentralised clinical management is preferred, in response to an increasing awareness that no single professional, general manager or clinician can be, in isolation, an effective manager of clinical resources.

The reality is that 10 years ago the number of provider organisations who had adopted a clinical directorate model of management were few and far between. Today those who have not adopted some variation of this model are in the minority.[2]

The Northern Ireland scene

Introduction

The Provider Support Unit (PSU) provides management development, training and organisation development services to a range of health and social care organisations in Northern Ireland. Our core clients include ten Trusts and the major purchaser within the province, the Eastern Health and Social Services Board, who collectively have responsibility for approximately 50% of the health and social care expenditure in Northern Ireland.

Northern Ireland absorbed the introduction of the general management model and the major reforms instigated by the NHS and Community Care Act 1990 simultaneously (circa 1990). The fact that our (current) core clients all achieved Trust status within four years of the introduction of the above reforms into Northern Ireland provided additional impetus to the clinicians in management agenda here. The degree, pace and time scale of the changes has been considerable, as have the associated challenges and developmental needs to be addressed at an organisation and individual level.

Current position

There are currently more than 75 clinicians involved in management, as medical directors, clinical directors or chief executives. This excludes those clinicians closely involved in service issues within directorates. All Trusts have established mechanisms for the involvement of clinicians in management and have adopted a clinical directorate model based on a clinical director, nurse and business manager (or directorate manager).

The clinical directorate model, as it has developed within Northern Ireland, could be said to have the characteristics shown in Box 24.1.

Box 24.1   Characteristics of Northern Ireland's clinical directorate model

- Directorates are becoming the 'natural business' units within the organisation and are structured around a compatible range of services.
- There is a distinction between the 'revenue generating' directorates and those providing services to the latter. Ultimately, service level agreements may be deployed to manage these relationships as the internal market develops.

- Directorates are the natural focus for business planning in line with the Trust's strategic direction.
- Directorates are linked managerially to an operational management team within the Trust which has day-to-day responsibility for operational issues and policy development/implementation.
- The majority of staff will consider directorates to be their 'natural unit of organisation'.
- Clinical directors are responsible for managing the overall affairs of the directorate. However, the day-to-day responsibility for running the directorate is devolved to either a directorate manager or a nurse and business manager.
- There is a desire to move towards a more conventional means of selecting clinical directors whilst retaining clinical colleague support/involvement in the process.

Although these are early days, there are a number of factors which impact on the development of the clinical directorate model within Northern Ireland. These include:

- the developing internal market — need for service rationalisation
- the need to control costs
- performance issues
- the need to embrace new approaches to service delivery (e.g. business process re-engineering, vertical disease management, managed care)
- the prevalence and implications of 'split site' working for clinicians and their organisations
- growing emphasis on accountability.

Arising from this, the issues to be addressed include:

- configuration, size and number of directorates
- key roles/relationships within the organisation
- organisational support arrangements for clinical directorates
- the clinical management team and its effectiveness
- succession planning arrangements
- career management/planning
- the training and development of clinicians involved in management.

Training and development of clinical directors

Clearly, even if all of the above issues are addressed, there remains the crucial issue of ensuring that prospective clinical directors are provided with training and development which meets their needs and will equip them to undertake the role of clinical director effectively. The range of developmental initiatives undertaken for clinicians within Northern Ireland with which the PSU is associated are discussed below.

PSU management development programmes

The PSU organises a range of management development programmes, primarily for its core clients, ranging from those working at supervisory level to the most senior managers. As far as clinicians are concerned, attendance has been most significant on the (formerly) Senior Management Development Programme and its successor the Director Challenge Programme. This is a multi-disciplinary programme aimed at those working at director level or equivalent within our core client organisations.

To date, an increasing number of clinicians are attending these programmes, particularly as far as medical directors and clinical directors are concerned. Clinicians found participation in this programme particularly useful; some of the benefits for them are shown in Box 24.2.

Box 24.2 Benefits of management development programmes

- Opportunity to meet other professionals and share experiences and ideas
- Understanding other professionals and what they have to offer
- Exploring current themes and changes within and outside the health care environment
- Learning about the theory and key concepts of management
- Clarifying strengths and development needs
- Developing personal action plans based on individual needs
- Building relationships and networks.

Clinicians, mainly at consultant level, also attend our other management development programmes, including 'Managing for Success', aimed at those senior managers working below director level, and 'Managing Health Services', which is organised on an open learning basis and supported by a structured programme of tuition and group learning activity.

Individual coaching

In addition to attendance on the management development programmes, clinicians avail themselves of coaching on a one-to-one basis. This has taken place before, during and/or after attendance on a programme. It is very often stimulated by participation on a programme and related to issues either in managing their own directorate/organisation or based on individual development needs they wish to address.

Clinicians also attend short course programmes organised by the PSU (e.g. communications, marketing, business planning, finance for non-financial managers). They also attend their own in-house programmes and a range of conferences and workshops organised internally, by the PSU, or externally.

Directorate-based activities

Increasingly, clinical directors are taking time out with their directorates to take stock of the issues facing them and plan ahead. These events normally take place outside the organisation and involve external facilitation (i.e. PSU and others). The workshops are normally attended by the clinical director, directorate manager(s), consultant staff, and other senior heads of department. They are very often attended (in whole or in part) by the Chief Executive, the Trust Chairman, and/or members of the Trust Board. They provide an overview of the wider issues facing the Trust and participate in the ensuing discussion.

The format normally involves a combination of input and group work and tends to focus on:

- Where are we now?
- Where do we want to be?
- How do we get there?

The output of these workshops is an action plan, involving a range of staff within the directorate and with built-in review mechanisms. The challenge is to harness the energy and commitment of staff into a cohesive agenda/plan of action for the directorate in line with the Trust business plan and strategic direction. The benefits of using the directorate workshop as an agent for change and a tool for development include:

- greater understanding of issues facing the Trust
- getting to know key players outside the directorate, including Trust Board members
- joint identification and ownership of directorate issues
- better understanding of the problems, needs, fears and expectations of directorate colleagues
- improved communications and relationships within and outside the directorate
- empowerment of participants to address real issues facing the directorate and to 'make a difference'
- involvement of medical staff on work-related issues in a multi-professional setting.

In-house training and development programmes

In an effort to 'engage' clinicians, particularly at consultant level within Trusts, in-house programmes are being organised for consultants and clinical directors (with no previous management training). The aim of these programmes is to provide an opportunity for participants to develop knowledge and skills in order to make them more effective in managing the internal and external environment in which they are working. These programmes comprise a number of modules, each with a key theme. The programme is designed and organised by the PSU in conjunction with the Trust in question.

Typically the first module of such a programme would involve looking at NHS policy issues, organisations and organisational culture, the role of the clinician within the organisation, participants' strengths and personal development needs, and projects to be pursued during the course of the programme. Thereafter the programme is designed in conjunction with participants to meet their needs and would normally address the following issues:

- business planning/contracting
- funding issues/financial management
- negotiation skills
- leadership and leadership styles
- team working/effectiveness
- power and influence
- dealing with difficult people

- personal effectiveness
- career development/planning
- performance.

Attendance on these programmes is providing a variety of benefits on an individual and organisational level: these are shown in Box 24.3.

Box 24.3   Benefits of attending in-house training and development programmes

> - Enhanced networks amongst clinicians and with other key staff within the Trust
> - Increased awareness of the external environment/context in which participants are working and the challenges facing their organisation
> - Understanding of systems and processes as well as the key roles and players within the Trust
> - Increased awareness of participants' strengths and development needs
> - Participants' awareness of the complexity/pace of change and their exposure to tools and techniques to help them manage this better in their work environment
> - Improved communications within the Trust.

Looking to the future, a number of other Trusts are considering running these programmes in-house. Although they are uni-disciplinary in nature, they have proved to be a very valuable way of engaging clinicians in issues and affording them an opportunity to learn about management with other clinical colleagues in a 'non-threatening' environment. The likelihood is that this process will also provide Trusts with a 'critical mass' of clinicians to enable them to address issues such as the future selection of clinical directors and succession planning. Clearly, for these programmes to be successful in the long term, participants need ongoing stimulus and involvement within their own directorate/organisation and, as appropriate, attendance on multi-professional management development programmes.

Organisation-based development initiatives

With the establishment of Trusts and the growing emphasis on performance, most Trusts, as part of the 'rhythm' of management activity, take time out during the year to review progress and to plan ahead. This normally involves either the Operational Management Board within the Trust (including clinical directors) or the Operational Management Board and the Trust Board together. To date the emphasis is on:

- key issues facing the Trust
- the Trust's strategic direction over the next three years
- role clarification at an individual and collective level
- team working/effectiveness issues
- development of an action plan to take issues forward.

The PSU has been involved in the facilitation of these workshops; some of the benefits for clinicians and others are shown in Box 24.4.

Box 24.4 Perceived benefits of the workshops

- Reinforcement for clinicians of their corporate role within the organisation and the reality of being a 'clinician involved in management'
- An opportunity for clinicians to keep abreast of key issues facing the Trust and to be involved in its future direction
- Time away from the 'coal face' to develop relationships and to get to know key individuals, particularly Trust Board members
- It complements other developmental initiatives being undertaken at individual and organisational level, referred to above.

Northern Ireland Clinicians in Management Group

Although a number of clinicians have participated in management development/training, for a significant number their management skills have been principally learned 'on the job'. In view of the number of clinicians now involved in management, the emerging agenda and the continuous pace of change within Health and Social Services, a number of clinicians met informally to discuss how best to address their growing development needs in this respect. They decided to create an informal support group amongst clinicians in Northern Ireland which could be used as a vehicle to discuss critical managerial and clinical developments affecting them and the development of their managerial role within the service. This group became known as the Northern Ireland Clinicians in Management Group; the role of the PSU has so far been one of facilitation and support. The objectives of the Group are:

- to provide a forum for the discussion and exchange of information on professional and management issues relevant to clinicians involved in management
- to discuss matters of concern and interest to members with government departments and organisations concerned with issues pertaining to clinicians.

Since October 1993 a number of meetings have been held, involving primarily clinical and medical directors. Each meeting had a theme which was considered to be relevant and current: to date these have included:

- the role of the clinician in management
- the Calman Report
- the future of acute services
- performance
- managing difficult colleagues
- consumers' expectations of health care.

At the first AGM in June 1995 a committee was elected to organise events and activities on behalf of the Group. A constitution has now been adopted to underpin its future activities.

Future activities

It is anticipated that the work of the Group in the future will include:

- organisation of meetings and workshops
- maintenance of an accurate database with membership information on issues such as training qualifications, current responsibilities, and training and development needs
- identification of training needs analysis and sources of training available to doctors
- research activities
- preparation of advice/information papers on subjects of interest to clinicians
- liaison with the DHSS and other organisations concerned with issues pertaining to clinicians.

Meetings are organised on the basis that there should be minimal disruption to clinical and managerial activity. They normally take place in the evenings, with the exception of the AGM or meetings where a key theme is being addressed and additional time is required. So far, the benefits of membership would appear to be:

- the provision of advice, information and support on issues which are mutually beneficial
- the existence of an extended network of clinicians, particularly for those who are becoming involved in management
- a vehicle for communication, both within the group and with government departments/external organisations as appropriate
- a way of keeping clinicians informed on some of the key issues which affect them in a way which causes minimal disruption of their clinical and managerial duties.

Attendance at externally organised courses

In addition to the above range of developmental activities organised either in-house or in conjunction with the PSU, clinicians do avail themselves of opportunities to attend external training and development activities. These are very much based on the individual's development needs and will be supported by the organisation in question. They provide another source of training and also an opportunity for participants to meet with colleagues from outside Northern Ireland to share experiences and ideas.

Conclusions

The range of developmental initiatives referred to above is not comprehensive in that there are clearly other initiatives, both within Trusts and externally, which are being undertaken and which are addressing the needs of clinicians in a variety of settings. However, my experience in assisting clinicians involved in management within Northern Ireland has led me to a number of conclusions about emerging patterns and the benefits to be derived.

a. Clinicians need to understand the context in which they are working and the major issues to be addressed, irrespective of whether they are clinical directors, consultants or junior medical staff. The research carried out recently by the Wessex Region[3] supports this in that two of the five key areas relating to clinician development concern wider contextual and strategic issues.

b. To be effective in the long term, clinician development requires a variety of approaches which will enable them to manage:

- themselves
- within their directorates
- across the organisation
- the external environment.

In some cases this can be done more effectively in-house. In others it can be more fulfilling to meet with people outside the organisation and learn about others' experiences. Development can also take place on a one-to-one basis (coaching), within the directorate setting, or with work colleagues in or outside the organisation itself.

c. Because of the traditional divergent paths that managers and doctors have taken en route to the management process, there is a need to address the underpinning 'medical' and 'managerial' value systems. Otherwise, knowledge and skills-based training can be superficial, and perhaps even counter-productive.

d. To encourage clinicians to be involved in management requires support and leadership from within the organisation including:

- chief executives who have a vision of the future and are prepared to motivate others towards the achievement of that vision
- medical directors who have the respect of their managerial and clinician colleagues and can, amongst other things, be an effective link between clinicians and key decision-making fora, particularly the Trust Board
- clinical directors who have the support of their colleagues within the directorate, can display leadership skills, and can make the clinical directorate model an effective vehicle for ensuring that high quality care is provided to patients and clients and a conduit for managing change.

e. Because of the deep-seated nature of the most recent health care reforms, the ongoing reality of cost containment within health care provision, and the increasing involvement of clinicians in management, new issues and challenges will continue to present themselves. One of these is the issue of accountability within the NHS. Consequently, the engagement of clinicians in management in the future will require arrangements which are much more explicit, open and accountable as far as both they and their organisations are concerned. It is to be hoped that this will also encourage new and imaginative approaches in motivating and retaining clinicians in management in ways which are mutually beneficial. This will prove helpful in encouraging clinicians to become involved in management and will also secure the obligations required of Trusts in relation to corporate governance and other issues.

REFERENCES

BMA, BAMM, IHSM, RCN. Managing clinical services. A consensus statement of principles for effective clinical management. 1993.
Rea C. Managing clinical directorates. Harlow: Longman, 1993.
Gatrell J, White T. Medical student to medical director. A development strategy for doctors. Bristol: NHS Training Division, 1995.

25. Continuing medical education and professional development for clinicians — the Welsh experience

Stephen Prosser   Christopher Potter

Introduction

As a result of the changes brought about by the introduction of the NHS internal market within Wales there was a recognition that management education and personal development opportunities for clinicians had to be further improved (Table 25.1). There were

Table 25.1 Some factors which have significantly impacted on the nature of the NHS in Wales in regard to organisation development and management development

1. The new NHS internal market:
a. New structures, with further amalgamation imminent. New organisations; new responsibilities; old relationships between providers and their districts changed.
b. Competition between providers, making provider units more wary of open communications and collaboration.
c. The need to be economically successful, demanding new skills and exerting more pressure on posts and people.
2. Changed governance:
a. The influx of many new non-executive directors (including the Chairs).
b. New responsibilities of executive directors, demanding new skills, and new methods of working with the non-executives.
c. Decentralisation of power and responsibilities; less dependence on centrally organised systems and programmes.
3. Breakdown of professional boundaries:
a. Greater emphasis on clinicians in management, with more managers recruited without administrative backgrounds, and more doctors and other health professionals taking responsibility for delegated budgets, etc.
b. Skill mix reviews, changing old boundaries and responsibilities.
4. Economic climate:
a. People reluctant to move or take risky career steps, partly because of changing contracts of employment, and partly because of housing problems.
b. Blocked avenues of progression, so more thought given to 'climbing frame' career development, instead of 'ladder climbing'.

so many new approaches to financing and managing the service that not only was old course material too dated to be useful, but the programmes and courses themselves were often inappropriately focused. New opportunities for clinicians to lead health organisations as chief executives — as well as the introduction of clinical directorates, the need for better resource management, coping with waiting list initiatives, and greater emphasis on quality, including greater emphasis on clinical audit — meant that consultants and potential consultants had to be prepared to play their expanded roles in the new organisations. The new NHS Staff College Wales was ideally placed to address this challenge in cooperation with the various employers around the Principality, health care professionals themselves, and the University of Wales College of Medicine.

The NHS Staff College Wales

The Staff College was established after several years of discussions with the various interested parties, and is now the lead organisation within the NHS in Wales for all aspects of management development and training. Based at Morriston NHS Trust, Swansea, it serves the whole of Wales. It is not a traditional residential training centre, nor does it have a large faculty. Indeed, some have described it as a 'virtual organisation' because it offers so much without having the normal trappings of extensive buildings, faculty libraries, and so on. It is a 'college without walls', a commitment to high standards of management and organisation development shared by a wide array of people who together form the network which is the NHS Staff College Wales.

In fact, it is perhaps best thought of as a commissioning body in its own right: a 'champion of the people', in this case the staff of NHS Wales, identifying their health needs and commissioning activities from a host of potential providers. It helps development specialists, including technical experts in many fields, to develop programmes and services which meet the needs of staff; at the same time, it helps staff and employing organisations to focus their development needs, and identify how and where to meet those needs.

The Staff College has a small core of health management and organisation development specialists, including one of the authors of this chapter, who is the Chief Executive. It also has an equally small administrative staff who are available to organise workshops, process applications, send out literature, and so on. It provides a wider range of expertise through four specific mechanisms which enable it to draw on a wide breadth of experience while keeping down costs.

Firstly, the Staff College has a Management Group, largely made up of representatives of various commissioner and provider organisations in Wales. This group currently includes a GP and a consultant surgeon who help to ensure that doctors' needs are not forgotten. Similarly, on the 'Advisory Forum' the presence of the University of Wales College of Medicine's Provost is a constant reminder of the medical profession's needs. The Advisory Forum draws from specialists outside the Principality and outside the NHS, as well as from internal experts. This helps to give the Staff College a broader frame of reference, and keeps it up to date on wider developments. All the Management Group and the Advisory Forum members are highly experienced recognised specialists in different aspects of development, management and health service organisation, and inter alia represent several academic institutions. These links with academic institutions are very important to the Staff College, because although it does not seek to be an academic centre itself, nor to award its own qualifications, it is part of its philosophy to maintain rigorous academic standards for itself, for its programmes, and for the services it sponsors.

The third mechanism for widening the College's spectrum of expertise is through the appointment of Fellows, including at least one visiting International Fellow at any one time (currently from the University of Minnesota, Minneapolis, Centre For Health Services Administration). All the other Fellows are drawn from senior staff within the NHS in Wales, and are either experts in some particular field of management or health services delivery who act as the Staff College's source for advice and input on that topic, or are pursuing developing such an area of expertise, linking it to post graduate work.

Fourthly, a number of 'Associates' have been appointed. Again, they are topic specialists with wide experience of the NHS. Associates may be drawn from any organisation, inside the NHS or outside it. They are individuals whom the Staff College recognises as being sympathetic to its aims and values, and whom it can call on to give informed advice, commission to undertake work on its behalf, or recommend to others. The main difference between Fellows and Associates is that the former would be fully employed in a recognised role within the NHS and seconded to the Staff College for a given number of days a year, whereas the Associates may be in a part-time or self-employed role, called on to offer assistance as and when required. In the provision of actual training services the Associates would normally be expected to tender for work as would be required of any other third party.

The work of the Staff College

What of the work of the Staff College, especially as it relates to medical staff development? The Staff College carried out an extensive consultation exercise with the NHS in Wales early in 1995. From this consultation with all the Trusts and bodies throughout Wales emerged five areas of work which the Service considered to be priorities:

- 'All Wales' schemes (e.g. graduate entry programmes, 'Widening Horizons' — a middle management programme aimed at clinicians)
- development programmes, including programmes for specific groups such as new board members, commissioners, and doctors (and other health care professionals) in management
- helping health organisations with 'learning and change' through a variety of support activities
- providing consultancy services in the areas of individual development, team performance and organisational effectiveness
- developing partnerships with academic centres already providing programmes and specialist services to the NHS.

Right from the start, the Staff College's remit has been to give high priority to the needs of doctors in management; in October 1995 a number of board chairmen, managers and senior doctors met specifically to discuss how best to meet the management needs of clinicians. In fact, the NHS in Wales already had considerable experience of management training for medical staff. The University of Wales College of Medicine (UWCM) has insisted for a number of years that all medical undergraduates receive management inputs, provided by the Department of Epidemiology and Public Health Medicine. This is an examined topic, and is taught in the fourth year. The same department provided management training as part of the Inter-Regional Training Scheme for Public Health Medicine for several years. It has also been involved with the Cardiff Business School in teaching the MBA(Health), the first such course in the UK when it was started, originally designed and sponsored by people associated with the Staff College. This MBA(H) is still supported by the Staff

College, although it is now just one course among several in which the Staff College takes a close interest. Over the years several consultants have been sponsored from NHS Wales funds to undertake masters courses in management, as well as a variety of other senior clinical staff. Their development has been as much a product of learning and interacting with representatives from other disciplines as it has been a result of specific course content. This year a consultant psychiatrist will be starting the MBA(H) in Cardiff, while altogether 16 staff are being sponsored for masters courses in eight different English and Welsh universities.

In addition to undergraduate and masters programmes, the Staff College had worked closely with the Post Graduate Dean in organising a Welsh Office-funded management programme for senior registrars for many years. Every senior registrar in Wales takes part in two modules, giving them an appreciation of the way the NHS is organised, as well as an understanding of many management concepts. This year the Staff College took the opportunity to put the senior registrars' programme out to tender. The tender document described the overall purposes of the programme as helping senior registrars become more effective consultants through:

- an understanding of the fundamental systems, roles and policy issues that shape the NHS
- an understanding of the interaction between, and interests of, different parts of the NHS
- an awareness of the non-medical knowledge and skills that they will require to manage themselves, manage others, and manage resources
- practising some basic skills, such as team working and negotiating
- learning how to plan and carry out their own management development.

Several well-known organisations bid for the work; from a number of strong proposals it was decided to give responsibility for delivering the programme to a consortium made up of commercial management consultants and a national academic centre, on the basis that this combination should provide a sound theoretical appreciation of the NHS as well as ensuring good understanding of commercial management requirements. The exercise demonstrates the way the Staff College works. Having identified senior registrars' training as a priority within the service, a working group from the Staff College and the Post Graduate Dean's department worked on the specification. A variety of potential providers were identified and invited to tender. The proposals were evaluated, and ongoing evaluation will be provided by the Staff College to ensure that the specifications are being met, and that any required adjustments to content or approach are introduced (Fig. 25.1).

It is not just hospital doctors who are benefiting from the work of the Staff College. The Staff College participated with the Faculty of the Royal College of General Practitioners and the Centre for Applied Public Health Medicine to organise an Autumn Conference entitled 'Translating evidence on care into local action'. It has also helped to organise three 3-day modules which attempted to anticipate what primary care will look like in the next decade. Participants from health and social services came together to share a vision of the future for services in Wales. Attempting to break the mould of traditional thinking about professional roles, the participants considered new relationships embracing multi-disciplinary approaches to matters such as continuing professional education.

The Staff College has also been involved with a unique Primary Care Management Development programme run by the Director of the Valleys Health Group, one of the Staff College's associate

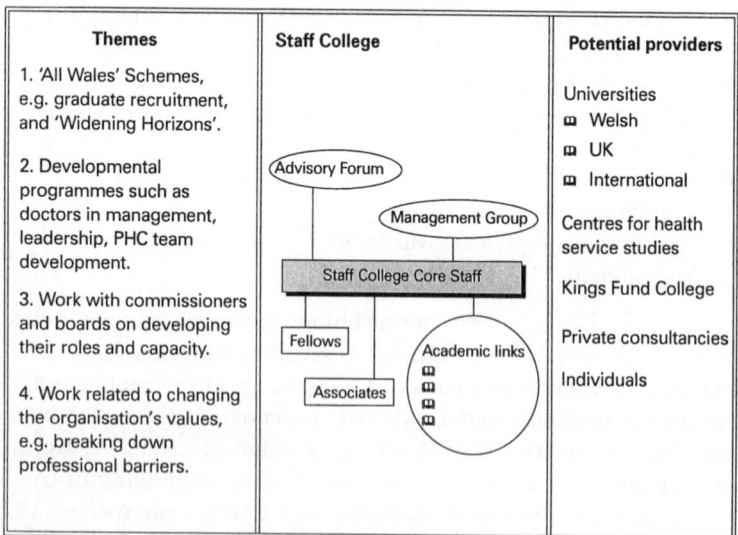

Themes	Staff College	Potential providers
1. 'All Wales' Schemes, e.g. graduate recruitment, and 'Widening Horizons'. 2. Developmental programmes such as doctors in management, leadership, PHC team development. 3. Work with commissioners and boards on developing their roles and capacity. 4. Work related to changing the organisation's values, e.g. breaking down professional barriers.	Advisory Forum — Management Group — Staff College Core Staff — Fellows — Associates — Academic links	Universities ▯ Welsh ▯ UK ▯ International Centres for health service studies Kings Fund College Private consultancies Individuals

Fig. 25.1 The conceptual model for the Staff College of the NHS in Wales, and the themes identified through consultation

consultants. The programme brings together the best of two very different development pathways — traditional academic teaching with national performance standards — in an attempt to help participants acquire both the knowledge and the skills needed to manage effectively in today's NHS. The aim was to avoid concentrating solely on theoretical knowledge, and to ensure that participants developed practical skills. Made up of four modules, the certificate is for general medical practitioners and practice managers who work alongside each other. It is the outcome of a long-established relationship between various commissioning bodies, FHSAs, the UWCM and the Staff College. It has led to the creation of a new postgraduate diploma in Health Services Management at UWCM, which started in January 1996. Initial evaluations were very positive and one GP declared, 'I wish I'd done it years ago!'. The diploma programme builds on the operational level competence acquired at certificate level, to enable participants to acquire the strategic level skills they will need to meet the challenges of tomorrow. Because of its early success a masters level programme is now being planned, to build on the certificate and diploma stages.

Another important aspect of the Staff College's work is consultancy, and at least two of its Associates have been heavily involved in providing consultancy services directly to clinical directors. In their work they have engaged with medical consultants in identifying training and development needs, how to meet those needs (given the busy lives such people lead), and the specific learning approaches best suited to adult professionals. In helping clinicians determine their own development needs, important areas for clinicians moving into management have included change management, financial management, conflict resolution, communications, team building in multi-disciplinary settings, and, most frequently mentioned, managing people.

All levels of the service have shown an interest in leadership skills. Chief executives and medical directors, as well as medically qualified non-executive directors, will be involved in the Staff College's work on training board members. Leadership programmes for senior staff will include medical staff, and discussions have been held with organisations such as the British Association of Medical Managers to try to identify the profession's perspective on development needs. The Staff College's work assisting commissioners will certainly involve the public health and other medical staff involved in determining local health needs and contracting for care.

The NHS in Wales has taken seriously the idea of 'the learning organisation' (see, for example, Senge)[2] and believes that individuals and organisations must take responsibility for reflecting on their growing experience, and rigorously seeking to improve their performance as a consequence. The Staff College tries to facilitate that process in some of the ways described in this chapter. There is a positive attempt to create a culture in which professional development is ongoing, and where individuals try to develop themselves with assistance and guidance from the wider organisation, but not limiting 'development' to attendance at courses with predetermined content, aimed shotgun fashion at a multitude of individuals in different circumstances and at different stages of development. It also recognises that professional and managerial values may not always be congruent, and seeks to expose professionals to new perspectives.[2] That climate of learning through change is exemplified by the work of the Staff College done on behalf of doctors in Wales. It is also supported by the role the Staff College plays in working with others to try and envision the demands of the future; workshops and seminars are designed to bring multi-disciplinary groups together to consider common problems and challenges.

An example of the latter is the Executive Seminar series run by the Staff College. Now in its eighth year, this series of monthly seminars brings together managers and professionals, civil servants, academics, and non-executive directors from throughout Wales to listen to a lecture from a prominent expert and to discuss the implications for the NHS locally. The speakers for 1995/96, for example, were from the media, professional bodies, academic institutions, and from the USA.

Conclusion

This description of the work of the NHS Staff College Wales will have given a flavour of the range and scope of work carried out for doctors in Wales, from undergraduate to board level. At key points in doctors' career paths specific training courses are provided in order that they will be able to function more effectively as clinicians within the NHS. The aim is not just to wait until people are in post, but to try to improve the understanding and effectiveness of all doctors before they reach consultant level. Those who gravitate towards specific functions which may need management training — such as board members, public health specialists, clinical directors, or doctors involved in functions needing high levels of management skill (e.g. blood transfusion services) — can take part in specific management and leadership courses, can seek sponsorship on an appropriate masters course (not necessarily in Wales), or can look to the Staff College for consultancy support. They can approach the Staff College with requests for information or advice about any aspect of management, organisational or personal development. They can take part in the many seminars, workshops and conferences provided. There is no excuse for any doctor in Wales not to be as well prepared for management responsibilities as he or she would like to be. Much is happening, and there will be much more to come.

REFERENCES

Senge PM. The fifth discipline: the art and practice of the learning organization. New York: Doubleday, 1990.
Morgan P, Potter C. Professional cultures and paradigms of quality in health care. In: Kirkpatrick I, Lucio MM, eds. The politics of quality in the public sector. London: Routledge, 1995.

26. Organisation development in health care — reflections on a decade of practice

Margaret Attwood

Beginnings

On 1st May 1986 I became Director of Organisational Development at Mid Essex Health Authority. This involved leadership of both the personnel and the service planning functions and a role as internal change agent. I had little prior knowledge and no experience of the NHS, having spent most of the previous decade as a principal lecturer in personnel management and industrial relations in a polytechnic. It was expected that I would bring a fresh approach to the Authority as it strove to improve its efficiency and effectiveness following the Griffiths Report (see endnote 1).

Mid Essex was an average District Health Authority, both in size and in range of services. There were (and are) no teaching hospitals. From the early 1980s extra money had been received from the redistribution of funds from inner London; however, this had enabled services only to do a certain amount of catching up. The view amongst managers and certainly amongst doctors was that services were still under-resourced. Employee relations had been low key. Unions were not strong. There was a fairly passive relationship between managers and staff.

During my first week with the Health Authority, a meeting was called to 'talk about how we might change the culture'. I had not expected this and was unconvinced despite the current hype surrounding *In Search of Excellence*[1] that organisational cultures are not readily susceptible to change.

Probably the most intriguing aspect of the organisation was the apparent lack of involvement of the consultant medical staff. It was as if managers and doctors inhabited different organisations. At a workshop for the District Management Board and senior consultant medical staff, we drew pictures of the organisation. One doctor drew several tables at each of which someone was sitting. In the corner of the picture was an indeterminate blob. He explained: 'These (the figures) are my colleagues and myself. We are traders bartering with each other for resources. If I do more of these operations, he has to do less of these. Otherwise we run out of money. The shape in the corner is management. It's not really got much to do with the way we work'. This person also defined management as something consultants 'do between gin time and ten o'clock at night!', indicating that it was a rather low grade and unimportant administrative activity. Another consultant told me that he had met the manager in charge of his unit three times in two years (see endnote 2).

I could see that organisational development (OD) work that did not involve doctors would be fairly fruitless. It seemed as if 'structured dialogue must occur before change objectives ... could be ... firmly clarified'.[2] We recognised that doctors and managers often had differing views about improving services. Politics in this sense was central to our understanding of change, but was this understanding sufficiently embedded in our practice?

Workshops to facilitate change

During 1986 and 1987 we ran strategy planning workshops with a wide range of doctors and managers to develop proposals for change, including a statement of purpose and values. There was much commitment to change. The results were consulted upon widely, first as a 'green paper' and then as a 'white paper'. However, in retrospect, this was a largely top-down initiative involving a few doctors. It hardly entered the consciousness of other doctors or front-line staff, probably because it was distant from the reality of clinical services.

We were keen to make the emerging definitions of organisational purpose and values and emerging plans for change concrete by defining their implications for managerial behaviour. We therefore embarked on a management development initiative for 180 managers. The strategy for change clarified the scale and nature of the managerial task, but did not define the attendant competencies. The design of this initiative is described elsewhere.[3] What is relevant to this chapter is the underpinning principle of both developing managers and developing managing by providing a framework within which individuals and groups can work through a series of questions such as those shown in Box 26.1.

Box 26.1 Personal and organisational development questions

Personal development questions	Organisational development questions
Who am I?	What kind of organisation is this?
What stage have I reached in my life so far?	What are its current characteristics /the issues it faces?
Where do I want to go in the future?	What needs to change?
How am I going to get there?	How can change take place?

The outcome of the workshops was both organisational and individual. The organisational outcomes emerged from small group activities in which participants identified information about the organisation which they would like to share with the Board. These covered the identity of the organisation, its functioning, managerial roles and relationships, and strategies for managing change. At the individual level the workshops assisted managers to diagnose development needs to improve their current effectiveness and to support career progression. They also enhanced identification with the organisation and provided a framework for decision-making about improvements in work systems and processes which participants could make. Figure 26.1 shows the emerging organisation and management development strategy.

The aspiration to become a learning organisation

The connection between individual and organisational development was a cornerstone of our emerging aspiration to become a learning organisation (see endnote 3). Another key theme was that of a 'learning effectiveness' bargain where the Authority's expectations of and obligations towards its managers were defined in its *Guidelines for Management Practice*. Managers were expected to take responsibility for their own development within the framework of organisational resources and processes. The senior management team tried to establish the appropriate climate for learning, both by paying attention to its own individual and collective development and by using learning as a major method of organisational development.

We also placed emphasis on the 'riddle of liberating structure',[4] recognising that our efforts to encourage self-directed learning

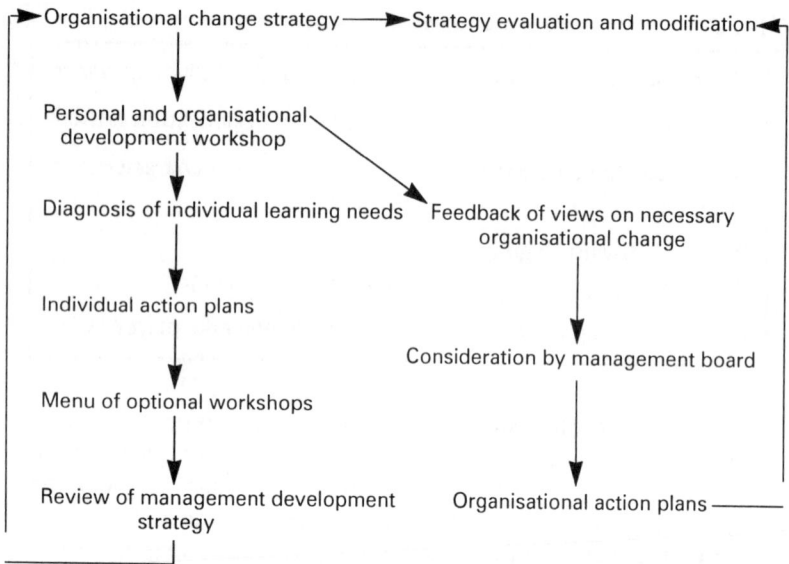

Fig. 26.1   The emerging organisation and management development strategy.

were organisation-led and that any activity therefore existed within the power structure of the organisation. Individuals both had, and did not have, the freedom to manage their work and learning. We concluded that managers' actions were likely to be guided by high levels of personal integrity. 'Responsible freedom' was core to the enactment of learning organisation principles in a health setting.

Reflections on organisation development in health care in the late 1980s from the perspective of the mid 1990s

Reflecting on these efforts to assist change is salutary. Many of the underpinning principles remain valid. What was unhelpful was the failure to involve doctors adequately. We recognised that: 'it is important to develop mechanisms for active and continuing debate ... including ... evolving strategy for improvement to patient care ... in such a way that legitimate concerns of both doctors and managers are recognised, even where those diverge'.[2]

The rest of this chapter reflects an understanding that working at the interface between doctors and managers is central to the development of health care organisations (see endnote 4). Here there is much tension but also much potential for learning.

Working within only the management sub-culture of health care organisations may be comfortable for OD consultants in the short term, but is unlikely to produce real service improvement.

There are a number of important issues for health care organisations that take an integrated approach to organisational and individual development and learning; these are shown in Box 26.2.

Box 26.2 Important issues for integrated development and learning

---

- The need for ongoing work on vision and purpose linked clearly to real clinical or service development issues in ways which require managers, doctors and other health professionals to work together
- A 'learning board' which in its behaviour demonstrates the importance of managing change through learning
- Emphasis on 'integration' as well as 'segmentation' in internal relationships (between doctors and managers or between directorates or departments) and with other organisations, notably purchasers (see endnote 5)
- Recognition that individual and organisational development and learning are at their most powerful when mutually supportive and reinforcing.

Developing a sense of shared vision and purpose which drives clinical and service development

In the mid 1980s much of the management literature emphasised the importance of cultural change. Implicit in this was the benefit of single corporate cultures to organisational effectiveness. Peters and Waterman[1] identified the 'loose–tight properties' of their 'excellent' companies. However, this is somewhat different from welcoming the inherent pluralism of the NHS.

The organisation development work in Mid Essex was in many ways an attempt to develop a management subculture pre-eminent over the professional subcultures. In this sense, it was typical of the inadequacies of traditional organisational development that have 'for too long been pursuing harmony, wherein a singular rationality is universal and human empathy never ending. The reality of life, however, involves experiencing contrasts ... as well as a positive stimulation to getting things done'.[5]

Those attempts to develop a shared vision, sense of purpose and plans for change, whilst recognising the importance of doctor involvement, tried to encourage change from within the prevailing assumptions of the emerging managerial subculture.

The need to involve consultant medical staff and other professionals in dialogue about organisational ethos, values and vision is still very much a live issue. These issues appear nebulous and irrelevant to many doctors, whose reality is one of the unremitting pressures of increasing caseloads. How can management best encourage involvement in thinking about the future? Health care organisations draw their strength from the differing perspectives and interests of their internal stakeholders. 'Participative policy making' and 'a learning approach to strategy' lie at the heart of the challenge for aspiring 'healthy' learning organisations (see endnote 6). If policy and strategy are made in isolation by boards, future clinical services are likely to be impoverished and management will struggle to get commitment to change; bringing together managerial and clinical perspectives will not be comfortable. Handling conflict or tension constructively is a key skill for all those involved.

Many health care organisations have sought a structural solution to these dilemmas — instituting clinical directorates or something similar, where doctors are drawn into managerial decision making. In one Trust where I worked recently, the clinical directors are members of a Clinical Policy Board that meets for two hours per month. Most accept this as a 'rubber stamp', being unwilling to release the additional time that would be needed to be more fully involved in strategic issues. The Trust, whilst on the face of it having a structure that involves doctors in management, in reality is unlikely to carry its clinicians with it in its future plans, nor has it enjoyed a rich clinical contribution to those plans. Some clinical directors are involved in high quality thinking about their own services, but there is inadequate dialogue across directorates about changes involving more than one directorate. Most integrated thinking about the future occurs between the executive directors, and there is a danger that a 'gulf' develops between them and the rest of the organisation.

Another Trust, keen to involve its doctors in planning, set up a team consisting of its younger consultants chaired by the Medical Director. This team did the thinking which is now core to the Trust's strategic plans. Initially there was a fear that the team might be over-supportive of the status quo. What has emerged, however, is a plan to 're-engineer' the Trust's services, stratifying patient care, for example by developing an assessment unit, critical care unit and a low dependency day unit. These are not novel plans — the important point is that they carry the commitment of a sizeable group of the consultants. This initiative demonstrates the political nature of change in health care organisations. As the team's thinking emerged, some difficulties were experienced in getting the commitment of other key internal stakeholders. There were complaints about the composition of the group, particularly from consultant 'elder statesmen'. Some managers felt the team was trespassing into their areas of power and responsibility. There are no magic solutions to these problems. In this case, quiet, informal involvement of others in developing thinking is encouraging wider ownership. A successful meeting with purchasers and other key groups has gone as far as is reasonably practicable at this stage to secure external commitment.

Learning boards

Since the implementation of the NHS reforms in 1990, health care organisations have had more clearly-defined responsibilities. The establishment of boards of Health Authorities and Trusts has involved the recognition of the need for 'policy making' at local level. Though the expected freedoms have proved somewhat illusory, there is in many places an understanding that the Board has the responsibility to define the basic rules within which others can plan the allocation of resources and tactics to achieve these broad objectives.

In my experience, those boards that are seeking to foster learning have some or all of the characteristics shown in Box 26.3.

Box 26.3 Characteristics of learning boards

- They spend time thinking about the ethos, vision and values of their organisations.
- They ask good questions of others rather than passing judgement on them.
- They seek to define appropriate success criteria for their organisation and translate these into performance measures.
- They resist the temptation to become 'hands-on'.
- They put a lot of energy into selection processes for executive directors and other top managers and, having selected good people, tend to trust them to run operations effectively.
- More nebulously, they put out messages that 'it's OK to be

learning around here' and monitor to ensure that learning is embedded into organisational systems and procedures. They ask questions about what was learned rather than who was to blame for failure.

- They exemplify their commitment to learning by being seen to have 'time outs' or other means of addressing their own learning needs.
- They are open about the dilemmas which the organisation faces and involve others in deciding on the organisation's direction.
- They ensure that good learning is rewarded.

Emphasis on integration as well as segmentation

Many health care organisations have developed structures designed to enable them to be big and act small. Clinical directorates are one way of achieving this. However, managing the 'fit' and 'split' paradox[6] requires the development of integrative learning and development processes between the corporate centre and directorates or departments, including the definition of the freedoms that the latter have to manage their own affairs. This is particularly important given the cultural pluralism of health care organisations. Involvement of the professions, particularly of doctors, in learning at the 'seams' between different parts of the organisation is vital if there is to be a coherent whole as well as energetic parts committed to continual service improvement. This paradox was embedded in our attempts in Mid Essex Health Authority to define managerial freedoms and obligations. Unfortunately, because these guidelines applied only to managers, many of the shibboleths of both the managerial and the professional cultures went unchallenged and the Authority lacked the vitality that can come from the creative tensions that both fit organisations together and split them apart.

Here are some examples of health care organisations seeking to optimise being big and acting small by managing the resultant tensions creatively:

a. A large provider of hospital-based services has established an executive board comprising corporate directors and doctors, as leaders of clinical services, where the members have roles both to lead and manage clinical services (in the case of the doctors) and to ensure that the organisation makes sense as a whole to its stakeholders (in the case of the directors). All those involved recognise that managing their differing agendas will inevitably cause conflict. The Trust has an ethos of managing change through learning, and the Board has begun a series of away days to enable it to develop effective ways of managing these tensions.

b. A provider of services for people with learning disabilities which is developing 'satellites' or locally-based services is taking care to define the freedoms of satellites and the responsibilities of the centre.

c. A very large provider of community services has begun pilot projects in two localities with the aim of assisting a wider group composed of executive directors and other locality managers to learn about the most productive way of managing the newly-devolved organisational arrangements.

Mutually supporting and reinforcing individual and organisational learning

The parallel personal and organisational development questions listed in Box 26.1 (p.000) were at the heart of efforts to develop managers and managing in Mid Essex Health Authority. Though we involved doctors peripherally, we made no sustained effort to encourage consultant medical staff to take responsibility for their own personal (as opposed to professional) development. At that time I did not question this, probably because I had accepted the prevailing assumptions of the managerial subculture.

Eight years later, in Mid Essex Hospital Services we recognise that it is necessary both to afford opportunities for the development of individual consultants and to involve consultants in the changes necessary to improve the Trust's organisational arrangements. There are clear parallels here with the recognition years earlier of the importance of developing both managers and managing (see Fig. 26.1 for a summary of this process). I now believe that efforts to improve service delivery and generally to involve doctors in organisational decision making will be greatly strengthened by paying attention to the personal development of consultants.

We offered residential personal development workshops to all 75 of the Trust's consultants, having discussed the principles underpinning this activity and the design with a small task group. We expected about 20 to volunteer to attend. In the event more than 50 took up the offer, and most expressed a wish for support for further development. The Trust is therefore running further skills development workshops on topics such as conflict handling, assertiveness, managing meetings, and time management. We have also started a number of action learning Sets, for doctors and general managers in 'learning partnerships' to develop roles and relationships, and, for a group of clinicians including the Medical Director, to progress the implementation of the Trust's Strategic Direction, including the aspirations for culture change. In embarking on action learning, the Trust is hoping that it will assist those involved to 'use the abilities of each team member and to welcome differing views'.[7]

In all these personal development activities we have provided opportunities both as part of learning events and in subsequent evaluation for doctors to give feedback to management on developments within the Trust. In this way we are putting into practice the recognition that personal development for doctors and the increasing involvement of doctors in the organisation are inextricably intertwined. I hope that we are doing this not in an attempt to encourage doctors to think like managers, but rather to strengthen the pluralism of the organisation's culture in ways that will improve patient services.

Why did it take so long to make this connection? Firstly, the external circumstances are now more favourable. The increased emphasis placed on continuous medical education and continuous personal development by the Royal Colleges has changed the perception of some doctors of the legitimacy of personal development. Secondly, there is less of a sense of doctors and managers inhabiting different territories. Current financial and activity pressures impact on both doctors and managers, creating in receptive cultures, a sense of 'comrades in adversity'. This was expressed by the Mid Essex consultants during the discussions about ways of more fully involving doctors in decision-making. Thirdly, these changes, if successful, should build more effective relationships between doctors and managers, including better understanding of each other's perspectives and orientations. Fourthly, doctors are not immune to the changes in career progression experienced by most people. No longer do they all expect to stay in one place once they become a consultant. Career choices are more apparent, particularly as entry into a full- or part-time managerial role becomes an option for many. These four factors seem to be assisting the development of a more receptive context for change. Increasingly, I understand that the 'energy and capability which underpin it (change) cannot be conjured up over a short period of time through the pulling of a single lever'.[8] We shall continue to develop understandings about the context for culture change as well as to take appropriate action.

Conclusions: reflections on the last decade

Thinking about my work as an OD consultant over the last decade has been something of an indulgence. Many of the principles which underpinned my work a decade ago are unchanged. There is still value in attempting to integrate individual and organisational learning. The principles of 'split' and 'fit'[6] are present today as they were then, though with increased emphasis on the need for creative contention between doctors and managers.

However, I am less naive about the NHS than I was when I started to work within it. This carries the danger that I take some of the barriers to change for granted. It is easier as an external consultant to maintain sufficient distance to protect a certain independence of view. Working in other sectors has also assisted me. In Mid Essex I have tried to work with the paradox of being both inside and outside the Trust. This has been supported by the organisation. I work from home and am not part of the formal reporting structure linking directly to the Trust Chairman.

I hope that having both independence and some personal security from a permanent contract are giving me the courage to work developmentally at the 'seam' between managers and managing and doctors and clinical practice. This is sometimes uncomfortable or even lonely, but is perhaps more likely to be of assistance in achieving real improvements to health services.

ENDNOTES

1. According to Griffiths,[9] the NHS lacked a clearly-defined general management function — 'the responsibility drawn together in one person, at different levels in the organisation, for the planning, implementation and control of performance' (p. 11). Prior to this, management was undertaken by consensus teams composed of a doctor, a nurse, an accountant and an administrator. Each member had the power of veto. 'If Florence Nightingale were carrying her lamp through the corridors of power of the NHS today she would almost certainly be searching for the people in charge' (p. 12). Griffiths felt that a strong general management process, stimulating 'initiative, vitality and urgency' (p. 13) and capitalising on the dedication and expertise of staff should lead the search for better service delivery.

2. These descriptions fit well with Handy's view[10] of professional cultures in which professionals expect to do complex technical work, participate in policy making, and leave the rest (lower level tasks) to administrators.

3. At that time our work was influenced by Argyris and Schon's work on organisational learning,[11] Garrett's work on the learning organisation,[12] and Pedler et al's early work on the learning company.[13]

4. Much of my experience of working at this interface has been in Mid Essex Hospital Services. The detail of the first few years of OD work there is covered in *The Never Ending Journey*.[14]

5. These terms are derived from the work of Moss Kanter,[15] who describes segmentalism as anti change — concerned with compartmentalising actions, events and problems. By contrast, in integrated organisations problems are treated as wholes, and their wider implications are considered.

6. These are two of the features of the 'learning company' suggested by Pedler et al.[4]

REFERENCES

Peters TJ, Waterman RH. In search of excellence. New York: Harper and Row, 1982.

Attwood ME, Johnson DB. Making general management work. Conference paper, Centre for the Study of Management Learning, University of Lancaster, 1987.

Attwood ME, Beer N. Development of a learning organisation. In: Pedler M et al, eds. Self development in organisations. McGraw Hill, 1990.

Pedler MJ et al. The learning company. McGraw Hill, 1991.

Kakabadse AP. Politics in organisations, re-examining O.D. Leadership and Organisation Development Journal 1982; 3(3): 3–28.

Pascale R. Managing on the edge. Penguin, 1990.

Moore JK, Neithercut WD, Mellors AS, Manning CA, Jones H, Alman RJ, Al-Bachari M. Making the new deal for junior doctors happen. British Medical Journal 1994; 308: 1553–1555.

Pettigrew A et al. Shaping strategic change. Sage, 1988.

Griffiths Report. NHS Management Enquiry. London: DHSS, 1983.

Handy C. Understanding organisations. 3rd ed. Harmondsworth: Penguin, 1988.

Argyris C, Schon D. Organisational learning. Addison Wesley, 1978.

Garratt B. The learning organisation. Fontana, 1987.

Pedler Boydell Burgoyne 1988

Attwood ME, Minett C. The never ending journey. In: Burgoyne J et al, eds. Towards the learning company. McGraw Hill, 1994.

Moss Kanter R. The change masters. Unwin Hyman, 1983.

Index